How Language Works:

Cohesion in Normal and Nonstandard Communication

Jonathan Fine
Bar Ilan University

Volume LI in the Series
ADVANCES IN DISCOURSE PROCESSES
Roy O. Freedle, Editor

ABLEX PUBLISHING CORPORATION
NORWOOD, NEW JERSEY

Printed in the United States of America

Library of Congress Cataloging-in-Publication Data

Fine, Jonathan.
How language works : cohesion in normal and nonstandard communication / Jonathan Fine.
p. cm. – (Advances in discourse processes : v. 51)
Includes bibliographical references and index.
ISBN 1-56750-044-7
1. Cohesion (Linguistics) 2. Language and languages. 3. Communicative disorders. 4. Language acquisition. 5. Social interaction. I. Title. II. Series.
P302.F537 1993
415–dc20 93-31527
CIP

Ablex Publishing Corporation
355 Chestnut Street
Norwood, New Jersey 07648

Contents

Tables and Figures

Preface to the Series

Roy O. Freedle
Series Editor

This series of volumes provides a forum for the cross-fertilization of ideas from a diverse number of disciplines, all of which share a common interest in discourse—be it prose comprehension and recall, dialogue analysis, text grammar construction, computer simulation of natural language, cross-cultural comparisons of communicative competence or other related topics. The problems posed by multisentence contexts and the methods required to investigate them, while not always unique to discourse, are still sufficiently distinct as to benefit from the organized model of scientific interaction made possible by this series.

Scholars working in the discourse area from the perspective of sociolinguistics, psycholinguistics, enthnomethodology and the sociology of language, educational psychology (e.g., teacher-student interaction), the philosophy of language, computational linguistics, and related sub-areas are invited to submit manuscripts of monograph or book length to the series editor. Edited collections of original papers resulting from conferences will also be considered.

Volumes in the Series

Vol. I. Discourse Production and Comprehension. Roy O. Freedle (Ed.), 1977.

Vol. II. New Directions in Discourse Processing. Roy O. Freedle (Ed.), 1979.

Vol. III. The Pear Stories, Cognitive, Cultural, and Linguistic Aspects of Narrative Production. Wallace L. Chafe (Ed.), 1980.
Vol. IV. Text, Discourse, and Process: Toward a Multidisciplinary Science of Texts. Robert de Beaugrande, 1980.
Vol. V. Ethnography and Language in Educational Settiings. Judith Green & Cynthia Wallat (Eds.), 1981.
Vol. VI. Latino Language and Communicative Behavior. Richard P. Duran (Ed.), 1981.
Vol. VII. Narrative, Literacy and Face in Interethnic Communication. Ron Scollon & Suzanne Scollon, 1981.
Vol. VIII. Linguistics and the Professions. Robert J. DiPietro (Ed.), 1982.
Vol. IX. Spoken and Written Language: Exploring Orality and Literacy. Deborah Tannen (Ed.), 1982.
Vol. X. Developmental Issues in Discourse. Jonathan Fine & Roy O. Freedle (Eds.), 1983.
Vol. XI. Text Production: Toward a Science of Composition. Robert de Beaugrande, 1984.
Vol. XII. Coherence in Spoken and Written Discourse. Deborah Tannen (Ed.), 1984.
Vol. XIII. The Development of Oral and Written Language in Social Contexts. Anthony D. Pellegrini & Thomas D. Yawkey (Eds.), 1984.
Vol. XIV. What People Say They Do With Words. Jef Verschueren, 1985.
Vol. XV. Systemic Perspectives on Discourse, Volume 1: Selected Theoretical Papers from the 9th International Systemic Workshop. James D. Benson & William S. Greaves (Eds.), 1985.
Vol. XVI. Systemic Perspectives on Discourse, Volume 2: Selected Applied Papers from the 9th International Systemic Workshop. James D. Benson & William S. Greaves (Eds.), 1985.
Vol. XVII. Structures and Procedures of Implicit Knowledge. Arthur C. Graesser & Leslie F. Clark, 1985.
Vol. XVIII. Contexts of Reading. Carolyn N. Hedley & Anthony N. Baratta (Eds.), 1985.
Vol. XIX. Discourse and Institutional Authority: Medicine, Education, and Law. Sue Fisher & Alexandra Dundas Todd (Eds.), 1986.
Vol. XX. Evidentiality: The Linguistic Coding of Epistemology. Wallace Chafe & Johanna Nichols (Eds.), 1986.
Vol. XXI. The Acquisition of Literacy: Ethnographic Perspectives. Bambi B. Schieffelin & Perry Gilmore (Eds.), 1986.
Vol. XXII. Cognitive and Linguistic Analyses of Test Performance. Roy O. Freedle & Richard P. Duran (Eds.), 1987.
Vol. XXIII. Linguistic Action: Some Empirical-Conceptual Studies. Jef Verschueren (Ed.), 1987.
Vol. XXIV. Text and Epistemology. William Frawley, 1987.
Vol. XXV. Second Language Discourse: A Textbook of Current Research. Jonathan Fine (Ed.), 1988.
Vol. XXVI. Systemic Functional Approaches to Discourse. James D. Benson & William S. Greaves (Eds.), 1988.
Vol. XXVII. Language Development: Learning Language, Learning Culture. Ruqaiya Hasan & James Martin (Eds.), 1989.
Vol. XXVIII. Multiple Perspective Analyses of Classroom Discourse. Judith L. Green & Judith O. Harker (Eds.), 1988.

Vol. XXIX. Linguistics in Context: Connecting Observation and Understanding. Deborah Tannen (Ed.), 1988.
Vol. XXX. Gender and Discourse: The Power of Talk. Alexandra D. Todd & Sue Fisher (Eds.), 1988.
Vol. XXXI. Cross-Cultural Pragmatics: Requests and Apologies. Shoshana Blum-Kulka, Juliane House & Gabriele Kasper (Eds.), 1989.
Vol. XXXII. Collegial Discourse. Allen D. Grimshaw, 1989.
Vol. XXXIII. Task, Talk, and Text in the Operating Room: A Study in Medical Discourse. Catherine Johnson Pettinari, 1988.
Vol. XXXIV. The Presence of Thought. Introspective Accounts of Reading and Writing. Marilyn S. Sternglass, 1988.
Vol. XXXV. Japanese Conversation: Self-contextualization through Structure and Interactional Management. Senko Kumiya Maynard, 1989.
Vol. XXXVI. Cognitive Assessment of Language and Math Outcomes. Sue Legg & James Algina (Eds.), 1990.
Vol. XXXVII. Pragmatics, Discourse and Text: Some Systematically-inspired Approaches. Erich H. Steiner and Robert Veltman (Eds.), 1988.
Vol. XXXVIII. Conversational Organization and its Development. Bruce Dorval (Ed.), 1990.
Vol. XXIX. Developing Discourse Practices in Adolescence and Adulthood. Richard Beach & Susan Hynds (Eds.), 1990.
Vol. XL. Text and Texture: Patterns of Cohesion. Sally Stoddard, 1991.
Vol. XLI. Conversation Analysis of a Marital Therapy Session: The Pursuit of a Therapeutic Agenda. Jerry Edward Gale, 1991.
Vol. XLII. Medical Discourse and Systemic Frames of Comprehension. Ronald J. Chenail, 1991.
Vol. XLIII. What's Going On Here? Complementary Studies of Professional Talk. Allen Day Grimshaw et al., 1993.
Vol. XLIV. Ambiguous Harmony: Family Talk in America. Hervé Varenne, 1992.
Vol. XLV. American and Japanese Business Discourse: A Comparison of Interactional Styles. Haru Yamada, 1992.
Vol. XLVI. Scientific Discourse: An Analysis of Biomedical Journal Articles' Discussion Sections. Betty Lou DuBois, 1993.
Vol. XLVII. Repetition in Discourse: Interdisciplinary Perspectives, Volume 1. Barbara Johnstone (Ed.), 1993.
Vol. XLVIII. Repetition in Discourse: Interdisciplinary Perspectives, Volume 2. Barbara Johnstone (Ed.), 1993.
Vol. XLIX. Word Choice and Narration in Academic Lectures: An Essay on Artistic Language Use. Barbara Strodt-López, 1993.
Vol. L. Discourse in Society: Systemic Functional Perspectives. Peter H. Fries and Michael Gregory (Eds.), 1993.
Vol. LI. How Language Works. Jonathan Fine, 1993.
Vol. LII. Naturalistic Text Comprehension. Herre van Oostendorp & Rolf A. Zwaan (Eds.), 1994.
Vol. LIII. Empirical Approaches to Literature and Aesthetics. Roger Kreuz & Mary MacNealy (Eds.), 1994.

Acknowledgments

This volume is the product of research on cohesion on several bodies of data and in several locations. I would like to thank my collaborators, funding agencies, and especially the subjects and their families who have permitted us to make tape recordings for research purposes with no prospect of immediate return. Without funding and the cooperation from speakers, it would be impossible to carry out the labor-intensive analyses on spontaneous conversation that work on cohesion requires.

Chapters 2, 3, and 4 are the result of collaboration with Drs. Giampierro Bartolucci and Peter Szatmari of the Department of Psychiatry, McMaster University and the Chedoke-McMaster Hospitals. The data were gathered and initially coded under grants from the Medical Research Council of Canada and the Roy C. Hill Foundation to Dr. Bartolucci, and from the Medical Research Council of Canada and the Ontario Mental Health Foundation to Dr. Szatmari. These colleagues have permitted me the generous use of the data they collected and have always challenged me to provide motivated, precise and informative insights from linguistics into the problems of psychiatric populations. Their intellectual and methodological rigor and friendly relations have helped and continue to help me towards bridging the gap between psychiatry and theoretical linguistics. However, these colleagues have no responsibility for the analyses in the volume and the conclusions I have drawn from the data.

Chapters 5 and 6 are based on data originally gathered under a grant from the Ontario Ministry of Education. Chapter 7 is based on data gathered by Debra Farbey as part of her master's thesis in the Department of English, Bar-Ilan University. I have relied on her background in the sociolinguistics of Hebrew language acquisition. I am grateful for her kind permission to use the data she carefully gathered. Most of the data have been reanalyzed for this chapter and so the analyses, questions, and conclusions differ from those presented by Farbey in her thesis. Chapter 8 is the result of a fruitful collaboration with William Greaves and James Benson of the English Department of Glendon College, York University. They first interested me in the analysis of bilingual data in a "real" setting. They provided me with research facilities, a unique living example of language in use, and great freedom to pursue my interests. They also probed for the right questions to be asked and the best answers to be given. The research was supported by the Interministerial committee on bilingualism in education and facilitated by Kathryn Manzer, chair of the LeCamp Committee. They psychopharmacological case study reported in Chapter 9 is based on data gathered at the University of Medicine and Dentistry of New Jersey—Rutgers Medical School under grants from UCB (Pharma) Ltd. and the National Institute of Child Health and Human Development to Rutgers Medical School. I am greatly indebted to Dr. Colin Wilsher now at UCB (Pharma) Ltd. and the University College of North Wales for writing the technical sections on experimental procedures and the background on the psychopharmacology of Piracetam. He has no responsibility for the cohesion analyses and for the conclusions that I have drawn about the subjects.

Most of the writing of this volume was done when I was on sabbatical at the Research Institute of the Hospital for Sick Children in Toronto, Canada. I appreciate the generous support of the institute and of the Psychiatry Department and its head, Dr. Susan Bradley. Drs. Russell Schachar, who organized my stay at the hospital, Rosemarie Tannock, Michael Merriott, and my office partner, Patricia Fulford, shared office space, car pool, coffee, tea, subjects, patience and ideas freely and constructively. I had the advantage of superb working conditions and technical support. The research atmosphere was stimulating, with the opportunity to discuss my work formally and informally, hear about other projects, and have undisturbed periods of work, all at my own choice.

The secretarial services of the Faculty of Arts at York University directed by Patricia Cates undertook the word processing of the first and second drafts of the volume. Annette Sotto carefully typed and corrected the drafts under pressure and at personal inconvenience to meet my intercontinental deadlines. The scheduling was done by Susan Raimey. I am very appreciative of the efforts this team made that went well beyond their duties, showing their care and understanding for the importance of getting academic work done well and efficiently.

This volume and the accompanying volume *Laterality Effects* were conceived together with Gerald Young of the Psychology Department of Glendon College, York University. I am indebted to his reading of parts of the manuscript and his thoughtful suggestions of concept and organization. His earlier work on cohesion in collaboration with Lelia Young initially suggested the current project of two volumes on cohesion. They have both widened my notion of what cohesion can contribute to an understanding of cognition. Less directly, I am indebted to Michael Halliday, Ruqaiya Hasan, and Jim Martin for setting the theoretical and analytical groundwork in cohesion that so many have followed. Their writings, lectures, and, where possible, conversations have initiated much work in the areas of systemic functional linguistics, text study, and cohesion.

Although I have tried to acknowledge the contributions of my collaborators and colleagues, any shortcomings are the result of not recognizing or taking advice proffered and are so my own responsibility.

The most important acknowledgement is to my wife, parents, and children, who have suffered the consequences of the long hours, impatience, and distraction that academic work involves. Their continued support is insufficiently returned by a few words of thanks.

Introduction

This volume is chiefly about key devices available in English that hold language together. Cohesion is used in the technical sense of Halliday and Hasan (1976) to include the nonstructural text-forming characteristics of language. Our interest is in how cohesion is used in conversation to construct interpretable messages. The main title of this volume, *How Language Works,* is intended to have two meanings: how language operates and how language accomplishes communicative work when it is used. Cohesion involves a number of specific relations (lexical, conjunction, reference, etc.) that together form text. In dialogue, cohesion indicates how the speaker's contribution is constructed and how it must be interpreted. Cohesion, though, does not exist in a vacuum. Cohesion is created within the context of other patterns of linguistic resources and the use of those resources. In the following chapters, the emphasis is on the relationship among the various resources for creating cohesion and between cohesion and a number of structures in the language. In particular, the construction of clauses into theme–rheme and given–new is related to the use of cohesion. The theme–rheme and given–new systems are structural text-forming devices and so function with cohesion in the creation of text.

As well as explicitly linguistic structures, cohesion also operates in the context of the organization of conversation.

Turn-taking mechanisms organize the contributions of speakers and thus form a framework for the construction of text. Related to the structure of conversation is, of course, the social identity of the speakers. Teachers, clinicians, and camp counselors have a status and a set of rights in conversation quite different from their students, patients, and campers. These social relationships interact with how text is created by cohesion. The studies that follow take into consideration both symetric and asymetric relations between speakers in conversation and the use of cohesion. If the construction of text in general and the use of cohesion in particular are bound to context, then the use of cohesion should reflect the important social relationships of speakers. Understanding the relationship between speaker status and the use of cohesion is relevant both for linguistic theory and for possible applications involving students and speakers with communication difficulties.

Cohesion also is the product of cognitive processes. The companion volume, Gerald Young's *Laterality Effects,* examines this cognitive aspect in detail. The present volume considers some cognitive hypotheses in the use of cohesion as those hypotheses pertain to how cohesion works in interaction.

To understand how cohesion works implies a comparative methodology. The relation of cohesion to social factors such as the interaction of speakers and to cognitive factors requires comparisons across situations and speakers. Each of the following studies deals with one or more comparisons among speakers or the situations they speak in. Although "cohesion" has been used as a convenient coding scheme for many comparative studies, it has generally not been considered in the appropriate linguistic and interactional contexts. Without this necessary reconnecting of cohesion to context and to the creation of text, cohesion is a measure without its essential functional values. The studies that follow thus focus on prior investigations that emphasize the functional role of cohesion in context, rather than on the many studies that use cohesion scoring to show differences between two groups of subjects. By taking a broad contextual and functional approach, the goal is to study how cohesion works as well as what the differences are among groups of speakers. Such a functional basis helps to bridge the gaps from descriptive analyses to explanations of how language works and from theoretical understandings of language to designing various teaching, diagnosis, or remedial programs.

The chapters on the language of psychiatric syndromes present both qualitative and quantitative data. These data aim to show that close examination of the language of the speakers can reveal a great deal about how the speakers fail to communicate adequately and thus why they are regarded as socially atypical. As some of the current research into the syndromes shows, there is an increased focus on functional approaches to the communication skills of these speakers. Systemic linguistics, of which cohesion is only the most widely known part, starts with the functions of language and develops a motivated and comprehensive account of functions and how they are related to specific surface linguistic features. Systemic linguistics can thus be applied to a number of problems in the language of psychiatric patients to illuminate how the speakers communicate.

The volume has been designed with two basic readerships in mind: linguists interested in empirical data that show how cohesion works, and those interested in the topic areas of first and second language development and the language of psychiatric syndromes. To serve these different readers, a certain amount of redundancy has been introduced to make the chapters that present data on specific speakers relatively independent of each other. In all chapters, the reader should keep in mind that there are objectives in terms of studying the functioning of cohesion and objectives in terms of the speakers whose language is the object of investigation. The reader may occasionally feel that the objective that he or she is most interested in at a particular point is receiving less than full attention. This is an inevitable consequence of trying to balance the two objectives and the needs of the two readerships. The reader is urged to be patient with what he or she may regard as the nonfocal objective and to appreciate why it is necessary to combine the two objectives.

1

THE FUNCTION OF COHESION IN SOCIAL INTERACTION

INTRODUCTION

People use language to communicate to each other. They do this on many occasions and for many purposes. In turn, language is organized in various ways to enable it to function as a means of communication. Systemic theory sees language as organized into distinctions of meaning with corresponding reflexes or realizations of those distinctions in the lexicogrammar. Language is used in verbal and nonverbal contexts, and those contexts have a central role in the functional use of language. It is a legitimate heuristic to simplify by studying phenomena out of context. However, there is also a cost in terms of ignoring possibly important relations between the phenomena under study and other phenomena. The current study attempts to place cohesion as part of the organization of language into the contexts of its use. Of course, there are a great number of possible aspects of context that can be related to the organization of language. This study is concerned with some aspects of language and some aspects of situation. For the many areas of language and context left out, the following studies can be seen as examples of the many further investigations needed. Despite these necessary limitations, the goals are (a) to provide an understanding of the functional organization of language in relationship to other aspects of language and in relationship to verbal and nonverbal contexts; and (b) to provide an understanding of the functional use of language in psychiatric disorders involving communication, and first and second language development.

Cohesion is a good candidate for a functional study of language use. Cohesion occurs relatively frequent in spontaneous discourse; it has a crucial role of signaling the relation of one stretch of language to another and to the nonverbal situation of language use, and has been the subject of both theoretical and empirical investigations. The study of cohesion is only one part of a functional approach to linguistic organization and to language in use (Halliday, 1985; Halliday & Hasan, 1976). Although there are an increasing number of studies of the functions of language in psychiatric cases and language development (e.g., Landry & Loveland, 1989; Sudhalter, Cohen, Silverman, & Wolf-Schein, 1990), many such studies focus on one linguistic variable or use an *ad hoc* system of categories. Cohesion, rooted in systemic theory, provides exhaustive paradigmatic contexts for each of the options. Each category of cohesion, at whatever level of delicacy, is in paradigmatic contrast with other categories and their realizations. In this way, the analysis systematically includes each of the paradigmatically related functions. The use of one option specifically excludes other options and so describes what is meant as a choice of what could have been meant but was not.

An example of such paradigmatic contexts and how they specify meaning are the different possible systems for number. Consider Language A that has two morphological forms for expressing number: one, more than one (usually called singular and plural, respectively). Language B has three forms for number: one, two, more than two (singular, dual, plural). The meanings for the plurals, that is, the forms realizing the choice "plural," are different in the two languages: one means "2 or more," the other means "3 or more." This difference in meaning is a result of the paradigmatic contexts that the two plural morphological forms operate in. More fundamentally, the morphological forms realize different functions. It is the paradigmatic systems of these functions that determine the distinctions that can be made in each language. Language A has a contrast between "one" and "more than one" in a paradigmatic set. Language B has a three-way contrast in the paradigm for a number such that a selection of "3 or more" necessarily excludes "two." Cohesion, then, must be seen in a paradigmatic context that relates options in language.

Cohesion is, though, just one of the resources that contributes to the formation of text. "Text" is language that is operative in situations, as opposed to language that is quoted out of context (Halliday & Hasan, 1976). Text is a semantic unit that gains its unity from the connections to both verbal context and to the physical circumstances of the situation language is used in. Therefore, cohesion must be considered in the context of its use.

Cohesion has thus far been introduced as serving social functions of interaction, of having an interorganism perspective. However, language is also the product of cognitive functioning, and so a functional account of language can also be taken as an account of the cognitive requirements of the speakers who use it: an intraorganism perspective. The potentials of meaning built into language and their means of realization are constructed within two sets of constraints: (a) what speakers in a society have to communicate about, and (b) what minds can process in real time. As well as independent constraints, each perspective can be seen as constraining the other. Cognitive abilities constrain social interaction through factors such as memory limits for faces and names, the rate at which verbal information can be decoded and encoded, and the number of conceptual or phonological distinctions that can be made. On the other hand, social interaction specifies the need for certain cognitive abilities. Phylogenically and ontogenically, the cognitive and social abilities must develop together. The same mental structures serve both surface forms of language and the functions that language serves in social communication. Social interaction takes place in the context of the available cognitive abilities, and cognitive abilities must develop to serve social functioning.

The argument is parallel to that of Edwards and Middleton (1986a) concerning Bartlett's view of language. They claim that there is a unity of mental functioning, and that language bridges individual mentality and social context. One should, they argue, not just see the influence of the social on cognition, but also the social basis of mentality. Mentality arises for social functioning, and language is the means that enables social activity to take place. As well as a unity of mentality, we can also claim that there is a unity of language. The same sequence of units (a) conveys meaning and fits the social constraints of the society (see Halliday, 1973, for a discussion of "can do," "can mean," and "can say" as potentials), and (b) is the output of mental processing of the speaker and input to the processing by the hearer. Is there a primacy of either social or cognitive factors in shaping language? The question has to be framed differently. Both these sets of factors influence the way language can be structured and formed into text. One can, of course, say that all things being equal, social group A speaks differently than social group B or speakers with syndrome C speak differently than speakers with syndrome D. However, the research question is how and over what systems of language do social and cognitive factors have influence. The two sets of factors operate simultaneously. Although heuristically the focus may be on one or the other with reasonable empirical control of the second, the fundamental unity of mentality and unity of language cannot be forgotten.

Service, Lock, and Chandler (1989) outline a similar social constructivist perspective. They claim (p. 23) that "an individual's abilities do not arise from the exercise of individually possessed 'cognitive processes,' but are constructed out of the social interactions an individual is immersed in." Service et al. (p. 45) see language as having "basic rules or steps," but that when language is used, the rules or steps "constitute social interactions that cannot truly be described as rule regulated, but as rule constitutive, these rules emerging from the negotiations made by the partners as they try to sustain the interaction." It is important to see language as a negotiation between speakers of what can be meant and how it should be said. From these negotiations in functional communicative contexts, the rules emerge. Of course, the rules are always open for renegotiation, but the existing rules form a background of expectations and describe the initial point for the renegotiation.

Social reality is then built up through language. The process is dynamic such that each successive utterance is in the context of prior utterances. Speakers signal their continuing agreement to the way language is constituting the social relationship. Language in use is organized by simultaneous systems. For example, turns in a dialogue are organized by mechanisms such as adjacency pairs, repair strategies, and the conventional and nonconventional encodings of speech functions. The language within those turns is also organized by syntax and cohesion. The speaker is required to adjust to the ongoing construction of context and to fashion utterances that realize a number of simultaneous systems. Cohesion is therefore not an isolated patterning available in language, but a functional resource that is used in the context of other components of language to create social interaction.

The social and cognitive perspectives on language and specifically on cohesion require that empirical studies include nonlinguistic data. Social roles, class membership, turn-taking, choice of language, and the specific task are variables outside of cohesion that provide information about social interaction that can then be related to particular cohesion variables. On the other hand, standardized neuropsychological texts and detailed clinical descriptions can provide information about cognitive processing in order to study the cognitive influence on cohesion use.

Given an empirical study involving samples of spontaneous speech, the question is how should the data be interpreted. The data themselves are the rates of using the various options of cohesion and other linguistic variables. As one sample is compared to another sample, there will be differences in frequencies on some variables. It is difficult to simply attribute the differences to either the cognitive or social sphere. Any given difference in the use of cohesion must be considered with respect to other differences in the use of language and nonlinguistic social and cognitive factors. The functions of the cohesion, and more generally, of the linguistic differences among speakers help suggest plausible social and cognitive associations. Since the theory is functional, the rates of specific variables can be related to aspects of social and cognitive abilities established by means other than the close analysis of conversation. Of course, it may be the case that the social and cognitive abilities are themselves correlated, as, for example, with high-functioning autistics (Szatmari, Bartolucci, & Bremner, 1989).

Insisting on both cognitive and social perspectives in language analysis presents considerable challenges; however, as the work of Edwards and Middleton (1986a, 1986b) and von Tetzchner, Siegel, and Smith (1989) suggests, it is a necessary approach to avoid oversimplification in understanding the use and organization of language. The social and the cognitive aspects are both aspects of human behavior and cannot be sealed in separate compartments.

The encoding-decoding perspective is another apparent dichotomy that must be reviewed before presenting the analysis of cohesion. Speakers must encode in language so that they will be interpreted and in doing so make assumptions about the social relations and history of the interactants.

The decoding process involves an interpretation of the functions encoded in speech that are produced in context. The context can help direct the decoding since hearers will have built up expectations about how one stretch of language is related to another. The decoding process can then be studied indirectly by analyzing productions. Typical patterns in language productions and the strength of those patterns suggest the decoding strategies that are needed for interpretation. Rochester and Martin (1977) take this position in suggesting that there are different strategies for interpreting different categories of speakers with and without psychiatric difficulties. As well as relying on typical associations of language options that have been built up in the speech community, decoding can also rely on the nonarbitrary combining of functions. That is, hearers expect certain functions to co-occur because of the nature of those functions. For example, information coded as "given" by the given-new information system involving word order and intonation is also likely to include anaphoric reference which also functions to signal that information is recoverable.

The expectations of hearers develop from the language that those hearers have used and interacted with. To create suitable text, the speaker must use these expectations in two ways. First, the speakers must be able to appropriately parse the verbal and nonverbal context into emic and etic components. Emic components are those differences that the community perceives of as relevant and contrastive. These differences serve to identify and distinguish behavioral units. Etic differences, on the other hand, are differences that the community does not regard as capable of carrying functional contrasts. To take a nonlinguistic example, the hand used to proffer a gift may be emic in one society (the right hand being typical, the left hand the sign of an insult or disrespect for the receiver), but merely etic in a second society. In this latter society, which hand is used may be hardly noticed, and even if noticed, will not convey any particular message. This parsing is in terms of the patterns built up in the linguistic community. For example, the speaker who does not use formal speech because he does not recognise the need for it in a particular context can be seen as not having parsed the context in the way it is typically parsed by other speakers. The speaker has missed the emic nature of formality in the context.

The second kind of expectation requires the speaker to take the parsing of the context and adjust the use of language accordingly. The appropriate adjustment is the use of specific language options according to the probabilities built up in the community. One simple corollary of this argument is that less effective speakers may show less variation in their use of language. The more limited variation may derive from either restricted ability in parsing contexts or the mapping from context to language options. In language development and psychiatric pathology, there may well be limitations and/or skewing of the linguistic interactions that must form the basis for learning the patterns of the language community.

Learning and following the patterns of the language community involves the approximation by individuals to the established patterns. These patterns can be seen in quantitative terms as the rates for using certain linguistic options under given conditions. Text, language operative in situation, is constructed in typical ways (cf. Firth's recurrent meanings in recurrent situations). The probability of meaning "x" in a given situation helps create the typicality of the situation. That is, language helps constitute the situation and the typicality of the situations. Specifically, it is the probabilities of using certain language options that contributes to the building of typical situations (the role of probabilities is more fully developed in).

Departures from the expected probabilities indicate that the speaker is not following the social and linguistic norms of what can be meant and how it can be meant. For the hearer, the question is: Why is the speaker not following the typical pattern? That is, we expect a reason for atypical uses of language. The reason may be that the speaker is not part of the linguistic community or has some social or cognitive impairment. For example, a speaker who asks an unusual number of questions, given the apparent social roles of speaker and hearer, may be understood, by sensitive interlocutors, as an outsider to the community. Probabilities can be seen as encoding the mediation between selections of linguistic options from networks and the verbal and nonverbal contexts in which the selections are made. The probabilities indicate the strength of the typical relations from one language option to another or from one language option to a feature of situation. The strength of the typicality will then account for the force of an atypical choice (see Fine, 1988, in press-a, in press-b).

Since linguistic options are established in functional terms, differences among speakers in using a given option are not merely convenient measures of individual or group differences. Rather, the quantitative differences indicate what speakers typically mean and how they mean in relation to other speakers and from context to context.

TYPES OF COHESION

The following outline of cohesion presents the major categories that are used in the empirical studies of later chapters. Halliday and Hasan (1976) developed the systematic study of cohesion with its categories. Since the original publication of *Cohesion in English* there have been revisions to many of the categories and greater levels of delicacy specified. The following sections summarize how cohesion fits into a broader understanding of language and then briefly describe the specific cohesion categories.

Aside from citational uses, language has a value in context. It is used to achieve effects desired by speakers. Language thus must be operative. There are various structural means that make language operative. For example, subject-auxiliary inversion, or a declarative word order with rising intonation, can be used to demand certain information. The yes-no question that is created must fit into the prior context and can be expected to be followed by responses of a certain kind. Aside from such structural resources that created a matching of language and context, there are nonstructural resources, namely, cohesion. Cohesion devices have the function of linking language to its verbal and nonverbal context, making the language operative—noncitational.

The systems of cohesion, like other parts of systemic theory, present options in paradigmatically defined sets. The options are defined as semantic functions that contrast with other members of the set. These functions are then realized or actualized by options in the lexicogrammar. This paradigmatic nature of the sets provides the background for quantitative studies. The rate of any option can be calculated in contrast to the rate of other options in the same set. To take a very simple grammatical example, the rate of using singular nouns is calculated against the rate of the plural option for all nouns that involve a contrast between singular and plural.

The functions in cohesion as in systemic linguistics in general are represented in system networks with the functions to the left being entry conditions for the systems to the right. For example, the choice of the function "participant" usually leads to a system that demands a choice of "one" or "more than one." These latter two options may then be realized in English by a contrast in grammar between singular and plural realized in the inflectional morphology.

As well as having a theoretical importance in showing the relationships among related systems, the scale of delicacy (see Butler, 1985, for a review) is very helpful for quantitative studies. The concept of delicacy emerges from the organization of systems being dependent on other systems. The option from one system can be the entry condition for a second system. This second system is thus dependent on the first system with the options of the second system specifying the subvarieties of the option selected from the first system. The second, dependent system is at a more delicate level than the first one. Very delicate distinctions will result in low frequencies of occurrence in running text. For some theoretically justifiable distinctions, very large amounts of data still show only a handful of instances (for example, the various types of substitution outlined in Halliday & Hasan, 1976). In these cases, a less delicate distinction can be used, such as combining substitution with ellipsis. A category that is reasonably frequent can then be compared to other reasonably frequent categories within the same paradigmatic set. It is also desirable to be able to link the quantitative data on the use of cohesion to the use of other linguistic systems and to nonlinguistic factors such as cognitive development. Highly specific (i.e., very delicate) functions and their realizations are difficult to relate to other parts of language use or to underlying cognitive processing. Ultimately, the most delicate options and their interactions will have to be studied. For the moment, the approach of using less delicate and more frequent options in cohesion has proven useful in various quantitative studies (for example, Bartolucci & Fine, 1989; Martin 1983b). In each case, what is important is the system in which the cohesion option is functioning and thus the method of computing the rate of use of that option.

Cohesion links language to other stretches of language and to the nonlinguistic environment. The terminology to refer to these various links needs to be clear. Following in part Gregory (1967) and the common use of the words, *situation* refers to the nonverbal environment of a stretch of language. *Context* refers principally to the verbal environment, but is used in phrases such as *verbal context* and *nonverbal context* to show the contrast between links to the verbal and nonverbal environments. Just as *situation* emphasizes the nonverbal environment, so too *co-text* is used to emphasis the verbal environment. Stretches of language become operative (become text) by virtue of the relation to situation and co-text that are built by cohesion.

PHORICITY

Phoricity is a system in nominal groups that directs the hearer to the interpretation of the utterance. Phoricity is a more general term than the term reference used by Halliday and Hasan (1976) and includes nominal ellipsis and substitution. Nominal groups that are interpretable on their own are nonphoric. For nominal groups that are phoric and thus set up a link, the location and clarity of the necessary information that is to be used for interpretation determine the network. The network and examples are given in Figure 1-1. The unclear options of ambiguity and additioning do not contribute to the formation of text, but rather make interpretation difficult. The hearer is signaled that a nominal group is phoric and so is interpretable only in terms of some further information. However, for ambiguity and additioning, the hearer cannot determine what that information is. (For further delicacy and related systems of phoricity, see Martin, forthcoming.)

CONJUNCTION

Unlike phoricity, *conjunction* is not a search command to the hearer to use information from elsewhere. Rather, conjunction is an instruction to interpret what follows in a given way in relation to what has gone before. The major subtypes of conjunction are additive (*and*), adversative (*yet*, *however*), causal (*therefore*, *because*), and temporal (*next*, *soon*, *afterwards*). Additive conjunction is the unmarked option: it merely specifies that the

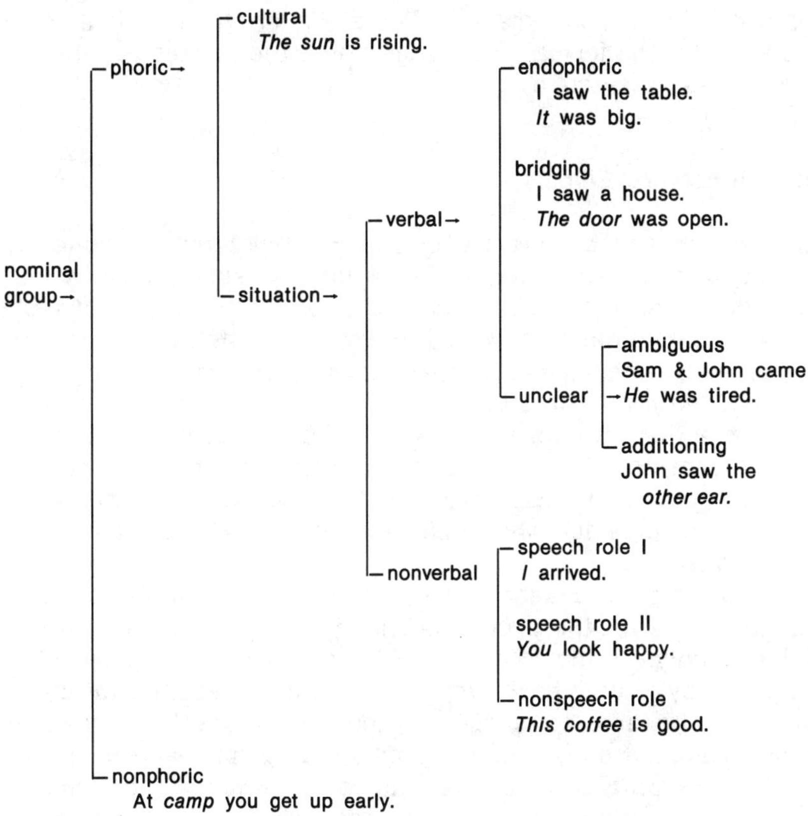

Figure 1-1. Phoricity system and examples

two stretches of language are related and part of the same text. The other options add more information about how the two stretches of language are related. (For much further delicacy in the conjunction system see Martin, 1983a.)

LEXICAL

Lexical cohesion creates ties within a text by the selection of vocabulary (that is, selection from relatively open sets of choices). The direct repitition of a lexical item indicates that the speaker is continuing to talk about roughly the same thing and is continuing in the same text. However, the use of synonyms, superordinates and general item (such as "thing") also create cohesion by lexical means. There is often no identity or reference with lexical cohesion, but the cohesive link is nevertheless created.

Substitution and Ellipsis

Substitution and ellipsis are closely related forms of cohesion that occur relatively infrequently in running texts (generally less than 3% of all cohesive links). For *substitution*, a grammatical signal ("grammatical" because the signals are from relatively closed sets of choices) is used to indicate that the linguistic form needed for the interpretation is found elsewhere in the text. If the question "Do we have paper clips?" is answered by "No, do you want one?" the item *one* refers the listener to a previous item in the text (paper clips) for the full interpretation. Substitution provides an explicit examle of the item that is to be searched for.

Ellipsis implies a search command to the listener similar to substitution, with the exception that the specific structural slot is left empty. If the question "Do you have your rocket?" is answered by "I only have his," the listener is required to supply a nominal head to complete the nominal groups *his rocket*. As these examples show, nominal substitution and ellipsis set up phoric links parallel to demonstrative or personal pronouns.

Phoricity, conjunction, and lexical cohesion are the major forms of cohesion that can themselves be seen as options in a system of cohesion. Given that text must be created, the different forms of cohesion are the resources that can contribute to the building of text. Texts may be created with relatively more or less of each of these major forms, so text may differ in how the speaker encodes the language as being connected to the verbal and nonverbal contexts. In each of the quantitatve analyses, the level of delicacy of the cohesion analysis and the options at risk are made clear.

The quantitative and funcional approach to cohesion implies a comparative method. The comparisons are not only from one speaker or group of speakers to another but also from one situation to another. In addition, there may be an interaction of speaker differences and situation differences. Since there are no absolute levels for the use of the cohesion, the levels of use must be compared and conclusions drawn from the differences found. These conclusions pertain to individual speakers, classes of speakers, and situation types.

The comparisons in the use of cohesion reveal different mappings of the resources of language with elements of the verbal context and nonverbal situation. These differences indicate the strategies hearers need in order to interpret the speakers. These strategies may be far from the hearer's the general expectations for the use of language. The greater the departure from the expectations of the hearer, the greater will be the difficulty in interpretation and surprise at unusual use of language. As well as mere difference from one speaker to another or from one situation to another, the direction of the difference is important. Since cohesion is based on the functions of language, relatively greater or lesser use of a cohesive relation encodes a different meaning relationship in the texts. These differences in what different texts mean can then be related to the social and cognitive abilities of the speakers and to aspects of the context in which the language is used.

The quantitative approach to cohesion has several aspects. Case studies are used to show the specific functional effect of cohesion and the detailed relationships to other language systems and nonlinguistic factors. By comparing individual speakers or small numbers of speakers, many variables and their interrelationships can be associated with the abilities of speakers. Suggestions can then be made about the functions of cohesion and the characteristics of speakers. The case studies form the basis for hypotheses about group diferences, but they also suggest hypotheses about the mechanisms of using cohesion in relation to other systems.

Representative sampling of developmental and psychiatric groups permits conclusions about differences. The quantitative data are frequently backed by statistical tests in the following chapters. When tests cannot be performed becaused of small sample sizes or because of the data gathering and processing procedures, relatively conservative interpretations are drawn with a circumspect confidence in the results. However, such data are valuable in suggesting trends in the data. Interpretations are contained not just by the descriptive statistics but by the coherence of the pattern that emerges. Even in studies based on a large number of statistical tests, common sense and an overall view of the data are needed to avoid conclusions based on possibly spurious "statistically significant" findings. All the quantitative procedures are important as examples of techniques that can be used to explore the use of cohesion.

The following chapters of empirical studies of cohesion are grouped as follows: The first three chapters (2 to 4) deal with the language of psychiatric patients. Chapter 2 is based on detailed case studies and Chapters 3 and 4 follow up with studies of a larger number of speakers. The next four chapters (5 to 8) concern the language of children. Chapters 5 and 6 have a specifically developmental focus, comparing the language of 5-, 7-, and 9-year-olds. Chapter 7 explores a possible class difference in the use of cohesion on a number of tasks. Two groups of Hebrew speakers are compared on picture description tasks and narrative recall. Chapter 8 is a study of first and second language use in a naturalistic setting. The interplay of cohesion within and across speakers and languages in different situations leads to conclusions about the social interactions of speakers. The final chapter draws general conclusions about cohesion and presents a case study of the cohesion of a speaker under drug treatment. This study is included to give an example of the relation of cohesion to cognitive processing.

There is an intentional redundancy across the chapters to increase the independence of the studies so that specialists in one area can focus on the relavant studies. Given the range of speakers examined and the consequent different backgrounds of readers, technical terminology and symbols are avoided when possible. This approach inevitably introduces further redundancy in wording.

2

TWO CASE STUDIES OF DEVELOPMENTAL DISORDERS

INTRODUCTION

Cohesion contributes to the creation of text by signaling the continuity of meaning from one stretch of language to another and the connections to the nonverbal context. Cohesion, then, is a means of presenting information that is being fitted into the verbal and nonverbal contexts. The given-new and theme-rheme systems are, like cohesion, part of the textual metafunction with respect to the context of the speech event, including the addressee. There may be cases of misuse of the systems of the textual function that lead to messages that cannot be interpreted. The data from Rochester and Martin (1979) indicate that some speakers use cohesion inappropriately by not constructing interpretable links from one stretch of language to another. Reference items such as *he* with more than one plausible antecedent, comparatives such as *another* when the first of the category is not mentioned, or exophora such as *today* when speaker and hearer do not share the same time frame lead to uninterpretable language. The hearer faced with such use of language cannot determine what meaning the speaker is presenting.

However, total breakdown in communication happens relatively infrequently in a speech community. Rather, speakers may use linguistic systems to create text in different ways. The differences in texts (or, in their property of texture) are differences in how the meaning of a text is constructed with regard to the verbal and nonverbal contexts of the speech event. An examination of the linguistic systems that create texture is thus an examination of how the speaker is fitting his or her language to the context. There is not a necessarily "right" way to do this. As mentioned, there are some uses of language that are uninterpretable and so inappropriate if interpretability is the objective, as it usually is. Speakers may differ from each other in how various systems are used and how the use of one system relates to the use of another. It is this variation in the range of interpretable language that is the subject of this chapter. The language of psychiatric patients, particularly schizophrenics, has been the focus of considerable study using analyses of cohesion. Psychiatric patients are of interest since there is abundant clinical evidence that the speakers do not communicate normally and in some cases fail to communicate at all.

Study of this language is important to learn more about how individuals and groups of speakers communicate and to learn which linguistic systems carry the variation. Since systemic theory is a functional theory, identifying the location of the variation within the linguistic system indicates which meanings are at risk in the language of different speakers. A functional account of the differences between speakers is then an account of the differences in how their language should be and can be interpreted in context. It is this study of how speakers construct language in context that is important for studies of language in use. The functional perspective enables specific parts of the linguistic system to be related to specific elements of contexts or abilities of speakers. If we know that a speaker does or does not use a certain linguistic option under given contextual conditions, then statements can be made about the interpretability of that speaker and the meanings that are presented to the hearer. Cohesion consists of a set of options that can be used to form text. There are, though, options from other systems that signal consistency in text. Consistency in (a) what the text is about (field), and (b) in the interpersonal relationships encoded by language operate with cohesion to create text. This chapter examines cohesion along with some systems not directly connected with cohesion to show how text is differentially constructed by speakers with two psychiatric syndromes.

This chapter presents two case studies of young speakers with psychiatric disorders. The following chapter then examines quantitatively the language spoken by a sample of speakers with these two diagnoses. Chapter 4 introduces both qualitative and quantitative data on the language of speakers with other psychiatric disorders. These three chapters are concerned with psychiatrically characterized patients from two perspectives: (a) the description and characterization of the communication and social difficulties of the speakers and how they relate to other characteristics of the syndromes, and (b) the way selections of linguistic options from various systems are made. The study of psychiatric patients can highlight linguistic processes that may not be apparent in the language of other speakers.

Studies of the language of psychiatric patients have been comparative. Usually, a specific syndrome is the focus of the investigation and is compared to clinically similar or contrasting syndromes and/or to a normal control population. This method is necessary since there are no absolute standards of how text should be created. The interesting aspects of these studies are what effect the measured difference in language has on communication and how that difference may be useful in pointing to more basic social and cognitive differences between the groups.

FUNCTIONAL APPROACHES TO THE LANGUAGE OF DEVELOPMENTAL DISORDERS

Linguistic Issues

A number of specific linguistic issues are relevant for examining the social difficulties and associated use of language in children with psychiatric developmental disorders. Recent studies have included the linguistic aspect of interaction in characterizing the developmental disorders. Prizant and Wetherby (1987, p. 472) use communicative intent as the basis for describing autism. Communicative intent is defined as "the ability to use expressive signals in a preplanned manner in order to affect the behavior or attitudes of others." Thus, communicative intent must involve social engagement and social causality. Prizant and Wetherby clearly indicate that the meaning of signals must be shared in a social community. They see conventional meaning at two levels: (a) pragmatic intent having to do with the use or function of language as a social tool; and (b) semantic intent having to do with "referential meaning, or the objects, persons, actions, locations, and so forth that particular words denote." Semantic intent can be seen as part of pragmatic intent. Referential meaning implies agreement on the labeling of the environment. That is, there must be a social convention that is recognized by the speakers in a speech community. Even referential acts are social in that they imply that the intended listener shares the speaker's conventions of naming.

Prizant and Wetherby (1987) find that the intents of autistic speakers are homogeneous in regulating adult behavior for a purpose (such as requests and protests), but the autistics seldom use language to attract and direct adult attention to objects or the speaker himself. The authors speculate that "the development of idiosyncratic and unconventional means to communicate results from the autistic child's limited participation in social exchanges from early in life" (pp. 476–477). Here we have a measurable deficit in the functional use of language that may be related to the early learning of social interactions. Communicative intent is a broad functional concept that links language to the social interaction of the speaker by specifying that signals affect others. In a functional theory of language, each account of linguistic choice represents the effect of the realization of that choice on the receiver. As with the Prizant and Wetherby findings for communicative intent, it may well be that other aspects of linguistic usage by developmentally disordered children may be affected by atypical social interaction at a young age.

Another set of functional approaches to developmental disorder is presented by Sudhalter et al. (1990). They studied retardation and autism by examining language in naturally occurring conversation. Their analyses of conversational interaction include the functional categories of direct response, initiation, and topic maintenance. As a measure of deviance they considered inappropriate repetition both across speakers (echolalia) and within the speaker's own speech (phrasal, sentential, or topic preservation). Their three subject groups were: Down syndrome, fragile X syndrome, and autism. They found that the autistics had more immediate and delayed echolalia, whereas the fragile X group displayed more preservation. Another comparison showed that the autistics do little topic maintenance and do not add new information in contrast to the fragile X speakers who do better at sustaining topics and adding new information. Sudhalter et al. suggest that repetition is an indication of discomfort in interaction and so may be the result of social deficits. They also consider the possibility that for some speakers with cognitive deficits, repetition may provide time for the verbal processing needed in interaction. The study in this chapter uses a number of functional systems to provide valuable information about the likely social capabilities of the subject groups in social interaction. The functional systems include the conversational status of speaker turns, the value of repetitions (deviant or not), and the source of material that is repeated (from the speaker or interlocutor).

The analysis of the language of the developmentally disordered presented in this chapter also uses a number of functional distinctions, including some quite similar to those of Sudhalter et al. However, the functional distinctions are motivated by a comprehensive and systematic linguistic theory and are designed to capture the atypicalities in form and function that are relevant to the specific developmental disorders under study.

A third approach to the development of the functional use of language is to study the combinations of vocalizations and gestures as language appears in normally developing children. Martinsen and Smith (1989) studied vocalization in combination with gesture longitudinally as children's first words emerged. They found that the combination of vocalization and gesture was more perceptually salient and therefore more interpretable than either vocalizations or gestures in isolation. The combinations were generally more often followed by parental reactions. It follows that the child must present signals that can be easily interpreted and then reacted to. Different communicative signals produced by children will be associated with different parental reactions. For example, Martinsen and Smith (1989) found that gestures or gestures in combination with vocalizations, are more often followed by a parental answer containing names and pronouns compared to parental responses to vocalizations alone. Although it is impossible to know about the precise early interactions of the developmentally disordered, the atypicalities noted for these groups include a variety of language variables (see, for example, Howlin & Rutter, 1989; Oshima-Takane & Benaroya, 1989; Szatmari, Bremner & Nagy, 1989) that could be associated with different parental reactions. Ultimately, the resulting atypicalities from both sides in the communication setting would impair the development of a communication system and the shared social reality that the child is normally expected to build and enter.

The above functional studies of language in developmentally disordered children relate the particular language patterning of a group to the level of social functioning of the speakers. Links can also be made to the early social behavior of the children and possibly to deficits in cognitive functioning that may shape social interaction.

Diagnostic Categories

The study of the language of psychiatric developmental disorders is dependent on the diagnostic categories initially used to group subjects. The criteria for grouping subjects may exist at different levels of generalization and involve quite distinct conceptualizations. The categories that establish the clinical coherence of psychiatric groups must be explained and the relation between the diagnostic criteria and linguistic variables considered. Autism, Asperger's syndrome, and, in a minor way, language development in general are considered in terms of the clinical characteristics and the language component of the categorization.

Autistic disorder is described by DSM-III-R as being a severe developmental disorder with (a) qualitative impairment in reciprocal social interaction, (b) qualitative impairment in verbal and nonverbal communication, and in imaginative activity, and (c) markedly restricted repertoire of activities and interests. Landry and Loveland (1989, p. 283) specify the particular linguistic problem for autistics as "using language in relation to the context of discourse." The difficulty is in adapting language to a variety of social situations. Landry and Loveland note a disagreement over whether the optimal situation for successful interaction of autistics is highly structured interaction or adults merely responding to the initiations of the subjects. The details of this study will be discussed in a later section. However, it is important to note here that attention-directing behavior separates the autistic group from the control groups in two ways. Autistics use less attention-directing behavior than the other groups and show less variation across social contexts. These findings help demonstrate the relationship of the impairment of autistics to the context. Autism is not a difficulty in communication or behavior that exists outside specific contexts. Thus, studies of the language of autistics are most profitably studies in context.

As suggested above, language has been considered an important element in distinguishing the groups of speakers with developmental disorders. There is a strong link between early language use, its social value, and the diagnoses of developmental disorders. Smith (1989) studied the interactions of young developmentally retarded children and their mothers. The mothers of the retarded children were more directive than the mothers of normal children. Smith speculates that the retarded may provide few cues for parents to use or at least parents are less observant of the cues provided by their children. The data suggest that the normal development of interaction depends on mutual building of signals and interpretation strategies between child and parent. If either partner provides signals or interprets signals unusually, than the interaction can be affected in both directions.

These findings can be seen in light of the study of Szatmari, Bremner, and Nagy (1989) that shows that parental reports agree with clinical assessments of Asperger's syndrome. The clues in communication and social behavior that are apparent to parents are usually sufficient to indicate the underlying developmental disorder. Although the data from Smith (1989) and Szatmari et al. (1989) do not directly support a causal link between early interaction and the impairments that are part of the diagnostic picture, at least the presence of early atypical interaction would reinforce social withdrawal or odd behavior that are associated with developmental disorders. That is, the atypicalities in the use of language and nonlinguistic social atypicalities can contribute to even more developmental dysfunction. Szatmari et al. (1989) report that the presence of "bizarre behavior" in the Asperger's group separates that group from the socially withdrawn control subjects. This finding can be taken as further evidence that behavioral and linguistic factors may interact and contribute to the ultimate diagnostic criteria.

Diagnostic criteria may thus be built from a number of factors that interact with each other. The resulting diagnostic categories may involve criteria of various types and different levels of generalization. Factors such as etiology, outcome, and course contribute to the diagnostic categories and may have a direct or indirect relation to the interaction and specifically linguistics measures.

For one area of developmental disorders, Szatmari et al. (1989) propose a distinction between autism and Asperger's syndrome as one of severity. The Asperger's cases like the autistics have impairments in relating to peers. The impairments include both (a) social features: only approaching others to have needs met, clumsy social approaches one-sided interactions, difficulty sensing or being detached from feelings of others; and (b) specific communication features: limited use of facial expressions and gestures, talking too little or too much, abnormalities in inflection (either flat or exaggerated), or repeating out of context. In addition to these social and communicative features, signs of more basic cognitive and neurological deficits set the autistics apart as being more seriously impaired. These features for the autistics include more bizarre occupations, motor stereotypies, insistence on sameness, and less imaginative play. The detailed analysis of language use by these two groups and with a socially withdrawn control group adds another dimension to the necessarily multifaceted definition and diagnostic criteria of the groups. The linguistic analysis can help to understand the coherence of the syndrome with respect to the social and cognitive dimensions involved. If the groups are distinct in terms of severity, then the linguistic analysis should reflect such a difference. The linguistic analysis can also explore the link between the early social difficulties and etiology and perhaps also with cognitive processing, treatment, and outcome (see Howlin & Rutter, 1989).

The work of Szatmari and colleagues on Asperger's syndrome and autism fits into the model of Prizant and Wetherby (1987) in considering a range of variables that interact in the definition of autism. Diagnostic criteria may not be independent of each other, and the coherence of a disorder is understandable in terms of the interacting factors that produce a certain cluster of signs. Prizant and Wetherby (1987) find that the intents of the autistic speakers are homogeneous and are related to social dysfunction. The work of Szatmari on autism and Asperger's syndrome also suggests an interaction of different kinds of deficits. Specific problems in intonation in the Asperger's cases may influence the reactions of others and so contribute to even more atypical interactions. Furthermore, the bizarre behaviors of Asperger's cases, in contrast to socially withdrawn controls, may also contribute to specific and atypical interactions from others. Thus, some findings from apparently distinct realms may be related and help explain the coherence of a diagnostic category.

Relationships between language and nonlanguage factors also emerge from the work of Sudhalter et al. (1990) in their study of autistic and retarded boys. They find that the retarded group with fragile X syndrome, unlike the autistics, adds new information in conversation, but also produce more perseverative deviant language. Sudhalter et al. (1990) suggest that the deviant language of the fragile (x) group is related to a series of nonlinguistic cognitive difficulties, such as auditory reception, auditory sequential memory, hyperactivity, and concentration, and to general discomfort in social interaction evident in measures of social gaze.

The relations among age, IQ, and language are explored by Landry and Loveland (1989) for autistic and language-delayed children. The measures were attention-directing language that included both speech role (I, you, etc.) and nonspeech role (here, there, this, that) exophoric reference and attention-directing gestures including looking, pointing, showing, and touching. The groups of subjects were autistic children aged from 4:10 to 12:11, normal controls matched for language level and nonverbal mental age. In general, the autistic group used less attention-directing behavior than the other groups and showed less variation across communicative contexts. In terms of the question of diagnostic groups, Landry and Loveland show that the attention-directing behaviors do not vary simply as a function of age or nonverbal IQ. The developmentally language-delayed group was similar to the autistic group on IQ and chronological age. The communication pattern of the autistics, then, is separable from the age and IQ of the subjects. In comparing Asperger's and autistic cases, a further variable is introduced. The asocial features and the bizarre behavior of autism are also found in the Asperger's cases, but without the intellectual impairment found in autism.

The diagnostic categories in developmental disorders are subject to revision from the psychiatric perspective (as the changes from DSM III [American Psychiatric Association 1980] to DSM III - R [American Psychiatric Association, 1987] indicate). These categories are based in part on communication and clinically evaluated language factors, but also strive to attain coherence in history, course, treatment, and outcome. Detailed linguistic exploration of the categories permits the study of specific signs and parameters within and across diagnostic categories. Language variables can be related separately to age, IQ, and measures of social functioning. Taken as unanalyzed entities, the distinctness of the diagnostic categories can be tested by specific language variables. The differences in functioning from one diagnostic category to another can thus be specified. Diagnostic category A may be distinct from B on one linguistic measure but not another. The measures that show such a distinction between categories then become important in understanding the possible deficits—linguistic and non-linguistic—that combine to produce the clinical coherence of the diagnostic category.

Functional Development of Language

There is a body of recent research on the functional aspects of language development and on the particular functional difficulties of the developmentally disordered. These studies are relevant to the specific linguistic analysis of the speech of Asperger's, autistic, and socially withdrawn subjects that we have investigated. The review of empirical language studies first deals with general language development in order to outline some of the abilities that speakers must acquire. Second, specific studies of developmental disorders are discussed.

von Tetzchner et al. (1989) present a number of studies dealing with the interactions of normal and impaired children. These studies help to outline the normal development of interaction: What does it take to interact as a child? Schaffer (1989) investigated joint involvement episodes, "encounters between two (or more) individuals in which the participants pay joint attention to, and jointly act upon, some specific topic." In reviewing the literature on adult-child interaction, Schaffer notes the common opinion that language emerges from dyadic settings in which there is negotiation of meaning in frequent verbal interactions. Although Schaffer cautions that many studies have not adequately sampled a range of interactions and have not considered the nonverbal context and motivation, the pervasive impairment in interaction found in autistic and Asperger's syndrome will have strong influences on language development, even if the precise social correlates of particular language problems are hard to isolate.

Three studies show the importance of both verbal and nonverbal interaction in the development of language. Martinsen and Smith (1989) studied vocalization and gesture longitudinally as the first words emerge. They found that vocalization-gesture combinations appear just prior to the first words. The combinations are also generally more often followed by parental reactions than either vocalizations or gestures alone. They conclude that the combinations of vocalizations and gestures are perceptually more salient and therefore more interpretable than either alone. The particular kind of parental response is also related to the child's communication system. Combinations or gestures alone are more often followed by parental answers with names and pronouns compared to vocalization alone. These findings support the importance of interaction in providing the context for the development of language. A child who does not interact in a typical way from an early age is likely to be reacted to atypically. There is no detailed knowledge about the very early interactions of the developmentally disordered (it would be difficult to identify the cases at such an early age). However, differences in early interaction would be compatible with differences observed later in pronoun usage and exophoric references. Exophoric reference is the verbal equivalent of gesture in the Martinsen and Smith (1989) study. Anaphoric pronouns and exophoric reference help signal speakers that they are sharing a common reality. If interactions do not take place because of a language difficulty or social withdrawal, then the two-way development of interaction and the accompanying language and social skills will be further impaired.

In a related study, Martinsen and von Tetzchner (1989) investigated imitations in the language of mothers and their children. They found that mothers follow adult conventions in using imitation to confirm topics and understanding. Through such interactions, the child learns first a general dialogue strategy of imitating known words from the previous utterance of the adult and later topic-comment structures in which imitation serves adultlike functions of confirming topic. Again, the empirical study of conversation shows the importance of appropriate social interaction. Without interaction, or with odd early verbal participation in conversation, the normal development of functions of imitation and of associated turn-taking conventions will not develop. Martinsen and von Tetzchner also speculate that the development of syntax itself could be affected by the imitation skills of young children.

As outlined above, Smith (1989) investigated the use of directives by mothers of normal and retarded children. The relative infrequency of cues from the retarded children or perhaps just the expectation by parents that there are fewer such cues is related to the directive behavior of parents. Thus, specific functional uses of language by parents are relatable to the developmental status of their children. The precise reason for the parents' differential use of directives is not clear. However, the bizarre behavior of Asperger's syndrome compared to socially withdrawn children without such behavior can be considered a factor in early interaction that could affect the use of directives and, more broadly, the mutual influence on the speakers' conversation.

The language of autistic children has been studied from a number of functional perspectives. These studies provide information on quite a range of differences between autistic and nonautistic children. One area of study is the autistics' relation to others and to objects. Prizant and Wetherby (1987) in their review of communicative intent found that autistics have a more limited range of intents. Their intents were to do with regulating adult behavior for specific purposes (to change the environment), but they rarely used language to attract attention to themselves or to objects. Their language was thus instrumental with respect to other speakers. Prizant and Wetherby saw the autistics' use of language as serving instrumental but nonsocial ends. The autistics seek to regulate their environment rather than to interact by commenting on the interaction with others, labeling objects for others, or requesting information. Prizant and Wetherby suggest that social involvement increases as autistics develop, whereas normal children exhibit a wide range of intents early in language development.

Autistics' directing of attention is a clear measure of interaction with others. Landry and Loveland (1989) study of the language and gestures used for directing parallels an observation of Prizant and Wetherby that autistics show less variation in language use. The data of Landry and Loveland show a narrower variation across communicative contexts, implicating a deficit in sensitivity to social circumstances as well as a simple language deficit. The autistics are poor at using attention-directing behavior, but they are equally poor in both spontaneous and adult-directed contexts.

By training parents to interact more with autistic children, Howlin and Rutter (1989) showed how kinds of interaction are associated with changes in some areas of language, but not in others. Parents were trained to use questions, repetitions, and expansions of child language. The intervention lasted 18 months. In unstructured interactions in the home, parents did change their communicative style by increasing the number of utterances to the child, the proportion of language-directed utterances, and by decreasing incomprehensible utterances. The autistic children showed improvement in frequency of utterances, in inflectional morphemes, and in closed class words. These changes reflect an increase in the meaning options available. However, the use of phrase speech (a heterogeneous category including complex and simple sentences, verb, noun, and prepositional phrases) did not change. Over 18 months the speech of the autistics became more communicative, more frequent, and less echolalic. In general, the children's speech paralleled the communicative changes in the parents' speech. The encouragement of social interaction is associated with better communication by autistics. Howlin and Rutter (1989) found no relationship, however, between the children's use of "grammatically correct phrase speech" and mother speech. This finding is further evidence that autistics do not improve grammatical structures. Another finding that corroborates the importance of specifically interactional activity is the lack of relationship between the total amount of speech by mothers and changes in the children; however, there was a close relationship between "mothers' use of directed remarks and children's use of communicative speech."

Another empirical study looked at the conversation of autistic children and adults with respect to their direct interaction through language. Oshima-Takane and Benaroya (1989) examined the pronoun usage in French of autistics in games with adult experimenters. They found that learning of the second-person pronoun (toi) required attention by the autistic to the usage directed to another person. On the other hand, the first-person pronoun (moi) could be successfully imitated without the observation of its use being directed to a third speaker. Their study helps to specify the role of interaction in the learning of language by autistics. The data indicate that the learning of social roles in speech and the linguistic mapping of those roles may need both direct experience as a linguistically encoded interactant (the use of first-person pronouns) and experience as a noninteractant of how others assign themselves linguistic identities (the use of second-person pronouns when the autistic subject is not directly involved).

As well as measures of direct social involvement in conversation, autistics have been studied in terms of repetition, topic shifts, and echolalia. As outlined above, Sudhalter et al.

(1990) found that autistic speakers repeated more than the retarded control groups. They also showed little topic maintenance. This finding contradicts the data in Fine (1988, in press-a) that show a high-functioning autistic speaker maintains topics considerably beyond an Asperger's case. The deficit in the autistics in Sudhalter et al. (1990) is in immediate and delayed echolalia. This finding concerning echolalia can be related to the association between echolalia and comprehension (Roberts, 1989). Roberts found that echolalia accompanied by other stretches of language ("mitigated echolalia") is associated with better comprehension. The echolalia may be providing linguistic material when comprehension or other abilities that normally contribute to topics or conversational maintenance are impaired.

This review of functional language characteristics in autistic speech indicates a number of areas of specific weakness. Autistics show atypicalities in how they interact with other speakers and the objects around them. These atypicalities are directly reflected in the use of language that encodes or refers to speakers, their social roles, and the topics that speakers attempt to mutually maintain. Repetition and echolalia have been regarded as highly typical of autistic speech, but can also be seen in a broader framework of the social and cognitive deficits of autistics. Prizant and Wetherby (1987) and others have argued that echolalia is often communicative and therefore a part of a system, not just a deviation from the normal child or adult system.

The analysis of cohesion in the conversations of Asperger's and autistic cases is a systematic way of studying the socially relevant use of language. In particular, the study of speech-role exophora (references to the speaker and addressee in a conversation), nonspeech-role exophora (direct reference to objects accessible to the speaker and listener), personal reference, and lexical cohesion show the ways that different groups of speakers build up socially interpretable language.

The research on the language of autistics and related syndromes repeatedly points to social and interactional areas. Deficits found in specific social circumstances are associated with specific atypicalities in language. The autistic spectrum includes retardation in the central cases, but not in Asperger's syndrome. Thus, there is a cognitive factor that interacts with the social impairment largely taken to be central to the spectrum. A way to study effects in social interaction is by examining how speakers signal the continuity of discourse participants in conversation. The continuity of participants is important in terms of a unity of text and interpretability of the speaker. If a speaker shifts participants frequently, it changes, at least in local ways, what the speaker is talking about as well as requiring the hearer to follow the changes. The continuity of participants may also involve implying links from one mention of a participant to another. The methods of continuing participants can vary in quality, and this variation is a means of examining how speakers construct socially interpretable messages in conversation. Lexical repetition, endophoric reference, implication, and imprecise references suggest different levels of certainty in continuity of participants, but also different assumptions about the knowledge shared by interlocutors and the ability of hearers to interpret the discourse. Interpretability is a concept that encompasses continuity of participants, continuity of references, and the relation of language to the situation of the speech event. The unity of conversation is dependent also on the use of the nonverbal situation. Participants from the nonverbal situation, largely the speaker and addressee, may be drawn on in speech. The identity and coding of these participants and their relation to participants from the verbal context further characterizes how a speaker manages the specifically social elements in conversation. Behavioral factors such as social withdrawal should be exhibited in linguistic systems that select and continue the identity of participants in social interaction. Without such continuity the interaction itself is in jeopardy. There can be a difficulty in understanding a speaker and in agreeing on and building a common reality.

ANALYSES OF TWO CONVERSATIONS

The following detailed analysis of two conversations from psychiatric patients examines how cohesion is used to present information by two different speakers. These speakers are representative of different psychiatric syndromes, and the analysis of how they use cohesion and other parts of the textual metafunction and language in general illuminates the value of those linguistic systems and their relation to each other as well as the syndromes themselves.

The analysis first describes the subjects and the psychiatric syndromes. Then the conversations are analyzed. The first set of analyses deals with the overall consistency of the conversations in terms of field, mode and tenor. The specific focus is on how this consistency is achieved or not achieved. The second set of analyses deals with how information is presented in the two conversations by cohesion. Particular attention is placed on the role of nominal groups.

Subjects

The conversations are from an 18-year-old high-functioning autistic subject (HFA) and from a 14-year-old subject with Asperger's Syndrome (AS). Both subjects were male. Szatmari, Bremner, and Nagy (1989) described these two disorders, and it is their description that follows below that was used to classify the subjects. AS and autistics have similar social impairments with peers, but autistic subjects also show a lack of social responsiveness to the primary caregiver, deviant language development, such as echolalia and pronoun reversal and lack of imaginative play. Szatmari et al. (1989) suggest that AS and autism differ primarily on severity. The AS subject in this study was anxious and showed some psychotic symptoms (including verbal hallucinations) and was judged to be more impaired at the time of testing than the HFA subject. The data examined are 10-minute interviews the two subjects had with a familiar psychiatrist while they were in-patients in the psychiatric ward of a general hospital.

Field

The first set of analyses concerns the consistency of field, interpersonal, and textual text-semantic relations (see Lemke, in press). Texts usually exhibit a consistency in what they are talking about. "Field" has been used to characterize what a text is about (see an early review in Gregory, 1967). More precise formulations of field derive from the experiences of speakers in social contexts and the associated semiological options in situation (Gregory, 1988), and even more specifically, from the orientations to relevant institutions and objects (Ventola, 1987). Field thus reflects the subject matter of a text. Consistency of field contributes to texture by signaling semantic continuity and therefore the presence of one semantic unit of text. One clause is related to another in what is being said, and the relationship (either a signal of continuity or a signal of some kind of change) is generally evident in the text. Lemke's textproduction perspective is dynamic in that it accounts for the meaning of an utterance as it occurs in context, rather than after the fact in terms of the complete context before and after the utterance. Lemke understands that texts follow typical structural organizations reflecting what is typically said. The relationships between stretches of language, and in particular, clause complexes reflect the dynamic weightings of selection probabilities. Earlier selections may condition the probabilities of later selections, and thus the weightings are reported as "dynamically" set. Lemke sees the reweightings of selection probabilities as deriving from the social function of language. In terms of field, consistency is realized by the selections made from a number of systems in the context of each other as the conversation develops. Following Lemke and the earlier definitions of field, this consistency ultimately derives from the social, institutional orientation of the stretches of language. Field does not emerge in text as an abstract quality of the text. Field is constructed in an ongoing negotiation of the social function of the text. Field may broaden or narrow as speakers mutually accept the redefinition of range of meanings that are socially relevant. This dynamic perspective will be used in examining the consistency and changes in field.

The first case to be examined is the 18-year-old high-functioning autistic called WB (the full transcript is in Appendix A of this chapter). The interviewer asks, "Now, how long have you been seeing ah a doctor at X (name of the hospital)?" WB answers, "Well. I've been seeing such doctors on and off all my life because, my mother to make a long story short has always had concerns for me because of the fact that in my earlier childhood I had an unusual life I lived with my grandparents without a father." The interviewer's wh-question is quite specific and asks for information about a time period that starts some time in the past and continues to the present. WB generalizes the participant from the interviewer's "a doctor" to "such doctors." "A doctor" indicates a singular nonspecific nominal group (Halliday, 1985). "Such doctors" signals that the same class (of doctors) is being spoken about, but the whole class is now being considered. The lexical repetition of "doctors" contributes to the continuity of the field and adds to the link established by "such." "Such doctors" represents two links compared to "such people," which is only weakly linked to the field instantiated by "doctors." It is not only the identity of the participant (see Martin, forthcoming) that is widened by WB. His answer applies to the time period "all of my life" rather than the period in the current hospital. In terms of the information that was requested, WB uses causal conjunction to offer information that was not requested. The interviewer requests a time period, but WB uses "because" twice to give reasons for what he says. In fact, the second "because" is embedded within the first causal statement introduced by "because." WB moves further from the requested information by reentering the conjunction system and rechoosing "because." A choice of "and," for example, would merely conjoin the two clauses, rather than offer a cause of a state of affairs that is itself to be treated as a cause for the clause, "I've been seeing such doctors on and off all my life." The speaker is moving to a more general concept of field both in the structure of the nominal group and in the use of causal conjunction.

In WB's following turn, he continues to give further background, but the relevance of the information to his earlier turn, and especially to the interviewer's original question, must be built by the interlocutor. WB's turn is:

> At the age of seven my mother by that time had remarried and we moved into a house with my adopted father and ever since then I've been trying my best to get on the so to speak usual track.

In terms of time, WB specifies a time later than the time specified in the prior turn—"at the age of seven"—but the relevance of this time frame to the original question is not stated. In WB's first turn after the interviewer's question, WB extended the time frame from the time in the hospital to "all my life" and then "in my earlier childhood" to both periods of time. In the second turn, WB starts with a punctual specification of time. Later, in the turn WB creates a time period with the complex conjunction "and ever since then." None of these time references apply to the interviewer's question. On the other hand, WB introduces ideational material that will be followed up in his later talk. For example, WB considers a field of self-improvement to be relevant to the interaction. The need for improvement enters in his first postquestion turn through the "concerns" of his mother and his "unusual" life. In the second turn the field is continued by "trying my best" and "the so to speak usual track." Later in the conversation WB signals that the same field is continuing by "caught up" (turns 10, 130-twice), "normal person" (turns 10, 12), "in every respect" (10), "change my self-consciousness" (18), "to be much less self-conscious" (20), and "to not be so self-critical about things" (22).

There are a number of other examples of WB responding to a question from the interviewer and then broadening the field. In turn 41 the interviewer asks about WB's interests. WB responds with two distinct fields (broadcasting and Christianity).

41 - I: I see well what do you like what are you interested in.

42 - WB: Well I'm interested in Christianity

43 - I: um hmm

44 - WB:I find that to be very intriguing I'm interested in the aspect of radio and television broadcasting.

From the remainder of the conversation it is clear that "the aspect of radio and television broadcasting" is not associated with the field of Christianity, although such an interpretation is possible from turn 44. The difficulty in interpreting turn 44 derives from the use of the definite and apparently anaphoric "the." The listener assumes a cohesive link between this nominal group and "Christianity" in turn 42. Such a link is made quite plausible since "that" in turn 44 clearly links back to "Christianity" (turn 42). However, "Christianity" and "radio and television broadcasting" do not overlap as fields in the remainder of the conversation. Each field is spoken about separately. WB has not established the appropriate textual connection in turn 44. Once the field of broadcasting is established and then widened to electronic equipment, WB continues the field for about 20 turns (46–66).

Another example of WB widening a field of discourse occurs in response to the interviewer's change of field from electronic equipment to Christianity (turn 77).

77 - I: You're I see now what about Christianity how do you pursue that interest?

78 - WB: Well I go to church once every Sunday that's my major time out of the household.

WB answers the interviewer's question but also comments on the answer and broadens the field to time out of the household. However, in succeeding turns it is the narrower field of Christianity that is continued.

In constructing fields, WB uses both simple lexical means and a variety of other cohesive devices. Turn 82, for example, includes two uses of the personal reference item "it," the demonstrative reference "that advice," and the grammatical parallelism of "hard to put into practice," "hard to accept." Furthermore, in turn 84 WB uses the nominal substitute "ones" to link back to the interviewer's question.

82 - WB: well scripture gives you sort of an owner's manual approach to living it gives you practical solutions to your daily problems now sometimes that advice is hard to put into practice hard to accept but it does work.

83 - I: um hmm what parts of scriptures are you reading these days?

84 - WB: The New Testament ones. . . .

In the later part of the conversations, WB combines fields that have been present in the conversation. This combining is done in response to the interviewer's questions that tend to change the field or subfield. In turn 141 the interviewer apparently tries to change the field from WB's father to school. In his response, WB continues the field of schooling and combines it with that of technology which has dominated earlier parts of the conversation (turns 44–64).

141 - I: I see hmm hmm um what do you like best in school in what kind of things do you enjoy doing there

142 - WB: Well I like using technology such as the school's VCR

143 - I: Um hmm

144 - WB: I like using audio and video tapes for my education because I like learning from those sources.

A similar combining of material from different subfields occurs in turn 146 in response to another question from the interviewer.

145 - I: I see what do you read besides the scriptures

146 - WB: I'm not into non-fiction well I'll start that again I'm not into

fiction because it doesn't interest me. At school I read novels because it's part of the course but I don't do so voluntarily.

The interviewer changes the subfield from school and technology to reading in general. However, WB answers the question by relating reading to school, both subfields that have been present in the conversation.

WB establishes and continues a number of fields. He tends to broaden fields presented by the interviewer and to combine fields present in the conversation. An interesting element of WB's consisting and changing of fields is that the changes occur in response to changes in field initiated by the interviewer. There is thus a point of adjustment by interviewer and patient as the field is changed.

In contrast to WB, the Asperger syndrome patient JP is much less talkative. JP shows consistency of field but without the shifts shown by WB. Furthermore, JP does not show a shifting of field in reaction to questions from the interviewer. Two questions by the interviewer are found in turns 9 and 19. In response to the interviewer's question in turn 9, JP answers directly without changing fields and continues for four turns.

9 - I: Well tell me what's been happening since?

10 - JP: First I was in this class I started out at Chedoke School

11 - I: Um hmm

12 - JP: In Mr. Anderson's class but

13 - I: Ya

14 - JP: I found it difficult to and the kids were picking on me they were behavior kids they were kind of disturbed.

15 - I: Ya

16 - JP: And I didn't belong there now I've moved to another school it's Westwood and it's a I lot happier there

17 - I: Um hmm

18 - JP: Cause all the kids in that that school ah ah all everybody in that school including the kids are welcoming me to be part of that school.

Similarly in response to the interviewer's next question, JP gives specific information without shifting the field.

19 - I: That's good that's good and what are you doing there hm hm

20 - JP: Well sometimes me and Miss T (name of teacher) go shopping

21 - I: Um hmm

22 - JP: And I do some math tests and spelling tests and we have lunch in the classroom at lunchtime and ah we do the dishes after . . . I always play baseball with the kids outside at recess.

Thus, even though JP is less voluble than WB, when JP does speak at some length and in response to the interviewer, he does not shift fields as was typical for WB, the high-functioning autistic subject.

The consistency of field in JP's speech is such that JP ignores a direct question from the interviewer that would change the subfield. The speakers have been discussing JP's friends at school when the interviewer asks about JP's grade at school in turn 31. In the adjacent turn 32, JP continues the prior field of friends and ignores the question of the interviewer.

31 - I: Are you in any specific grade right now

32 - JP: No I made a few friends there too at Westwood.

Both the high-functioning autistic and the speaker with Asperger's syndrome show consistency of field in the conversations. However, there are clear differences in the kind of consistency. WB, the autistic, tends to extend the field presented by the interviewer and to combine fields once they are established in the conversation. JP, the speaker with Asperger's syndrome, continues a narrow field and even overrides an attempt to change the field. As pointed out by Lemke (in press) and detailed empirically by Fine (in press-a), the dynamic nature of the construction of text must be considered as well as a synoptic account of the linguistic systems. In the analysis of consistency of field it was seen that the reaction to the interviewer was a point where one speaker typically altered the definition of the field, whereas the other speaker showed considerable consistency. The cohesion set up within and across speakers is inherently a response to the language that has already been spoken. These differences can be accounted for by a dynamic system that specifies for each speaker what choices are likely to be made at a certain point in the creation of text. Speakers and, likely, classes of speakers will differ in how they construct conversation as conversation develops.

Interpersonal

As well as a consistency in field, text also exhibits a consistency in the interpersonal semantic relations expressed. The interpersonal component of language involves the choice of speech functions (including mood and intonation), the status of and syntactic choices in the turn, social distance, and the speaker's assessment and attitude to what he is saying (Gregory, 1988). The two speakers show rather different interpersonal orientations, but are quite consistent within their own speech. In general WB uses considerable numbers of modality markers and discourse adjuncts, whereas JP rarely uses modals and uses instead adjuncts of frequency. In addition, WB's interpersonal consistency is related to the interaction with the interviewer.

WB is generally hesitant to commit himself strongly to the statement he is making. This hesitancy is evident in the verbal group itself by the choice of modals: "it might be" (turn 14), "it might just be" (14), "I'd" (20, 22), "that I might make" (28), "which is going" (30), "I couldn't" (54), "I might" (54), and "seems" (stressed) (112). It is also expressed by adjuncts and within nominal and adjectival groups. Adjuncts such as "quite sure" (10), "really" (12), "just" (14), "really" (14), "so to speak" (30), "as much" (38), and "let's say" (60) have the effect of hedging the speaker's commitment. Similarly, nominal groups such as "somewhat of a difficult question" (10) and "a so-called normal person" (10) also encode the hesitancy. There are cases without this rather consistent pattern of interpersonal hedging. In turn 36, WB answers without hedging "No I haven't" to a question that asks for a simple fact. From later turns it is clear that WB has what he presents as adequate reasons for his behavior. In answer to another question of fact (turn 93: "What is your church?"), WB answers simply: "Covenant Belt State Christian Centre SCC." In this case little was at stake interpersonally, and WB did not include his typical coding of interpersonal hesitancy.

There seem to be changes in the interpersonal consistency as the relationship between patient and interviewer changes. From turns 42 to 52, WB uses no modal verbs and few markers of interpersonal hesitancy. However, turn 53 of the interviewer ("How much do you understand of the actual technology?") is apparently heard by WB as a challenge to his position. His answer, turn 54 ("Well I couldn't actually repair a TV set because I haven't gone that far in knowledge I might never ever do so") has two modal verbs, the adverb "actually" and the causal conjunction "because," all of which serve to mitigate WB's position. Thus, WB is sensitive to the movement of the conversation and chooses options that are consistent with his overall interpersonal orientation, but are also sensitive to the particular interpersonal demands of special points in the conversation.

A further consistent marker of WB interpersonal hesitancy is his use of "well" to start responses to wh-questions. Although the surface pattern is to start response to wh-questions with "well," there is an even more consistent pattern. Some questions request information without using the canonical wh-question form. The cases are turn 17 "is there anything about that you would like to ah change?", turn 125 "Maybe you could describe him [your father]," and turn 153 "Tell me one [novel] you enjoyed reading at least to some extent." The answers to these three turns begin with "alright" (18), "alright" (126), and "I'd say" (156). That is, in each case of a request for information, WB starts the response with a marker of preparing the answer ("well") or conceding that he is prepared to answer ("alright," "I'd say"). Furthermore, WB distinguishes between the canonical wh-questions, which are responded to with "well" and the noncanonical request forms. That is, the interpersonal relationship encoded in the speech function of the interviewer is responded to by a typical patterning. In fact, WB consistently distinguishes the different interpersonal values of canonical and noncanonical requests.

The patterning claimed above has some minor exceptions that are themselves illuminating. In turn 82 the interviewer embeds a wh-question within a yes-no question: "You said you find it fascinating can you give me an idea of what is it that you find fascinating about Christianity." WB treats this turn as a wh-question and responds with a turn beginning with "well." The ungrammaticality of the "is it" predicator-subject order may have contributed to treating the wh-clause as the operative interpersonal element of the interviewer's turn. Again we see considerable sensitivity of WB's speech to the form and function of the language of the interviewer.

Another apparent exception to WB's patterning of interpersonal relations is found in turns 93 and 94:

93 - I: What is your ah ah church ah are you what

94 - WB: State Convenant Belt State Christian Center SCC.

In this case the answer is clear, with no interpersonal face at risk for WB. This particular wh-question does not involve determining how the interviewer should be answered and how much information should be placed at risk.

A third apparent exception to WB's use of "well" in response to wh-questions occurs in turns 145 and 146:

145 - I: I see what do you read besides the scriptures

146 - WB: I'm not into nonfiction well I'll start that again I'm not into fiction because it just doesn't interest me. . . .

WB does not start his response with the typical "well." However, in just this case he starts with an incorrect statement. This example indicates that the "well" is a helpful hesitation marker that gains time for WB when faced with a question that requires ideational information.

JP, the subject with Asperger's syndrome, also shows a consistency in interpersonal semantic relations. However, these semantic relations are quite different from those used by WB, the autistic speaker. Generally, JP uses no modality within the verbal group. As a rule he does not explicitly signal his judgments about what he is saying. Put another way, JP does not indicate the levels of certainty in what he is saying and so does not allow the hearer to judge the reliability of the speaker's statements. Without a pattern of modality it is difficult to build trust in the speaker since all statements seem to have the same degree of reliability—unusual for most members of a speech community. English has a developed system of modality, and a speaker who rarely uses it would seem to violate the rules of expressing uncertainty when uncertainty is present. JP does qualify his statements, but this tends to be done by adjuncts of frequency rather than adjuncts of probability (see Halliday, 1985). "Sometimes" as an adjunct of frequency is used in turns 20, 58, and 97. The only apparent indications of modality occur after direct requests for feelings or opinions. Three such cases are examined individually.

The interviewer asks JP:

55 - I: What are the things you enjoy the most? You know the things you look forward to.

In response to this direct request for preferences, JP used the verbal groups "used to go to," "we'd go swimming," "we'd go to," and "we're gonna do" among others. These verbal groups contain an element that could be modal or merely temporal. In the context of the entire turn, these apparent modals should be treated as carriers of temporal marking and so be part of the ideational rather than the interpersonal function. They do not assist the hearer in discovering JP's attitude to the statements he is making. In this case, then, the direct request for preferences and thus some interpersonal meaning results in forms that on the surface could be modals but are in fact being used to code temporal distinctions within the ideational component of language.

A second example of a point in the dialogue that produces some element of modality in JP's speech occurs in turn 124 when the interviewer asks:

124 - I: Just these voices once in a while? What do you think they are?

125 - JP: I think they're I hear them they remind me of the people on soap operas the a they talk gossip.

In turn 124, as with turn 55, JP is asked a personal opinion. Typically, such opinions have some modal element to convey the speaker's attitude toward the ideational component. In turn 125, JP starts to give such attitudinal information by using the verb "think." However, the clause is aborted and the turn is completed with statements of fact that again avoid signals of speaker attitude or commitment. The interviewer's direct question invites a statement qualified in modality. However, the question is followed by a clause that starts to express modality but then is aborted in favor of clauses that express no interpersonal semantic relations—the typical pattern for this speaker.

A third example of a request for a personal assessment leads not to an attempt at modality but to a very specific response. In the context of a question about television the interviewer asks:

138 - I: And you have any favorite program then?

139 - JP: Oh ya *One Day at a Time*

There is little at risk in this question, and JP has a clear answer available. The minor clause, without tense, does not allow the expression of modality in the verbal group.

The three examples confirm the pattern that JP does not exploit the interpersonal function, except under strong constraints from the interviewer. Even under such constraints, the coding of interpersonal relations is ambiguous or aborted. Again, we see the importance of a dynamic view of the creation of text. The options available to speakers at certain points in conversation must be compared to the actual options chosen and the semantic relationship in the interpersonal function. Although both speakers have a consistency in interpersonal function and certain exceptions to the general pattern, even these exceptions should be interpreted in terms of the overall pattern for each speaker. The overall pattern of interpersonal meanings in fact explains the unusual and aborted uses.

Textual

The third kind of consistency of semantic relations in text according to Lemke (in press) is consistency in the textual function. As well as cohesion, the textual component includes the organization of the clause into given-new and theme-rheme segments. Textual consistency, then, is achieved by a combination of cohesion and other textual devices. As with interpersonal consistency, the two speakers achieve textual consistency in rather different ways. The comparison will start with WB, the high-functioning autistic.

WB uses a number of different kinds of themes that are coded both as given (the unmarked case) and new (marked themes). Themes that involve first-person speech-role references are common in both WB's and JP's dialogues. In WB's turn 6 there are a number of themes that all include first-person speech-role references.

6 - WB: Well I've been seeing such doctors on and off all my life because my mother to make a long story short has always had concerns for me because of the fact that in my earlier childhood I had an unusual life I lived with my grandparents without a father.

The sequence of themes "I," "my mother," "in my early childhood," "I," and "I" creates a consistency of what is treated as the "starting point of the message"—the gloss on the thematic position. Elsewhere in the conversation, anaphoric references occur in themes of clauses. In these cases, the function of theme, "the point of departure of the clause," and the text-forming character of cohesion are combined to encode that the speaker is speaking about what is knowable to the hearer from linguistic sources. For example, the anaphoric references in the following turns are within the clause themes and create continuity from clause to clause.

78 - WB: Well I go to church once every Sunday that's my major time out of the household

Anaphoric theme: that

82 - WB: Well scripture gives you sort of an owner's manual approach to living, it gives you practical solutions to your daily problems now sometimes that advice is hard to put into practice hard to accept but it does work

Anaphoric themes: it, it

96 - WB: That's at 350 Kenilworth Avenue North right by the Central Mall

Anaphoric theme: that

98 - WB: Um hmm it's a interdenominational church

Anaphoric theme: it

102 - WB: Different faiths, that's right

Anaphoric theme: that

In all these examples the theme combined with anaphoric reference creates continuity of text. Successive clauses depend on earlier clauses for their interpretation, and the text is consistent in how continuity is signaled. An exception to WB's use of first-person speech roles and anaphoric reference in themes is the use of generalized cohesion in turn 10:

10 - WB: Well it's a bit that's somewhat of a difficult question to ask . . . one I suppose is never quite sure whether or not he has caught up to a so-called normal person in every respect.

The use of "one" and "he" seems out of place since they do not set up cohesive links to earlier stretches of language, despite their thematic position and surface cohesive form.

In contrast to WB, there are few markers of specifically textual consistency in JP's speech. Overwhelmingly, JP uses themes of first-person speech roles. Thus, the consistency largely derives from the ideational consistency of the identity of the themes. This consistency is not generally created by the connection of one stretch of language to another. Rather, the consistency is in a repeated connection to the nonverbal situation. There are cases when JP uses anaphora in the themes of clauses. Turn 14 provides an example in which "the kids" is bridging anaphora to the mention of a class two turns earlier, and "they" is used twice to create links within the turn.

14 - JP: I found it difficult to and the kids were picking on me they were behavior kids they were kind of disturbed

Although JP is not voluble and there are therefore relatively few utterances with full theme-rheme structure, there is still a pattern of little exploitation of textual resources to create consistency in his speech.

Lemke proposes an organization of text semantics that mediates between social semiotic formations that indicate what is typically said and the selections from the lexicogrammar. Selections from the lexicogrammar realize the text semantics dynamically as conversation is built up by interlocutors. The review of the kinds of text-semantic relations proposed in Lemke (in press) has shown the two subjects to have rather different organizations of their text. For both subjects there is a consistency in field, interpersonal, and textual; however, the type and amount of signaling of the consistency varies. Patterns of semantic relations emerged for each subject, but there were also different conditioning factors associated with exceptions and subpatterns in the dialogues. Cohesion plays a role in establishing text-semantic relations, but this role is in the context of various lexicogrammatical systems.

PRESENTING AND CONTINUITY INFORMATION

The analysis of the two subjects will now turn to a series of specific questions about which information is presented and how it is presented in the interactive situation of conversation. The analyses focus on specific types of cohesion and the kinds of information that the cohesion presents.

Presenting and Presuming Information

The first specific question is whether the speakers use nominal groups to signal that information from elsewhere is needed to interpret the current nominal group. Martin (forthcoming) calls this the distinction between presuming and presenting nominal groups. Presenting nominal groups do not require further information for their interpretation. They present information as if for the first time. These categories are similar to the phoric-non-phoric distinction in Fine, Bartolucci, and Szatmari (1989) and Rochester and Martin (1979) where both sets of terms are used. The presenting-presuming distinction is cross-classified by the generic-specific distinction. Generic nominal groups specify that the "whole of some experiential class of participants is at stake rather than a specific manifestation of that class" (Martin, forthcoming). Thus, presenting and presuming nominal groups may be specific or generic. WB, the high-functioning autistic, uses the full range of presuming and presenting nominal groups, but by concentrating on certain options unusual messages are presented. JP, on the other hand, uses a more restricted range of nominal groups with a corresponding narrowing of the meanings typically conveyed.

WB's presentation of a variety of kinds of information is exemplified in turn 64:

64 - WB: But I make it a point to read owner's manuals and other helpful booklets to learn exactly how much you can do with a VCR.

Presenting generic nominal groups are: "owner's manuals" "a VCR." Presuming generic nominal groups are "you" and "other helpful booklets." The presuming specific nominal group is "I." WB uses a number of presuming generic nominal groups including "you" a number of times and the possessive in "your daily problems" (turn 82). These presuming generic nominal groups indicate that WB is making statements about classes of participants that he codes as already available or possibly available to the hearer. The presuming category establishes that the speaker can count on the hearer to establish a link to some information known by both speaker and hearer. WB not only uses language that presumes a specific participant is known to the hearer, but also that classes of participants are shared by speaker and hearer.

JP also uses presuming nominal groups, but they are

overwhelmingly specific. In the following example of turn 97, "I," "they," and "there" are specific and presuming.

97 - JP: I hear sometimes I hear voices talking they're not really there.

In turn 125 there are both presuming and presenting nominal groups. The presenting groups are generic ("the people on soaps operas," "soaps operas," "gossip"), whereas the presuming nominal groups are specific ("I," "they," "I," "them," "they," "me," "they"). JP does not significantly use presuming generic nominals (one example is possibly "the theater" in turn 56, although it is possible that this is also a specific presuming group). Thus, although the presuming-presenting distinction and the specific-generic distinction cross-classify, in fact the full range is not typically used by JP. His use of the systems indicates a narrowing of the kinds of meanings he presents to the hearer.

As well as a restriction in the kinds of meanings speakers use, we can investigate the effect of using some options with unusual frequency. As outlined, WB uses some presuming generic nominal groups. WB also uses presenting generic nominal groups with some regularity. In some instances there is a series of presenting nominals that together effect the communicative value of the speech. In turns 60 to 64 there are a number of presenting generics and specifics.

60 - WB: Some people are afraid to adjust the controls on let's say a VCR

61 - I: Um hmm

62 - WB: For fear of doing something wrong

63 - I: Um hmm

64 - WB: But I make it a point to read owner's manual and other helpful booklets to learn exactly how much you can do with a VCR.

The presenting generics are: "the controls on let's say a VCR," "a VCR," "owner's manuals," "owner," and "a VCR." The presenting specifies are: "some people," "something," and "a point to read owner's manuals." A similarly constructed stretch is found in turns 48 to 54. The density of these presenting nominals signals to the hearer that the speaker is not counting on the hearer to notice continuity of meaning from one participant to another. Furthermore, the speaker is using an unusual number of generic nominal groups which refer to whole classes of participants. Referring to classes of participants makes the speech sound somewhat vague and general. Such characteristics do not necessarily hamper communication. However, when they are used relatively frequently and in combination with other features (such as presenting) they may contribute to language that is less connected to its verbal and nonverbal context.

In contrast to WB, JP uses specific nominal groups almost to the exclusion of generics in some sections. Such a section is in turns 14 to 18:

14 - JP: I found it difficult to and the kids were picking on me they were behavior kids they were kind of disturbed

15 - I: Ya

16 - JP: And I didn't belong there now I've moved to another school it's Westwood and it's a I lot happier there

17 - I: Um Hmm

18 - JP: Cause all the kids in that that school ah ah all everybody in that school including the kids are welcoming me to be part of that school.

The specific groups are: "I," "it," "the kids," "me," "they," "they," "I," "I," "another school," "it," "Westwood," "it," "I." That is, nearly every nominal group is specific and most are also presuming. This use of nominal groups strongly creates semantic links to the verbal and nonverbal contexts and so is quite different from the pattern used by WB. The two speakers construct their contributions to conversation with different semantic relations. WB may seem vague by speaking in general terms, whereas JP clearly ties his language to the current verbal and nonverbal context.

To return to the question that was formulated, the analysis indicates that speakers do use nominal groups differently to signal that information from elsewhere is needed to interpret the current nominal group. Furthermore, what kind of information is presented (specific or generic) contributes to the overall interpretability of the speaker. The interpretability is not just a matter of successful or unsuccessful communication, but of the kind of interpretation that is necessary. Cohesion thus plays a role in the overall interpretability of nominal groups and must be seen as interacting with other systems operating in the nominal group.

Nominalizations

Nominalization creates nominal groups and participants that can then be linked to by cohesion. Martin (forthcoming) suggests further that nominalizations tend to be generic and abstract. These properties are investigated in comparing the speech of the high-functioning autistic and the Asperger's subject. The high-functioning autistic subject (WB) uses 12 nominalizations, while the Asperger uses none. Some of WB's nominalizations are as follows:

Turn 6 - my mother . . . has always had concerns for me (compare: was concerned about me)

38 - at this particular time (compare: now)

40 - I don't feel the need for . . . (compare: I don't need)

54 - to go into it as a job (compare: to go to work on it)

148 - I like gaining knowledge (compare: learning about).

Despite the nominalizations used by WB, they rarely contribute to forming chains of reference. Rather, participants are formed by nominalization, but the potential of using the nominal form so that it can be easily referred to in cohesive chains is not exploited. One example where the nominalization is continued in a referential chain occurs between turns 48 and 49;

48 - WB: and the aspects of signal broadcasting things of that sort that's my passion (compare: what I like)

49 - I: I see how do you pursue that passion what kind of things do you do?

In this example the referential link is not from the speaker of the nominalization back to that nominalization, but rather the referential link is established by the interlocutor. The nominalization's potential to create a referential link is not exploited by the subject but by the interviewer. The use of nominalizations by WB therefore does not directly contribute to the creation of cohesion. On the contrary, the establishment of more nominals not part of cohesive chains reduces the density of text-forming devices.

As well as being relatively uninvolved in cohesive chains, WB's nominalizations are abstract and so contribute to the vagueness of his speech. The following nominalizations in addition to those above are abstract:

54 - WB: I haven't gone that far in knowledge (compare: I don't know that much)

58 - WB: I can get maximum use out of it (compare: use it best)

148 - WB: I like gaining knowledge (compare: learning about)

156 - WB: lead as normal a life (compare: live as normally)

The nominalizations in WB's speech are largely uninvolved in cohesive chains and abstract. Nominalizations can be further characterized as specific or generic (Martin, forthcoming). Generic nominal groups indicate that the speaker is talking about "the whole of some experiential class of participants" rather than "a specific manifestation of that class." WB's nominalizations tend to be generic rather than specific as in turns 6, 54, 58, and 148 given above. The generic nature of WB's nominalizations further contributes to the vagueness of his speech.

Nominalizations are used in clause structure. How WB uses nominalizations in clauses reveals the tendencies in the meanings at stake in WB's conversation. Except for the field of Christianity, turn 80 and afterwards, WB rarely uses the subject "I" with verbs carrying substantive meaning. Rather, the "I" subject and first-person references in general are associated with nominalizations. For example, in turn 54 WB says "I haven't gone that far in knowledge." He combines the semantically relatively empty verbal group "haven't gone" with the nominalization "knowledge," instead of "I don't know that much." Similarly, in turns 40, 46, and 48, the subject or potential subject is "I" with a verb with little semantic content. It is the nominalization that encodes the ideational meaning from the verb in the unnominalized form.

40 - WB: I don't feel the need for (compare: I don't need)

44 - WB:... I'm interested in the aspect of radio and television broadcasting

45 - I: Um hmm

46 - WB: not the actual field itself to go into it as a job. . . . (compare: to work in it)

48 - WB: and the aspects of signal broadcasting things of that sort that's my passion (compare: that's what I like)

This use of first-person forms with nominals can be compared to the clauses WB forms with other participants as subjects. Clauses that refer to the speaker's father or to other participants in the subject slot do not have nominalizations. Note the clauses without first-person subjects in turns 110, 130, and 140.

110 - WB: Well my mother said that she loved my father and still does and I do believe that my father does look after my mother

130 - WB: my father was raised in a home where extreme mannerisms weren't taught. . . .

140 - WB: yes and my father while he was younger he practiced some sort of religion it was just that a religion rather than a faith I don't consider my religion if you want to call it that as true religion and it isn't a whole series of rituals which you have to carry out just for some sort of security measure.

The tendency to use nominalizations in clauses suggests a particular distribution of meanings and how they are expressed. When speaking about himself, WB uses wordings that tend to be vague. He uses nominalizations which tend also to be generic and abstract. However, in speaking about other participants, nominalization are not used, and correspondingly, more ideational meaning is found in other grammatical units such as verbal groups. The use of nominalizations associated with first-person subjects tends to reduce the density of cohesion, since the nominalizations are not part of cohesive chains that would signal continuity of meaning. The speaker's talk about himself tends not to be semantically connected and is furthermore difficult to follow, since it tends to be generic and abstract.

In clinical terms, the use of nominalizations by WB and his further typical choices of generic and abstract results in rather vague talk about himself, although not necessarily so when speaking about others. Although JB, the Asperger's subject, speaks much less than WB, the absence of nominalizations in JB's speech and their presence associated with first-person subjects in WB's speech contributes to the apparent directness of the Asperger's subject, JB, and the apparent indirectness and vagueness of WB, the high-functioning autistic. The use of nominalizations and the association of nominalization with clause subject helps to specify the difference in meanings typically expressed by the two speakers and how those meanings account for clinical judgments of the speakers.

Continuing Information: Reference

In analyzing nominalizations the issue of the continuity of participants was raised. When the autistic subject uses nominalizations, the participants so created are generally not referred to again. The following analyses look specifically at how the speakers signal the continuity of meaning. As well as the options in the cohesion system, word order which encodes the structures of theme and rheme, are considered. The theme of a clause is the element of clause structure placed first. Other clause elements then fall into the rheme. The theme is glossed as "the starting-point for the message; it is what the clause is going to be about" (Halliday, 1985, p. 39). The use of cohesion of different types in the theme results in a combination of meanings "this is what the clause is going to be about" from the encoding as theme and "retrieve meaning from a location I, the speaker, expect you the listener, to know about" from the meaning of reference.

In 15 out of 49 themes, JP uses endophoric reference. Although he speaks more, WB, the high-functioning autistic, uses endophoric reference in only 20 of 102 themes, a third less frequently than JP. The finding in this case is similar to the findings for groups of autistic and Aspergers in that autistics use comparatively less endophoric reference (see Chapter 3). Here we can see the specific effect of not using endophoric reference in themes. What is lost is the combination of the meanings of theme and endophoric reference. The point of departure of the clause is not linked by the available means of reference to what has already been verbally shared between speaker and listener. Examples of this use of anaphora to connect a theme to earlier language is found in turns 36 and 58 of JP's conversation.

35 - I: um hmm what about math

36 - JP: ya it's good too she always Miss Txxx gives me each night she gives me a piece a math page

58 - JP: and sometimes we'd jump on the trampoline and it's really fun.

In turn 35, "it" is an anaphoric reference item that creates a link to "math" in the prior turn. Since "it" is the theme of the clause, the meanings of anaphoric reference and theme are combined to let the listener know that the point of departure of the clause is something that is already available in the verbal environment. In turn 58, "it" functions similarly to a simultaneously link to "we'd jump on the trampoline" and uses that meaning to start the following clause. These two examples differ in that in turn 36 the endophoric link is within the speech of one speaker, but in turn 58 the link extends from one speaker to another. JP is exploiting the combination of endophoric reference and thematic position more frequently to display to the listener how the meanings in conversation are continuing.

Since speaker WB has relatively few themes with endophoric reference, it is useful to examine how WB's themes contribute to coherence. About 60% of WB's themes include speech role references to the speaker himself. Turns 42 and 44 contain examples of repeated uses of "I" as themes.

41 - I: I see well what do you like what are you interested in

41 - WB: Well I'm interested in Christianity

43 - I: Um hmm

44 - WB: I find that to be very intriguing I'm interested in the aspect of radio and television broadcasting.

Thus, there is considerable consistency and unity of meaning created by using speech-role references to the first person. JP places 79% of his first-person references in themes compared to 67% for WB. WB distributes first-person references more equally into themes and rhemes. Instead of using the theme and cohesion to signal a continuity of meaning, first-person references as theme signal to the listener that the identity of the speaker himself is the major factor relating what has gone before to the upcoming message.

Cohesion can be placed in the rheme as well as the theme. In the rheme, cohesion has a less clear role in signaling the continuity of meaning. The rheme stands in opposition to the theme as that part of the clause not chosen as what the clause is about. Typically, the rheme contains the new information in the clause and often some information that is coded as given or possibly given. JP, the Asperger subject, uses endophoric reference in the rhemes of clauses. In turn 16, the uses of "there" twice and "another school" are endophoric links in the rhemes that refer to earlier information. The words in capitals indicate the sentence stress, and thus the uses of "there" are coded as given. The stress on "another" is apparently contrastive and coded by the given-new system as new. Such a stress on a closed class item is marked and so represents an unusual combination of meanings. Closed class items and especially anaphoric ones are not likely to be encoded as new (see Fine, Bartolucci, & Szatmari, 1989). Here JP has created an unusual combination of meanings that WB rarely does. WB has little endophoric reference in rhemes, as he has little endophoric reference in general. However, the paucity of endophora in rhemes probably has less of a consequence for the hearer than the paucity in themes where the combination of endophora and thematic status plays a special role in signaling the continuity of meaning in conversation.

16 - JP: and I didn't BELONG there [Ch School] now I've moved to ANOTHER school it's W and it's a I lot HAPPIER there.

The interplay of endophoric reference and the given-new structure of clauses is not arbitrary in the conversations examined. Where there is a coinciding of the options to create texture, the interaction is facilitated. More marked combinations of options run against the expectations and interpretative strategies of hearers. A theme whose function is normally to indicate the starting point of a message can be constructed to be helpful to the hearer by signaling that some of the information is presumed to be available. Constructing themes that refer to first-speaker information creates unity in terms of the speaker's and hearer's shared understanding of the nonverbal situation (the identity of the speaker), but it is the continuity of meaning within the text that contributes to WB's more intact conversation.

Within the category of endophoric reference, personal reference specifically links participants in discourse. The third-person reference items "he," "she," "they," "it," "him," "his," and so on, set up links within the text that link participants by identifying information about number, gender, and case. The use of personal reference is thus a good indication of how participants are reidentified in a conversation and the presumptions a speaker can make about the hearer's ability to reidentify participants in context.

The autistic speaker, WB, tends not to signal the continuity of referents with personal reference. The personal reference chains are short and occasionally do not refer to participants. In turn 140, WB constructs a number of short personal reference links within the turn. There are no links beyond the turn. The personal reference items are italicized.

140 - WB: Yes and my father while *he* was younger *he* practiced some sort of religion *it* was just that a religion rather than a faith I don't consider my religion if you want to call *it* that as true religion and *it* isn't a whole series of rituals which you have to carry out just for some sort of security measure.

Rather than such personal reference, WB uses lexical repetition to sustain the identity of participants across speakers and across turns, although personal reference could be used unambiguously. In the following turns there is only one male participant introduced in the conversation, yet WB uses lexical repetition, except for two rather inappropriate uses of third-person reflexive pronouns in turn 114.

107 - I: Now you've been living with your adopted father for eleven years?

108 - WB: yes

109 - I: how do you think ah—what do you think your mother's choice has been was it was it a good choice or

110 - WB: well my mother said that she loved my father and still does and I do believe that my father does look after my mother

111 - I: um hmm

112 - WB: and as well my father seems to be a good father to my sisters

113 - I: um hmm

114 - WB: but I've never been able to have a strong relationship with my father because our beliefs our standpoints are widely varied as my father himself said himself and I are about as different as we can possibly be.

When WB uses items that apparently signal personal reference, closer examination shows that they are not used to create links that reidentify participants. Turns 10 to 14 provide examples.

9 - I: Yes well you seem to be ah fine person in what way do you feel you're not on the usual track?

10 - WB: well it's a but that's somewhat of a difficult question to ask one I suppose is never quite sure whether or not he has caught up to a so-called normal person in every respect

11 - I: Um hmm

12 - WB: cause very hard to examine the so-called normal person just exactly is normal no one can really say

13 - I: right very true

14 - WB: it might be a state of mind it might just be a minor deviation which really does not make any difference.

In turn 10, WB starts a clause with the personal reference item "it," but abandons the clause and restarts a clause with the demonstrative "that" referring to the interviewer's question and not to a participant. In the same turn "he" is used not anaphorically but generically for a class of individuals. In turn 14, "it" is used twice, apparently as a personal reference. However, the content of the clauses makes clear that the uses of "it" do not refer to "normal" or "the so-called normal person" of turn 12. Rather "it" refers to the absence of normality. Thus, even in cases that WB apparently uses personal reference, the effect is not to sustain participants in discourse.

Unlike WB, the Asperger's subject JP uses personal reference to sustain participants in discourse. He creates chains of more than one link both within and across turns. In turn 14, "they" is used twice to refer to and continue the identity of "the kids" from an earlier clause in the same turn.

14 - JP: I found it difficult to and the kids were picking on me they were behavior kids they were kind of disturbed.

Similarly, in turn 97, "they" refers to "voices" in the prior clause within the same turn. In turn 99, "they" continues the referential chain across turns from JP in turn 97 to the interviewer in turn 98.

97 - JP: I hear sometimes I hear voices talking they're not really there

98 - I: what do they say

99 - JP: they just have conversations.

The building of chains of more than one link in turns 14 and 97 to 99 demonstrates how JP sustains the presence of participant information in the conversation. By successively choosing to continue the identity of participants by personal reference, JP indicates that he is assuming that the hearer can interpret his message despite the retrieval operation necessary.

The placement of personal reference in the speech of JP further contributes to the sustaining of information in discourse. JP uses personal reference in themes to link to information in the rhemes of the interviewer's speech. This patterning is probably the most appropriate extension of information from one speaker to another. Examples of such uses of personal references are found in turns 36 and 99.

35 - I: um hmm what about math

36 - JP: ya it's good too. . . .

The "it" in turn 36 creates a link to "math" in the rheme of the interviewer's turn 35. JP uses the personal reference "it" to signal that he is continuing the identification of "math" introduced by the interviewer and, furthermore, making it the starting point of his own contribution. A similar use of personal reference in a theme is found in turn 99.

97 - JP: I hear sometimes I hear voices talking they're not really there

98 - I: what do they say?

99 - JP: they just have conversations.

"They" in turn 99 is in the theme of its clause and links back to "they" in the rheme of the interviewer's turn 98, which is itself part of a chain that starts with "voices" in turn 97. JP, unlike WB, contributes to these extended chains and, in particular, uses the personal reference as the starting point for the message of the upcoming clause. Turn 99 provides an example of personal reference in a theme creating a link to the rheme of a clause in the prior turn. The use of "they" in turn 97 is a similar use of personal reference to create a link to the rheme (specifically "voices") of a prior clause within the same turn. Thus, JP is using a personal reference to pick up and then add to information that is provided in either his own or the interviewer's contributions to the conversation. The semantic specificity of the personal reference (compared to demonstrative reference) helps create text that is easy to interpret and cohesive.

The analyses so far have shown JP's effective use of reference to continue participant information. However, JP also uses reference in an unclear way. A number of his nominal groups are ambiguous or require the listener to add information. In turn 58, JP uses "these" in a way that is ambiguous. It may be nonphoric, but if phoric it would signal a focal participant in the conversation (Martin, forthcoming). However, the skating rinks are not referred to again. The nominal group does not start a referential chain. "These" may also be taken as anaphoric, but without an available antecedent. In this case, the hearer must add an antecedent since the speaker does not provide sufficient information. The function of "these" is thus not clear, and one of the possible functions, as anaphora, is itself not properly realized.

58 - JP: and sometimes we'd jump on the trampoline and it's really fun but I also like roller skating and down to these big places roller skating.

In turn 125 there is some ambiguity in the use of "they" in the last clause. "They" could refer to either the "voices" that have been continued into turn 125 with the third-person plural personal reference items "they," "them," and "they" or to "the people on the soap operas." The chain of personal reference items linked to "voices" suggests that the final "they" is part of this chain. However, the proximity of "the people on the soap operas" suggests that nominal group is the antecedent. In this particular example, there is not a great difference in interpretation riding on the choice between the two possible antecedents. JP has fashioned a nominal group that in context leaves some slight doubt about its interpretation.

124 - I: Just these voices once in a while? what do you think they are?

125 - JP: I think they're I hear them the remind me of the people on soap operas the a they talk gossip.

In two other cases, JP starts to use a reference that is potentially unclear, but then he rewords the message. In turn 32, "there" is potentially ambiguous meaning either of the two schools that JP has attended. JP immediately eliminates the ambiguity by adding "at W," one of the two schools mentioned earlier.

31 - I: are you in any specific grade right now

32 - JP: no I made a few friends there too at W.

Similarly, in turn 36, the first use of "she" is without an antecedent and is uninterpretable at that point in the text. However, JP repairs the faulty personal reference by providing a fully identified nominal group "Miss T" right after the uninterpretable nominal group.

36 - JP: Ya it's good too she always Miss T gives me each night she gives me a piece a a math page.

The use of an unclear reference, but the elimination on some occasions, is consistent with the clinical description of JP. From Rochester and Martin (1979) and Bartolucci and Fine (1987) we know that unclear reference in interviews is produced by schizophrenics and especially thought-disordered schizophrenics. JP was diagnosed as having Asperger's syndrome, but also was judged to show mild psychosis. The association of some unclear reference with psychosis found in JP is thus consistent with findings from larger numbers of subjects. That JP stops to repair some unclear references indicates that he can take the hearer's needs into account, at least retroactively, if not in the first formulation of his talk. The autistic speaker, WB, is much more voluble than JP, but does not use any unclear reference. As Rochester and Martin (1979) demonstrated, unclear reference is disturbing to the hearer and accounts for judgments of thought disorder. The absence of unclear reference helps convey the impression that WB's speech is not impaired.

The analyses thus far have dealt with the kind and quality of referential links having to do with the interactive nature of dialogue. A speaker can create referential links to either his own earlier language or to the language of the interlocutor. In the following constructed example, the first "she" links back to "Mary" in the same turn. The second use of "she" links back two turns to speaker A's own speech. On the other hand, "there" links A's language to the antecedent "town" in B's language.

Cohesion thus may be within one speaker's language, either in one turn or across turns, or may be from one speaker's language to another speaker's language.

A: I saw Mary yesterday and she was cheerful.

B: Were you in town?

A: Yes, and she seems happiest there.

The balance of these two kinds of links indicates which semantic information is typically drawn on by the speaker. Is the speaker creating text across speakers, or is the texture principally built within the language of one speaker? Examinations of the balance of referring to one's own speech or to an interlocutor have shown that older children refer more to their own speech (Fine, 1978), and that referring to one's own speech characterizes the conversation of psychiatrically more healthy patients when compared to the more impaired (Fine, 1988). An index of referential links to the speaker's own language was created by dividing the number of links to the speaker's language by the number of links to the speaker's and interlocutor's language combined. The index is thus the number of links to the speaker's own language as a proportion of all referential links. JP and WB are very similar in their use of the two kinds of links (.88 and .89 respectively). Although the two speakers differ considerably in how they construct text and present meaning to be decoded by the hearer, they draw on information in the interactive verbal situation in an almost identical way. Hypotheses about differences in the attention to the interlocutor's contributions are therefore not supported in comparing these two speakers.

Continuing Information: Repetition

As well as reference, lexical repetition is a means of creating text. Lexical repetition makes the connection between two stretches of language explicit by using the same lexical item, even if there is not a specific identity of referent. Most of the lexical repetition involves nominal groups rather than verbal or other groups. Within the nominal group there are different functional roles, and the location of the lexical repetition with respect to those roles signals how the speaker is using lexical items previously used. The relationship of the functions of both repeated and nonrepeated items is at issue in the analysis of nominal groups.

Following Halliday (1985, pp. 159ff), the nominal group typically has the functional role of [thing] as head. Preceding the head the functions are from left to right: deictic (two possibilities), numerative, epithet (two possibilities), classifier. These functions are discussed as they are relevant to the description of the conversations at hand. The general progression from left to right is from the element that can specify the most. The leftmost elements of the nominal group have the greatest potential to indicate the relevance of the nominal group to what is available in the discourse. Lexical repetition within the nominal group but outside the head itself enables a continuity in the text by adding meaning often from another nominal group to the head of the nominal group in question. Unless the head of the nominal group is relatively empty semantically (e.g., "thing"), repetition in the periphery of the group enables a combining of ideational meanings. The Asperger's subject, JP, regularly uses lexical repetition as a text-forming device. Almost all the repetitions in the nominal group are in the head of the nominal group. Turns 32 to 36 provide examples of this lexical repetition in the head of the nominal group as well as JP's only use of lexical repetition in the periphery of a nominal group. (Lexical repetitions are in italics.)

32 - JP: no I made a few *friends* there too at *Westwood*

33 - I: um hmm um how good are you at spelling and stuff like that what what's your best ah

34 - JP: I think *spelling* is

35 - I: um hmm what about math

36 - JP: ya it's good too she always Miss Txxx gives me each night she gives me a piece as a *math* page.

In turn 32, JP repeats "math" from turn 35. In the nominal group "a math page," "math" is a classifier that specifies the subclass of the head of the group. It is the repeated lexical item that functions as a classifier. That is, lexical repetitions serve to link the speech of one person to another by supplying semantic material that narrows the meaning of the participant in the discourse.

Like JP, WB typically uses lexical repetition in the heads of nominal groups rather than in the peripheries. However, WB does use lexical repetition in peripheries with some frequency. These repetitions serve as classifiers. Some examples of nominal groups with the repeated item in italics are:

82 - an *owner's manual* approach to living

84 - State *Christian* Centre

138 - a *physical* person
electronic circuitry

142 - the *school's* VCR.

A closer examination of WB's use of lexical repetition reveals its use in terms of WB's idiolect. At least some of the repetitions used as classifiers seem to have a special or favored meaning for the speaker. The classifiers "extreme" (turn 130 "extreme mannerisms" —compare turn 20 "there is an extreme which isn't good"), "physical" (turn 138 "a physical person"—compare turn 138 "to a great degree a physical person"), and "electronic" (turn 50 "electronic equipment"—compare turn 138 "electronic goods," "electronic circuitry," turn 148 "electronics") repeat and signal some of the speaker's preoccupations. WB is interested in the world in terms of electronics and extremes, and so such items are repeated as classifiers in nominal groups. In larger samples of speech, it could be expected that repetition in the classifier function would be a useful indicator of what is salient to different speakers.

Continuing Information: Conjunction

As well as by relations of reference and repetition in nominal groups, cohesion is created by the use of conjunction. Conjunction links stretches of language together with the signal to the hearer that one stretch is to be related to the other in terms of a semantic function. The major classes of conjunction are additive, temporal, causal, and adversatives (see Halliday 1985; Halliday & Hasan, 1976; Martin 1983a). Out of 26 uses of conjunction by JP, 21 are additive. That is, JP rarely uses conjunction with explicit marking of temporal, causal, or adversative meanings. Turns 22 and 59 contain a series of additive conjunction, indicated by italics.

22 - JP: *and* I do math tests *and* spelling tests *and* we have lunch in the classroom at lunchtime *and* ah we do the dishes after . . . I always play with the kids outside at recess

59 - JP: *and* sometimes we'd jump on the trampoline *and* it's really fun but I *also* like roller skating *and* down to these big places roller skating

Some of these additive conjunctions could be replaced by other types of conjunction to state the conjunctive relationship more fully. However, it is not just the use of additive conjunction that creates the particularly unspecified (or underspecified) nature of JP's dialogue. It is the successive use of additive conjunction that creates relatively long stretches of language with little cohesive marking of temporal, causal, or adversative relations. JP rarely varies the semantic load carried by conjunction, using unmarked additive conjunction to signal merely that one stretch of language is to be interpreted in relation to another. This tendency to use unmarked additive conjunction can also be seen in several stretches of language in which JP does not use explicit conjunction at all. The conjunctive relations are left implicit. In turn 125, the clauses are not linked by explicit conjunction, but, rather, the hearer is left to infer the relationships among the clauses.

125 - JP: I think they're. I hear them they remind me of the people on soap operas the a they talk gossip

Thus, the tendency not to supply semantically rich conjunctive links can be realized by the choice of explicit additive conjunctions or by not stating the conjunctive relationship at all.

In contrast to JP, WB, the autistic speaker, uses a variety of causal, adversative, and temporal conjunctive links. Of 44 conjunctive links, 19 are additive, 13 causal, 11 adversatives, and 1 temporal. The relatively frequent use of "*but*," "*however*," "*because*," and "*so*" leads to a variety of semantic relationships being stated with no long series of successive additive conjunctions. Examples of WB's use of causal and adversative conjunctions are italicized in turns 130 to 136.

130 - WB: my father was raised in a home where extreme mannerisms weren't taught now when I was much younger I didn't have a whole degree of a mannerisms *but* I've certainly caught up at least I hope so in personal hygiene I know that I've caught up

131 - I: um hmm um hmm I think you do

132 - WB: *so* I believe myself to be more polished in that area than my father

133 - I:um hmm.

134 - WB: *but* I'm going to keep trying to be polished in that area.

135 - I: I see

136 - WB: *cause* you can't go too far.

WB is displaying to the hearer that what he has to say is related in specific semantic ways to what has already been said. His message is that it matters which conjunctive relationship is interpreted. The message is not merely of information connected to other information (the meaning of unmarked adversative conjunction). WB uses conjunction to signal that there is more meaning at stake in how stretches of language are related to each other. By contrast, JP signals that there is little at stake semantically in relating one stretch of language to another. WB is using more of the meaning potential of the conjunction system both qualitatively and quantitatively.

CONCLUSION

The close analysis of two conversations has shown that the high-functioning autistic (HFA) and the Asperger's subject differ from each other in complex ways. The HFA speaker is voluble, but uses language and particularly cohesion in ways that, suggest that text is being created vaguely. He uses a range of options from the specific-generic and presenting-presuming systems, but tends to choose generic nominal groups. He uses nominalizations that apparently create new participants in the discourse, but these nominalizations do not participate in cohesive chains and so do not help create texture. On the other hand, the Asperger's subject, RP, uses specific nominals and does not use reference to create cohesive chains of any substantial length. Furthermore, the Asperger's subject uses personal reference along with the information and thematic structure of the clause to formulate interpretable messages for the hearer. His creation of text is impaired, however, by the use of unclear cohesion. Sometimes, but not always, difficulties in cohesion are repaired before they hamper interpretability.

Analyses of the overall consistency of interpersonal systems also show substantial differences between the subjects. The HFA uses modality to encode the speaker's level of certainty about his statements and reveals considerable hesitancy. His use of such linguistic devices is sensitive to the interaction with the interviewer. The Asperger subject rarely uses modality to encode interpersonal information. That is, the entire modal system is rarely exploited, resulting in the expression of a relatively narrow range of meanings. Rather than using modals or adjuncts of probability, the Asperger subset uses adjuncts of frequency. This speaker thus has a different range of meanings compared to the HFA speaker, and typically only uses a specific subset of meanings available in the total meaning potential of English. As with the HFA speaker, the use of aspects of interpersonal meaning are dependent on the interaction with the interviewer.

The differences between the speakers must be characterized in terms of the interpersonal and cohesive systems they use and the context. There are three kinds of differences that are at issue. First, there is the use or nonuse of certain systems or options within systems. Second, the frequency of using certain options relative to other options may vary from speaker to speaker. Such variations characterize the typical meanings expressed by the speakers. Third, the use of language must be considered in the context of interaction. Each subject shows variability based on what the interviewer has said. However, which systems in the subjects' language show the variability and which aspects of the interviewer's language condition changes in the subjects' contributions are themselves variable.

Conversation is shaped by both speakers. However, speakers, vary in how they react to the contributions of their interlocutor. For speakers with psychiatric disorders related to communication and social interaction, this variation can be indicative of the locus of the impairment. Similarly, identifying which linguistic systems vary or fail to vary can account for the abilities and disabilities of the speakers to engage in normal social intercourse.

Case studies of speakers with psychiatric disorders combined with more extensive differences from one diagnostic group to another can explain the impairment in social interaction in precise semantic terms. The differences among speakers can be related to the meanings that can be expressed and that are typically expressed. At the next step of understanding, the differences of which meanings are at stake can be related to other aspects of the syndrome including etiology, family communication, and other measures of verbal and nonverbal functioning.

APPENDIX

TRANSCRIPT OF ASPERGER'S SYNDROME PATIENT (JP) (Turn Numbers Are Indicated on the Left Side, I = INTERVIEWER, J = PATIENT)

1.I: OK. Now the lady with you (hmm) I'm sorry the lady with you was you Mum wasn't she?

2.J: Yes

3.I: (Hm hmmm) And she said you remembered seeing me.

4.J: Hm Hm

5.I: Some time ago.

6.J: Ya

7.I: At Ch.

8.J: Ya

9.I: Well tell me what's been happening since?

10.J: First I was in this class. I started out at Ch. School

11.I: Um Hmm

12.J: In Mr. A's class but.

13.I: Ya

14.J: I found it difficult to and the kids were picking on me they were behavior kids they were kind of disturbed

15.I: Ya

16.J: And I didn't belong there now I've moved to another school its Westwood and it's a I lot happier there.

17.I: Um Hmm

18.J: Cause all the kids in that that school ah ah all everybody in that school including the kids are welcoming me to be part of that school

19.I: That's good that's good and what are you doing there Hm hm

20.J: Well sometimes me and Miss T go shopping

21.I: Um hmm

22.J: And I do some math tests and spelling tests and we have lunch in the classroom at lunchtime and ah we do the dishes after. . . I always play baseball with the kids outside at recess

23.I: That's good and ah have you made friends

24.J: ya

25.I: There are kids you see at times ah after school

26.J: ya I made a friend at Ch too

27.I: Um hmm

28.J: And I I've kept in touch with him

29.I: That's good

30.J: Ya

31.I: Are you in any specific grade right now

32.J: No I made a few friends there too at Westwood

33.I: Um hmm um how good are you at spelling and stuff like that what what's your best ah

34.J: I think spelling is

35.I: Um hmm what about math

36.J: ya it's good too she always Miss T gives me each night she gives me a piece a a math page

37.I: Um hmm

38.J: Sheet to do sometime in the evening I can do it

39.I: That's good How do you feel otherwise do you feel petty good?

40.J: Ya

41.I: Do you sleep well?

42.J: Um Hm

43.I: Your appetite is good?

44.J: ya

45.I: How do you find yourself when you're playing baseball. Are you good at it?

46.J: Ya

47.I: What what are you best at?

48.J: I'm best at baseball

49.I: Batting catching

50.J: Ya batting

51.I: Batting?

52.J: Um hmm

53.I: What are the things you enjoy the most?

54.J: Ah . . . ah

55.I: What are the things you enjoy the most? You know the things you look forward to.

56.J: Well I used to go to this program earlier in the year at they was held at NB. Center it's ACLD group and we'd go swimming and then we'd go to the theater and decide what we're gonna do

57.I: Um hmm

58.J: And sometimes we'd jump on the trampolene and it's really fun. I also like roller skating and down to these big places roller skating

59.I: You do like that huh

60.J: ya

61.I: How are you getting along at home?

62.J: Pretty good

63.I: Let's see there's you and do you have brothers and sisters I've forgotten

64.J: No

65.I: Just you

66. J: Um hmm

67.I: And your mom who works

68.J: Ya

69.I: And your father?

70.J: Ya he works

71.I: Ya so they both work

And what do you do in the evenings I mean do you go home from school

72.J: I come home and I'm the only one

[interruption]

73.J: Ah you know video games donkey kong there's donkey kong junior mousetrap

74.I: Are you good at it?

75.J: Ya

76.I: You're fast with your hands?

77.J: Hm hm

78.I: I can never do them so you play with your games do you read?

79.J: Sometimes

80.I: Do you enjoy reading?

81.J: Ya

82.I: What what books have you read ah lately you know what do you read?

83.J: I used to read a lot of lists and everything I just like to go through them.

84.I: Um hm

85.J: I have this Peanuts book it's it's

[interruption]

86.I: You know is there any kids in the neighborhood?

87.J: No

88.I: So when you're home you're pretty alone a good deal of the time.

89.J: Um hmm

90.I: have you ever had any problems like (hm hm) ah any problems with your hearing?

91.J: No

92.I: Ah hearing things that are not there?

93.J: Ya

94.I: What kind of problems are they hearing voices talking to you?

95.J: Ya

96.I: What kind of voices?

97.J: I hear sometimes I hear voices talking they're not really there

98.I: What do they say?

99.J: They just have conversations

100.I: Can you give me an example?

101.J: No

102.I: Confrontations?

103.J: Con conversations

104.I: conversations I'm sorry

105.J: ya

106.I: Are the conversations about you?

107.J: No

108.I: or something else

109.J: Just gossip

110.I: Just gossip about other people?

111.J: ya

112.I: (Hm Hmm) Are the voices familiar do they sound as if ah you've heard them before?

113.J: No

114.I: And ah when when does it happen. does it happen in the evening?

115.J: No

116.I: Or when you're alone or when you're in people's company?

117.J: No

118.I: What about your eyes? Do they bother you do you see anything at all?

119.J: No

120.I: Funny taste in your mouth?

121.J: No

122.I: Funny feelings in your body in any any way?

123.J: No

124.I: Just these voices once in awhile? What do you think they are?

125.J: I think they're. I hear them they remind me of the people on soap operas the a. they talk gossip

126.I: How do you do you have an explanation of why you hear them?

127.J: No

128.I: do they bother you?

129.J: No

130.I: So soap operas is something you do watch huh?

131.J: Um hmm

132.I: Which one is your favorite?

133.J: Well I don't actually watch them I just see them

134.I: You just glance at them when they're on

135.J: Um Hmm

136.I: But you do watch television?

137.J: Um Hm

138.I: And you have any favorite program then?

139.J: Oh ya *One Day at a Time*

140.I: Hm Hm

141.J: Um and

142.I: You like ah those short things

143.J: Ya

144.I: Little fun in it

145.J: Ya

146.I: Does the television or the radio ever bother you as if you know they were talking about something familiar or

147.J: No

148.I: Talking about you? You never get that feeling

149.J: No

150.I: OK well

TRANSCRIPT OF AUTISTIC PATIENT (WB)
(I = INTERVIEWER, W = PATIENT)

1.I: Your name is WB

2.W: Right

3.I: Right and ah . . . OK Today is May 23 and you are WB

4.W: Right

5.I: Now. How long have you been seeing ah a doctor at Ch

6.W: Well. I've been seeing such doctors on and off all my life because. my mother to make a long story short has always had concerns for me because of the fact that in my earlier childhood I had an unusual life I lived with my grandparents without a father

7.I: I see

8.W: At the age of seven my mother by that time had remarried and we moved into a house with my adopted father and ever since then I've been trying my best to get on the so to speak usual track

9.I: Yes well you seem to be ah fine person in what way do you feel you're not on the usual track?

10.W: Well . . . it's a bit that's somewhat of a difficult question to ask one I suppose is never quite sure whether or not he has caught up to a so called normal person in every respect

11.I: Um hmm

12.W: Cause very hard to examine the so-called normal person just exactly is normal no one can really say

13.I: Right very true

14.W: It might be a state of mind it might just be a minor deviation which really doesn't make any difference

15.I: Um hmm Well let me ask you in a different way

16.W: Um hmm

17.I: Is there anything about you that you would like to ah change?

18.W: Alright I'd like to change my self-consciousness

19.I: Um Hmm

20.W: I'd like to be much less self-conscious It's good to be self-aware but there is an extreme which isn't good

21.I: I see

22.W: And I'd like to be able to not be so self-critical about things

23.I: You are eh you criticize yourself a lot

24.W: In my mind yes

25.I: Um hmm so you feel kind of tense particularly in a social situation?

26.W: Um hmm

27.I: You feel (hmm hmm) that you may be judged by others

28.W: That I might make

29.I: Hm hmm

30.W: A mistake which is going to negatively affect my position so to speak

31.I: I see how old are you now eighteen?

32.W: Ya Yes

33.I: (hmm hmm) so it must be difficult particularly if you want to be with a girl that's always a situation where we are more self-conscious

34.W: Um hmm

35.I: Have you ever been out on a date?

36.W: No I haven't

37.I: You're too shy?

38.W: It's not so much that it's just that I'm not interested at this particular time

39.I: You're not

40.W: No I don't feel the need for a female companion as such

41.I: I see well what do you like what are you interested in?

42.W: Well I'm interested in Christianity

43.I: Um hmm

44.W: I find that to be very intriguing. I'm interested in the aspect of radio and television broadcasting

45.I: Um hmm

46.W: Not the actual field itself to go into it as a job but actually the technical aspects of it

47.I: I see

48.W: And the aspects of signal broadcasting things of that sort that's my passion

49.I: I see how do you pursue that passion what kind of things do you do?

50.W: Well, I like manipulating electronic equipment like stereo systems TV sets VCRs things of that sort

51.I: Um hmm do you have one at home?

52.W: Um hmm

53.I: How much do you understand of ah the actual technology?

54.W: Well I couldn't actually repair a TV set because I haven't gone that far in knowledge I might never ever do so.

55.I: Um hmm

56.W: However I understand the basic principles of how such equipment works and I know how to adjust the mechanisms the switches and such.

57.I: Um hmm

58.W: of such equipment so that I can get maximum use out of it

59.I: I see

60.W: Some people are afraid to adjust the controls on let's say a VCR

61.I: Um hmm

62.W: For fear of doing something wrong

63.I: Um hmm

64.W: But I make it a point to read owner's manuals and other helpful booklets to learn exactly how much you can do with a VCR

65.I: I see

66.W: For example

67.I: Um are you going to school?

68.W: Um hmm

69.I: In what grade are you now?

70.W: Well I'm in Phase I at C School have you ever heard of that?

71.I: Ya sure yes you like it?

72.W: Um hmm

73.I: It's a a good school

74.W: Um hmm

75.I: You get along with the other people in it?

76.W: Um hmm

77.I: You're I see. Now what about Christianity How do you pursue that interest?

78.W: Well I go to church one every Sunday that's my major time out of the household

79.I: Is it?

80.W: Um hmm. And. I study scripture about once a day or so

81.I: Um hmm You said you find it fascinating ah can you give me an idea of what is it that you find fascinating about Christianity

82.W: Well scripture gives you sort of an owner's manual approach to living. it gives you practical solutions to your daily problems Now sometimes that advice is hard to put into practice hard to accept but it does work.

83.I: Um hmm What parts of scriptures are you reading these days?

84.W: The New Testament ones the Epistles the letters written to the Church just after Jesus died

85.I: I see

86.W: Um hmm

87.I: I see you do it alone or ah are you ah helped by someone

88.W: Umm generally alone

89.I: Do you participate in any activities with the Church where yo/u/ g/o

90.W: m/m/m/ N/o/ I don't

91.I: Just go to ah what did you say to Church on Sundays right?

92.W: Um hmm

93.I: What is your ah ah church ah are you what

94.W: State Convenant Belt. (X X) State Christian Center SCC

95.I: Um Hmm

96.W: That's at 350 K Avenue North right by the Central Mall

97.I: I see

98.W: Um Hmm It's an interdenominational church

99.I: I see

100.W: Um hmm

101.I: So you have people from different kind of religions

102.W: Different faiths that's right

103.I: Background

104.W: Um hmm

105.I: And It's interesting

106.W: Um hmm

107.I: So now you've been living with y/our adopted father for eleven years?

108.W: yes

109.I: how do you think ah what do you think your mother's choice has been W/as it was it a good choice or

110.W: Well my mother said that she loved my father and still does and I do believe that my father does look after my mother

111.I: Um hmm

112.W: And as well my father seems to be a good father to my sisters

113.I: Um hmm

114.W: But I've never been able to have a strong relationship with my father because our beliefs our standpoints are widely varied as my father himself said himself and I are about as different as we can possibly be

115.I: I see. You're now talking about your natural father or your

116.W: Ummm

117.I: stepfather?

118.W: I'm talking about my stepfather now

119.I: But you call him father and

120.W: Um hmm

121.I: In what way are you different?

122.W: Well . . . I don't know the best way to start that

123.I: Um hmm

124.W: It's more or less how should I put it to you

125.I: Maybe you could describe him

126.W: Alright my father is in the physical aspect six feet tall just about my height he's to put it to you purely descriptively overweight

127.I: Um Hmm

128.W: While I'm thin which I thank God for

129.I: Um hmm

130.W: My father was raised in a home where extreme mannerisms weren't taught now when I was much younger I didn't have a whole degree of mannerisms but I've certainly caught up at least I hope so in personal hygiene I know that I've caught up

131.I: Um Hmm Um hmm I think you do

132.W: So I believe myself to be more polished in that area than my father

133.I: Um hmm

134.W: But I'm going to keep trying to be polished in that area

135.I: I see

136.W: Cause you can't go too far

137.I: Right

138.W: Another thing is that my father is to a great degree a physical person he likes to work on such things as train sets model airplane building building shelves sheds things of that sort while I'm more a mind person dealing with electronic goods electronic circuitry

139.I:I see you like concepts and ideas

140.W: Yes and my father while he was younger he practiced some kind of religion it was just that a religion rather than a faith. I don't consider my religion if you want to call it that as true religion and it isn't a whole series of rituals which you have to carry out just for some sort of security mesure

141.I: I see (hmm hmm) um what do you like best in school? um what kind of things do you enjoy doing there?

142.W: Well I like using technology such as the school's VCR

143.I: Um hmm

144.W: I like using audio and video tapes for my education because I like learning from those sources

145.I: I see what do you read besides the scriptures?

146.W: I'm not into nonfiction well I'll start that again. I'm not into fiction because it just doesn't interest me at school I read novels because it's part of the course but I don't do so voluntarily

147.I: I see

148.W: At home I like to read about electronics such as stereo systems and the like because I like gaining knowledge on that sort of thing

149.I: I see what novels (hmm hmm) have you had to read ah as part of your school courses?

150.W: Well they're rather varied but we've read novels such as *Never Cry Wolf* a book about a person who goes up North to examine the wolves in their habitat

151.I: Right

152.W: You see

153.I: Tell me of one you enjoyed reading at least to some extent

154.W: Um hmm

155.I: Hmm hmm

156.W: I'd say *Like Normal People* It's a book about two retarded individuals who grow up and get married and lead as normal a life if you want to put it that way as they possibly can

157.I: Um hmm they made a ah television show out of that

158.W: Possibly

159.I: I think so have you ever had any ah medical problems have you ever been in hospital for any reason?

160.W: mmm No No

161.I: have you had any problems with your perception like ah your vision your hearing?

162.W: No

163.I: Feelings in your body?

164.W: No

165.I: hmm hmmm have you ever heard voices where no one was there?

166.W: No I

167.I: Or had ah seen things that were not there have you ever had any experiences of that sort

168.W: No I didn't

169.I: Good any strange feelings in your body at any time?

170.W: No

171.I: Funny taste or smell?

172.W: Um Um

173.I: Anything like that? All right ah we'll stop now

174.W: Alright

3

QUANTITATIVE STUDY OF DEVELOPMENTAL DISORDERS

INTRODUCTION

The following study deals with psychiatric diagnoses in which problems in social interaction are prominent features. A problem in social interaction is also found in schizophrenic language. However, in the developmental disorders now being considered there are the additional elements of possible developmental delays and retardation.

The linguistic analysis of the speakers aims at providing generalizations about the signals that are sent to interlocutors. The nature of these signals over sustained conversation and a reasonable number of speakers from the diagnostic groups is at issue. The data then reveal which meanings are typically encoded and what kind of text is presented to the hearer. From the perspective of the hearer, the data describe the task of hearers in decoding each group of speakers. In large measure, the developmental disorders can be determined by interviews with parents that focus on the early history of the child. Thus, there are data available to those who regularly interact with the child that are sufficient to determine a diagnosis. Much of this early data is based directly or indirectly on language data. The argument is, then, that a child with certain developmental disorders displays language patterns to a nonlinguist observer that are indicative of the underlying psychopathology. If the child's linguistic interaction is clearly describable by a caregiver, then there is prima facie evidence for an atypicality in those interactions. The linguistic analysis of the data attempts to locate the atypicality in linguistic interaction and, by using a functional approach, to explain how the atypicalities affect the hearer's interpretation of the speaker.

As well as the relation between the subjective perception of the child's interaction and the linguistic analysis of the conversation, a quantitative analysis helps account for the typical reactions to certain groups of speakers and the social abilities of those groups of speakers in terms of their linguistic patterns. Such generalizations about groups should reflect clinical descriptions of the syndromes. The linguistic data should ultimately be considered with nonlinguistic clinical data to understand how the linguistic and nonlinguistic data may be related to each other and be suggestive of etiology, treatment, and outcome. For example, social withdrawal at an early age may affect language developmental in certain kinds of interactions. The resulting atypicalities in language use may in themselves contribute to further unusual interactions.

The method followed starts with the clinical categorization of subjects. This categorization reflects a variety of parameters that determine the coherence of the groups. As well as the current state of the subject, the clinical categories also reflect commonalities such as etiology, response to treatment, and outcome. The linguistic study then takes these groups and attempts to describe the communication patterns of the groups and how they compare to each other. In neurocognition there is a debate concerning the use of case studies or group data (Caramazza, 1986; Caramazza & McCloskey, 1988; McCloskey & Caramazza, 1988; Zurif, Gardner, & Brownell 1989). One of the questions in this debate is whether one can infer from behavior (including language behavior) to cognitive architecture (including cognitive deficits and their physiological correlates). The study of psychiatric categories and the language used by patients is different from the neurocognitive language studies in that the language of psychiatric patients is relevant data in itself. The patient's interaction with others is the issue to be studied. This interaction may reflect problems at cognitive or biological levels, but it is nevertheless the language in interaction that constructs the speaker's place within a society.

When the speaker does not relate to the society normally and is not related to as a normal member, then it makes sense to investigate the patterns of linguistic interaction involved. Furthermore, groups who interact in similar ways will be reacted to similarly. There is a generalization to be made from the language to the psychiatric syndrome that is different from the inference from language and other behaviors to neurocognitive organization. In using language to study certain psychiatric syndromes, the focus is on one of the manifestations of the speaker's atypical functioning, rather than on a behavior to be taken as a manifestation of some other process. It may be the case that a psychiatric syndrome has an underlying organic cause, and that the language may reflect that cause relatively directly or indirectly. However, it is still relevant in terms of clinical assessment and the understanding of the syndrome to study the language of groups of speakers. As a group, the speakers differ in typical ways from other speakers, and so differ in how they behave socially.

In studying the language of children with developmental disorders, it is relevant to consider the early socialization of children. This early socialization may be either part of the cause of the later use of language by the child or the result of other cognitive or social difficulties. Thus, the coherence of the early history of a group of developmentally disordered children is relevant to the study of their language. Language is a means of socialization and also a product of it. Children with difficulties in social relationships may well have atypical linguistic interactions. Furthermore, specific linguistic atypicalities may be associated with each other and with specific difficulties in social relationships.

The development of social problems in children and the relationship of these problems to atypicalities in language is open to numerous influences. It can be expected then that children will show considerable variability in both the psychiatrically described social problems and in the atypicalities in language use. Furthermore, diagnostic categories may themselves be rather loose and cover nonhomogeneous groups; for example, the use of disjunctive characteristics to define schizophrenia (a patient may be diagnosed as schizophrenic by having characteristics "a" or "b" or "c"). The linguistic measures associated with such diagnostic categories may show that, in the clearest cases, a range of values on a linguistic variable characterizes a diagnostic category. In less clear cases, two or more linguistic variables may show an atypical association or disassociation from each other. Outliers on these linguistic variables can also be expected as a result of the heterogeneity of the diagnostic categories. However, as argued above, the extent to which the members of the diagnostic category were classified on the basis of linguistically and interactionally derived criteria will create similarity within categories on the functional linguistic measures. That is, the clinical cohesiveness of a diagnostic category is created only in part by the verbal and social behavior of the patients. Each language variable may account for part of the characteristics of a group. The cohesion analysis of schizophrenic language in Rochester and Martin (1979), and the analysis of various components of cohesion and intonation in Fine, Bartolucci, and Szatmari (1989), show such specific relationships between language variables and diagnostic categories and subcategories.

SUBJECTS

Three groups of developmentally disordered children were studied. (See Szatmari, Bartolucci & Bremner, 1989, for a description of the recruitment procedures.)

1. *Asperger's Syndrome*. The inclusion criteria for this group were isolated behavior, impaired social interaction, onset before 6 years of age, and one of odd speech, impaired nonverbal communication, or bizarre preoccupation. There were 23 cases of Asperger's syndrome aged between 8 and 18. The average age was 14.

2. *High functioning autistics.* A group of high-functioning autistics was determined according to two criteria: a diagnosis of autism according to DSM III (American Psychiatric Association, 1980) and a score of above 70 on at least one of the Vineland Adaptive Behaviour Scales (Sparrow, Balla, & Cicchetti, 1984)—communication, socialization, or activities of daily living. There were 19 high-functioning autistics from 7 to 32 years of age with an average age of 23.

3. *Socially withdrawn out-patients.* This group had a variety of peer problems and were referred to a psychiatric out-patient team for social impairment. The children had familiar childhood psychiatric disorders with the added problem of getting along

with peers. This group was matched with the Asperger's group in age. There were 35 socially withdrawn subjects aged 7 to 17 with an average age of 14.

DATA COLLECTION AND PROCESSING

Each of the 77 subjects was interviewed for 10 minutes. The interviews were loosely structured and covered school, hobbies, and family topics. The interviews were done by a young research assistant in a relaxed atmosphere.

The interviews were transcribed, and then the cohesion analyses performed. The cohesion analyses were done by a research assistant blind to the diagnostic categories and the specific research questions of the study. Table 3-1 presents the cohesion variables. Proportions were then calculated to control for differences in volubility. A regression analysis was performed treating each group as a variable. Age and sex were included in the model so that the power of the linguistic variables to differentiate the groups was independent of age and sex.

RESULTS AND DISCUSSION

Language is used in the current study as a means of assessing the social functioning of speakers. Children with pervasive developmental disorders have a series of problems in relating to others. Some of these problems are noted as specifically linguistic and others are more generally behavioral. In addition, social problems in these children may result in secondary difficulties in using language for social ends. The data on cohesion in children with pervasive developmental disorders address three basic questions: (a) how do speakers continue the identity of participants in conversation? (b) how do speakers display a common understanding of the conversation? and (c) how do the groups of speakers differ in their use of cohesion?

The first measure of the continuity of participants concerns the frequency of making any connection with information outside the nominal group. A simple way to measure the frequency of connections is to calculate the nonphoric nominal groups as a percentage of all nominal groups. The percentage

Table 3-1. Cohesion categories, examples and sources for coding

Nonphoric reference
George saw *an airplane*
Endophoric reference
Mary was tired. *She* yawned.
Comparative reference
I have the red bag but where is *the other bag*?
Cultural reference
The moon was full last night.
Substitution and Ellipsis
Do you want paper clips? A large *one*.
Lexical cohesion
I have my cup. Where's your *mug*?
Exophoric non-speech roles
This newspaper is interesting
Exophoric first person speech roles
I prefer *my own cooking*.
Exophoric second person speech roles
You have *your book*.
Ambiguous reference
My brother and father are tall. *He* likes basketball.
Bridging references
The house was dark, but *the door* was green.
Additioning
Tom saw *the other man*.

Based on Rochester & Martin (1977), Bartolucci & Fine (1987), Fine (1985).

of nonphoric groups thus suggests the independence of nominal groups from the verbal and nonverbal context. Table 3-2 presents the percentages of nonphoric nominal groups for the three groups. The autistic group has the most independent nominal groups, whereas the other two groups are similar to each other. The autistic speakers make less use of the phoric resources of language compared to the other groups.

To determine more specifically how participants are contin-

Table 3-2. Nonphoric nominal groups as a percentage of all nominal groups

Asperger's Syndrome (AS)	*High-Functioning Autistics (HFA)*	*Control Patients (CP)*
40	46	41

Regression analysis
HFA > AS $p < .03$
HFA > CP $p < .05$

Table 3-3. Endophoric nominal groups as a percentage of all phoric nominal groups

Asperger's Syndrome (AS)	*High-Functioning Autistics (HFA)*	*Control Patients (CP)*
45	35	42

Regression analysis
HFA < AS $p < .005$
HFA < CP $p < .04$

ued, the nature of the phoric links for each group of speakers needs examination. Endophoric links indicate continuity of nominal groups from one part of the conversation to another part. Table 3-3 shows endophoric nominal groups as a percentage of all phoric nominal groups. Not only do the autistics have more nonphoric nominal groups, but among their phoric nominal groups they use fewer endophoric links. The autistics, than, less frequently continue participants from one stretch of language to another.

If the autistics tend not to build links to other stretches of language, then their phoric nominal groups must be creating other kinds of links. Table 3-4 presents exophoric nominal groups as a percentage of all phoric nominal groups. The autistics create links to the nonverbal situation and in that way create continuity of participants. Rather than continuing participants mentioned verbally, the autistics more frequently than the other speakers call on the nonverbal situation as a source of recurring participants.

As well as the continuity of participants in discourse created by links to the verbal or nonverbal contexts, there may be attempts to build continuity by inference (bridging). Since inference is not completely explicit, there may be cases of attempted inference for which the listener lacks sufficient information forcing the listener to supply the missing informa-

Table 3-4. Exophoric nominal groups as a percentage of all phoric nominal groups

Asperger's Syndrome (AS)	*High-Functioning Autistics (HFA)*	*Control Patients (CP)*
51	61	54

Regression analysis
HFA > AS $p < .005$
HFA > CP $p < .02$

tion (additioning). Table 3-5 presents attempted inferencing (bridging plus additioning) and successful inferencing (bridging) as a percentage of all phoric nominal groups. The Asperger speakers use more successful inferential links than the autistic speakers ($p < .04$ on the regression analysis). However, both developmentally disordered groups show a lower rate of successful inferencing compared to the control patients. Thus, the two disordered groups when attempting to create inferential links from one stretch of language to another fail somewhat more than the control patients.

The strategies used to continue participants in conversation can be described at a number of levels as indicated by the data available. There can be differences: first, in the use of language to signal continuity (phoricity); second, in the use of the verbal or nonverbal contexts as a source of participants; and third, in attempts and success in creating inferential links.

A second issue addressed by the linguistic analysis of the language of the developmentally disordered is how speakers signal a common understanding with their interlocutors. The data on bridging and additioning indicate that Asperger's speakers attempt to use nominal groups with implicit links. Such links demonstrate to the listener that speaker and listener share an understanding of the interaction sufficiently to relax the level of explicit signaling. However, the Asperger's and autistic speakers are less successful than the control patients in providing appropriate implicit links when such links are attempted.

Signaling common understanding can be accomplished by the choice of vocabulary as well as the use of phoric nominal groups. The number of nominal groups that are linked by lexical cohesion encodes the continuity of what is being talked about by overt means with little interpretative processing required by

Table 3-5. Bridging plus additioning and bridging as percentages of phoric nominal groups.

	Asperger's Syndrome (AS)	*High-Functioning Autistics (HFA)*	*Control Patients (CP)*
Bridging plus additioning	9.2	5.8	6.9
Bridging	6.4	4.3	5.6
Bridging (successful) inferential links) as a percentage of bridging plus additioning (attempted inferential links)	70	74	81

Table 3-6. Nominal groups with lexical cohesion as a percentage of all nominal groups

Asperger's Syndrome (AS)	*High-Functioning Autistics (HFA)*	*Control Patients (CP)*
8.8	7.2	6.0

speaker or hearer. Table 3-6 presents nominal groups with lexical cohesion as a percentage of all nominal groups. The tendency is for the developmentally disordered groups to use more overt lexical links. A similar pattern emerges from Table 3-7 in terms of phoric links: The disordered groups depend more on lexical links than phoric links compared to the control group. These results corroborate the findings on bridging suggesting that the developmentally disordered groups are impaired in their presentation of links that require some interpretation and also tend to avoid such links by using simple lexical cohesion.

To explore further the nature of the endophoric links, each link was coded as either a direct link to the earlier preceding information that is necessary for interpretation or as part of a chain with at least one link intervening between the endophoric item and the full information that the following links in the chain rely on. The following conversation illustrates the different kinds of links.

1. I: you got kidded out by who is particular?
2. P: my dad and it just—one night he walked in half a couple time over. I guess he was drunk or something I'm only fourteen at the time and he started something with me and everything . . .
3. I: oh
4. P: then I went to group homes for about a year which was sort of a pain, and then I went into Webber House downtown
5. I: Um hmm that's (indistinguishable) facilities are they?
6. P: oh it's for teenagers in between. . . .

Table 3-7. Nominal groups with lexical cohesion as a percentage of phoric nominal groups and nominal groups with lexical cohesion

Asperger's Syndrome (AS)	*High-Functioning Autistics (HFA)*	*Control Patients (CP)*
12.5	11.7	9.3

In turn 2, the speaker initiates a chain with the full nominal group "my dad." The next nominal group in the chain is "he" which refers directly back to "my dad." The two later occurrences of "he" are linked to "my dad" through a chain involving at least one intervening endophoric nominal group. All these links are within the language of the same speaker and, in fact, within a single turn. In turn 4, the patient introduces "Webber House." In the following turn the interviewer mentions a type of facility but uses the plural and so indicates that this nominal group is not in a chain with "Webber House." However, the singular "it" in turn 6 is a direct, nonmediated link to "Webber House" mentioned two turns earlier also by the patient. To study how these links are created, two ratios were calculated: (a) the direct nonmediated-endophoric links within a turn to the total number of such direct endophoric links in all turns; and (b) the chained, mediated-endophoric links within a turn to the total number of such chained endophoric links in all turns. Table 3-8 presents the data for these two ratios.

The ratio of direct links shows no difference among the three groups of speakers. The use of direct links within a turn is the same among the groups. However, for mediated chains of links, the two developmentally disordered groups use comparatively few chained links within turns. This measure points to other findings that indicate older and saner speakers link more to their own, compared to an interlocutor's, speech (see Chapters 4 and 5). The data here indicate that the difference between the developmentally disordered groups and the control patients is specifically in chained links within a single turn. Direct links do not distinguish the groups. The variation in the chained links is thus in a measure that sets up a weaker (chained compared to direct) link for which the distance in terms of changeovers of turn is relevant. Direct links are easy enough to interpret so that

Table 3-8. Chained endophoric links within a turn as a ratio of all chained endophoric links

	Asperger's Syndrome (AS)	*High-Functioning Autistics (HFA)*	*Control Patients (CP)*
Direct links	42	34	36
		no significant differences	
Chained links	54	58	68
		Regression analysis	

AS < CP $p < .05$
HFA < CP $p < .05$

the changeover of turns is apparently not relevant in revealing differences in the processing strategies of the speakers. The measure of linking across turns does not in itself show the difference in language of the developmentally disordered. Rather, the nature of the cohesive link as direct or chained is important in specifying the kind of processing required for production and comprehension. The more indirect processing required in chaining distinguishes the developmentally disordered. These speakers attempt chaining more across turns. The suggestion is that such chaining represents an inappropriate or at least an unusual strategy, since it increases the difficulty of interpretation despite no clear breakdown in communication. Such a finding of a linguistic pattern that reflects more complex processing is the kind to be expected with syndromes that do not greatly impair communication, but nevertheless are associated with reportable language abnormalities and cognitive and social deficits.

Cohesion, then, plays a role in displaying what is regarded as a common understanding of the interaction. Another part of language organization with a similar function is the encoding of given and new information by word order and intonation. In Fine et al. (1989) it is shown that the more highly marked encodings of new information do not discriminate among the groups of speakers. Rather, it is the communicatively more useful encodings of new information that discriminate the speakers. Furthermore, the high-functioning autistics seem more impaired in the use of intonation to signal the given-new distinction using more marked and less communicatively useful forms (Fine, Bartolucci, Ginsberg, & Szatmari, in press). Thus, the use of intonation to signal the distinction between given and new information parallels the functions of cohesion in encoding assumptions about the shared understanding of the unfolding conversation. The intonation data indicate that autistics tend to use intonation in ways that are least likely to be communicatively functional in displaying a shared understanding with the interlocutor. Both intonation and cohesion provide a speaker with the means of indicating shared assumptions to the interlocutor. The examination of the detailed ways in which cohesion and intonation are used suggests underlying social impairments that may be either contributing causes or effects of the psychiatric syndromes.

Given the specific findings on cohesion, a description of each of the developmentally disordered groups can be presented.

These descriptions consider the cohesion findings in the context of other studies of the language and interaction of the developmentally disordered. Autistic children have, in general, been the subject of a number of studies, and it is with this group that we start.

The high-functioning autistics use relatively more exophoric reference, more nonphoric nominal groups, and less endophoric reference. These speakers are not establishing links from one stretch of language to another, but rather are linking their language to aspects of the physical speech situation.

Landry and Loveland (1989) found that reference to speech roles in spontaneous interactions does not show group differences among autistics, normal children matched for language level, and a group of the developmentally language delayed matched to the autistics on nonverbal mental age. However, they found that the autistics used somewhat less non-speech-role exophora ("this"/ "that," "here"/"there" in Landry & Loveland, 1989) in spontaneous interaction with an adult. The autistics in the Landry and Loveland study were younger—mean age 105 months compared to mean age of 23 years in this study—and more retarded (mean mental age 66 months) than those in the current study. Landry and Loveland calculated non-speech-role exophora as a percentage of all communicative acts. However, even the verbal autistic children of their study would likely be less talkative and outgoing than either of the two control groups. Therefore, exophora taken as a percentage of communicative acts is probably underrepresented for the autistic group (see Bartolucci & Fine, 1987, for a similar finding on the effects of calculating the frequency of a linguistic variable in two ways). Another difference in the Landry and Loveland study is the kind of activity in the unstructured spontaneous situation. The child was with an adult with a number of toys and other objects so that non-speech-role exophoric reference could be quite appropriate depending on the focus of attention of the speakers. In the current study of high-functioning autistics and Asperger's syndrome, the subjects were engaged in conversation with a clinician in an informal clinical situation rather a play situation. The likelihood and appropriateness of non-speech-role exophora are therefore less than in the Landry and Loveland study. Although the two studies apparently show contradictory findings on non-speech-role exophora, there are significant differences in methodology. Landry and Loveland found, though, that the autistics showed the least variation in use of exophora across situation types. This lack of variation is most striking for non-speech-role exophora in the spontaneous interactions. In addition, Landry and Loveland found that the autistics use fewer of the more active communicative gestures of showing and pointing as well as little variation across situations. Overall, the studies suggest that verbal autistics refer to the physical setting of the speech event in atypical ways.

Martinsen and Smith (1989) suggest an explanation for the findings of atypical exophora in the language of autistics. In a study of normal children, Martinsen and Smith found that vocalizations and gestures appear in combination just prior to children's first words. Furthermore, such combinations, which are perceptually most salient, are more often reacted to by parents than either vocalizations or gestures alone. Early language development would seem to need perceptually salient attention and then reaction. Although we do not know the precise early interaction patterns of the developmentally disordered subjects (Martinsen & Smith studied the period of 10 to 17 months), the early onset and pervasiveness of the disorders suggest that even in the earliest interaction the children may have displayed atypicalities. The research of Martinsen and Smith then suggests that parental interactions would also be affected. If the autistic speakers tended to use exophoric reference as a perceptually salient signal, then an effect on pronoun use by children and parents could be expected. Exophoric reference is a verbal pointing to the physical environment and can be seen as a combination of the gesture and vocalization that Martinsen and Smith find as promoting parental reactions. Exophora for children is a way of verifying the encoding of the physical environment into language. If the encoding is shared by an interlocutor, the child has succeeded in relating the physical world to language—the means of sharing information with others. At a later stage language must refer to other stretches of language, and thus the presence of endophora in older children is important.

Oshima-Takane and Benaroya (1989) found that autistics must attend to language directed to third parties to correctly learn the use of "toi" (second-person exophora). The data from the three groups of developmentally disordered do not show differences in the use of second-person exophora. Because all three groups have difficulty in social relationships, any atypicalities in early observation and production of second-person exophora may be roughly similar. Oshima-Takane and Benaroya do not provide explicit explanation for possible differences in non-speech-role exophora. However, if their hypothesis of attentiveness as a factor in autistics difficulty with language is supported, then a similar line of reasoning can be applied to the finding that autistics underuse endophoric reference. Endophoric reference requires careful monitoring of the speech of both speakers in a conversation. If this monitoring is deficient, then the speaker may try to avoid endophoric reference (the autistic group) or to attempt to use it but fail (the Asperger's group).

The Asperger's group, compared to the autistics, seems to use cohesion appropriately. However, there are subtle indicators that a few linguistic systems are used atypically. The Asperger's speakers attempt the continuity of participants in language through endophora and even implicit reference (bridging). In a small, but significantly more frequent, number of nominal groups than the control subjects, the Asperger's speakers provide uninterpretable signals. Perhaps to avoid such signals the Asperger's rely on lexical continuity slightly more than the other groups.

The comparison of the autistic and Asperger's groups on linguistic measures relate to a number of issues in understanding the diagnostic differences and etiologies of the categories. Asperger's syndrome is characterized by the social impairments of autism, but without accompanying retardation. However, the greater linguistic impairment of the autistic group and their greater social impairment may be associated with cognitive factors. The complex linguistic tasks necessary for conversation may be compromised by more general cognitive impairments. Atypicalities in the use of functional linguistic systems that produce "odd speech" early in childhood contribute to unusual, difficult, or diminished ranges of interactions. The social difficulties of the developmentally disordered cannot be simply attributed to atypicalities in language, either as language emerges or later in childhood. However, it is likely that language effectiveness contributes to the responses of others to a child and thus to the child's integration into social interaction. Szatmari et al. (1989) found that the Asperger's group was less impaired that the autistic group in responsiveness to the primary caregiver, echolalia and pronoun reversal, and imaginative play. Such findings of an early history further suggest an interaction of social and linguistic factors. The social interaction needed for the development of functionally appropriate language in interaction is greatly impaired for the Asperger's.

The autistic group shows not only early social difficulty, but also a history including a range of symptoms implicating some basic cognitive abilities: motor stereotypies, insistence on sameness, and bizarre occupations (Szatmari et al., 1989). Such cognitive deficits are compatible with the autistics overuse of functionally inappropriate intonation patterns and the more frequent departures from the control groups in the use of cohesion. The autistics do not just say things in an unusual way, but produce language that does not fit into the situation, both in terms of intonation and cohesion.

LINGUISTICS CONCLUSIONS

The study of the language of the developmentally disordered contributes to understanding of how linguistic systems function. Linguistic systems work to produce interpretable language in context: text. By the use of specific parts of these systems, the developmentally disordered show two kinds of variation: (a) variation in the use of uninterpretable signals, and (b) variation in the use of interpretable signals. These two kinds of variation are linked to each other in a scale of atypicality and in terms of the risk of communication failure. Typical speech is both highly interpretable and in accordance with the expectations of hearers. Rochester and Martin (1977) found that the strategies for interpreting schizophrenic speakers are based on both increased difficulty in constructing interpretations and different expectations for the interpretable stretches of language.

For both intonation (Fine et al., 1989; Fine et al., 1991) and cohesion there are degrees of interpretability and atypicality that emerge from examining the probabilities of using various options. In the intonation data, the more severely impaired group, the autistics, uses options from various systems in highly marked ways. This high level of marking indicates that the utterances are compatible with highly restricted contexts. The less severely impaired group, the Asperger's, uses marked intonation patterns that could be appropriate in reasonably likely contexts. In the cohesion data, the study of frequencies produces a similar picture. The uninterpretable signals produced by the autistics are a limiting case of language which does not fit into context. The use of implicit reference is, on the other hand, a signal of a sharing of the context with the listener.

Both intonation and cohesion thus permit the expression of the degree of compatibility of language to its verbal and nonverbal context. The degree of marking in the combination of systems that express sentence stress and the degree of interpretability and assumption of common information in cohesion are indications of the quality of the text (or "texture") produced by different speakers. Similarly, the amount of marking in the realizations involving other combinations of systems should be a measure of language impairment. Although the amount of marking emerges as an indicator of functioning from the empirical data, it is also predicted by systemic theory. Marking in systemic networks indicates that there is some special reason for not choosing the unmarked options. Thus, marking is a realization of atypical choices derived from atypical meanings or combinations of meanings with each other or in the context. Increased levels of marking place increased constraints on the appropriateness of realizations. From the hearer's perspective, increased marking requires increased matching of the marked utterance with relevant aspects of the verbal or nonverbal contexts—interpretation involves more processing. The limiting case is the case for which no context explicitly accessible or implicit is available. Interpretation in this case fails. Thus, the fit of language into its context, the creation of the semantic unit of text, is characterized by systemic theory and can be used to describe both the impairments of developmentally disordered children and the interpretative processes of hearers.

In fact, a case can be made that the problem of language impairment, to a substantial extent, can be seen as parallel to the interpretative processes that hearers of such speakers must undertake. The language is regarded as impaired because the interpretation of it in context is atypical or impossible. Linguistic theory must be functional in the sense of predicting the degree of impairment evident from given stretches of language. These degrees of impairment should then also be compatible with the characterization of the speakers by other measures of social and cognitive functioning.

The analysis of the above quantitative data comparing groups of speakers leads to some necessary points about how linguistic systems in use should be considered. As a functional system that is always used in specific contexts, language is based on paradigmatic options. Included with these options is knowledge about the relative frequencies of the options and how these frequencies relate to aspects of the situation of their use. Members of a speech community know the common and expected things that can be meant and how they are typically said. Speakers also build up patterns of using options that indicate that some options are marked and used only when there is a specific reason not to use the unmarked or default option. The existence of marked options, however, is not just a probabilistic fact. The unmarked option is characterized paradigmatically with the other options in the system as the option that is chosen if there is no special reason to chose another one. Thus, marked options result from some special function that must be served, and so these options have a special appropriateness and fit to the verbal co-text and/or situation.

Within a society, speakers, by using language in similar ways, come to agree on the mapping of paradigmatic options onto the contexts that language is used in. These agreements are expressed by the frequencies of choosing various options under specific conditions. In terms of the individual speakers, the frequencies can be regarded as the expectations that a well-integrated member of the speech community has. Speakers will use and expect to hear marked and unmarked options with certain frequencies given certain conditions.

The role of difference in frequencies can now be considered. The departure from an expected option in a single instance in text is taken as reflecting Halliday's "good reason principle." The hearer will presume that the speaker has a good reason for not using the expected option and try to interpret the speaker accordingly. The speaker is either presenting an atypical meaning or combination of meanings or is perhaps suggesting that the context is not what it appears to be, and the hearer should reevaluate the context to make the utterance less marked according to some implied context. Repeated and consistent departures from expected patterns of linguistic choices suggest that the speaker does not fit into the apparently relevant speech community. Speaker/hearers in the wider community must try to assess and cope with the different set of probabilities they are called on to interpret. The speaker may seem excentric, part of another speech community (perhaps defined by geography, class, ethnic, or professional group) or, in some cases, pathological.

As well as an overall departure from typical patterns, certain speakers may depart from the expected patterns in only some contexts, defined by verbal or nonverbal elements of the context.

If the trigger for the atypical choices is the wider context of situation, then the speaker perhaps does not know the norms of the society and so, for example, inappropriately chooses options that reflect formality or informality or that reflect ironic or sarcastic compared to "straight" talk. On the other hand, the trigger for atypical choices may be the co-text that is jointly constructed by the participants in conversation. When the speaker's choices of options are atypical, only some of the time the speaker may appear even more unusual. If hearers can easily perceive the unusual pattern of linguistic choices, then it is relatively easy to attribute the atypical frequencies to some more or less permanent factor, such as regional or social dialect. However, if the speaker sometimes follows the typical patterns in terms of frequency and mapping onto elements of verbal and nonverbal context, then the hearer will assume that the speaker is following the "good reason principle" and will try to find the reason for the atypical choice of options. If such a reason is not supported by the context and what the hearer believes the speaker can and is assuming about the context, then the hearer will have difficulty in interpreting the speaker.

The discussion of atypical frequencies and conditions for using certain options in language helps explain the findings of the language used by children with developmental disorders. If children experience very atypical social interactions from an early age, then these may be insufficient and provide an atypical opportunity to discover the appropriate frequencies and conditions for various linguistic options. In particular, one-sided interactions, social isolation, or extreme shyness would skew the kinds of contexts from which a child would learn the patterns of language typical in the society. Such an argument does not preclude underlying cognitive or neuropsychological bases for a developmental disorder. Rather, the atypical interactions may mediate between underlying nonlinguistic factors and atypical linguistic productions. Such atypical uses of language then further contribute to odd interaction and atypical reactions by other interactants to the affected speakers.

The preceding line of reasoning suggests that early difficulties in social interaction may necessarily lead to atypical, if not seriously impaired, use of language. However, in their study of high-functioning autistics, Szatmari, Bartolucci, Bremner, Bond, and Rich (1989) find that early measures of social and linguistic impairment do not correlate well with later social or language behavior. Rather, it is full-scale IQ that correlates well with outcome in adolescence and early adulthood. It seems that sufficient underlying cognitive ability can overcome the disadvantages of unusual social interactions early in life. Similarly, the below-average cognitive abilities found in most autistic cases can then be seen as compounding the difficulty these children have in learning the linguistic and social skills needed for smooth interaction.

The quantitative study of cohesion and other linguistic systems is not merely a convenient statistical means for distinguishing groups of speakers. The study of frequencies, or probabilities, to look at the data in a slightly different way accounts for an essential way in which language functions to establish and continue social interaction. Quantitative data reveal the expected patterns of meanings and their realizations in society. The norms are built up in part by the frequencies of use that are then represented in the expectancies of speakers and hearers. The probabilities for using given linguistic options reflect agreements (more exactly, the range of agreements) among speakers that are then regarded as the background for identifying atypical choices. These atypical choices should account for the precise departure from usual communication that hearers experience. In clinical cases, the linguistic account, in terms of specific linguistic options and their probabilities, should reflect the clinical description of the speakers with respect to difficulties in communication and social interaction.

4

INTERPRETABILITY AND COGNITION IN PSYCHIATRIC SYNDROMES

INTRODUCTION

The study of the language of psychiatric patients provides information about how the systems of language are used and how they are related to each other, about the communicative abilities of the speakers, and about the social and cognitive processes associated with language use. Clear disturbances in how language is used, typically found in some psychiatric patients, highlight the specific ways that language is related to cognition. As well, these disturbances help focus on the specific contributions of different systems of language to successful communication. In clear cases of inadequate verbal communication, the specific linguistic system responsible for the difficulty can be isolated.

This chapter first reviews some of the basic issues in studying the language of psychiatric patients and in studying how the systems of language relate to social and cognitive issues. The first set of data concerns the language of schizophrenia and the relationship between thought disorder and language. The next topic is a study of the language of manic and depressed patients. The third topic is a case study of an amnestic syndrome as revealed in language. The clear cognitive deficits in this case are used as a starting point for examining the cohesion in the subject's speech and the social effect of her language. A fourth study looks at the use of cohesion longitudinally. Cohesion is examined in relation to changes in clinical state to understand the relationships between various measures of cohesion and cognitive processes and the effects of the cohesion on interaction.

Various psychiatric syndromes are associated with different disturbances in verbal communications. Typically, these syndromes are also associated with identifiable social and cognitive deficits. From the point of view of language, identification of deficits in specific functions provides rich hypotheses about the disturbances of social interaction and cognitive processing. If a class of speakers rarely uses a particular set of linguistic options that have a specific function, then a cognitive process underlying that function can be proposed and evidence for it sought in other realms of processing, both verbal and nonverbal. In a parallel manner, the social effect of rarely using a set of linguistic options can be related to the clinical presentation of the syndrome.

The linguistic approach to psychiatric syndromes can help characterize the particular atypicalities in the syndromes. The relation between linguistic descriptions and psychiatric entities is bidirectional. Linguistic systems, viewed functionally, must be processed by cognitive mechanisms that probably underlie other types of processing. Linguistic systems provide a means for communicating and cannot be seen as constructed and functioning independent of what they are used to achieve in communication. Similarly, those systems must be related to plausible processing mechanisms. In cases of psychiatric syndromes there are frequently problems both in social interaction and in cognitive processing. These associations of deficits may be the result of accidental impairments of different neurological systems (see Marshall, 1982). However, the precision of hypotheses about communication that systemic functional linguistics provides can suggest mechanisms common to social interaction and other cognitive deficits. In the other direction, hypotheses about cognitive state and psychiatric condition suggest lines for the investigation of linguistic systems. Although concepts of thought disorder, psychosis, and social impairment may be loosely defined and difficult to determine on the basis of specific, objective measures, they are stable and clinically valid generalizations about individuals and groups that can at least initially serve to suggest specific atypicalities in the use of language.

The recent literature on a number of syndromes discusses the possible associations of language with other kinds of processing. Examples of this line of research and the approach that has been taken will be given as a background to the more detailed discussions of language in a number of psychiatric syndromes. Lovett, Dennis, and Newman (1986) studied the use of pronouns in hemidecorticate adolescents. These subjects have had either the left or right hemisphere removed before five months of age. The study is thus an investigation of the hemisphere-dependent differences in the use of one kind of cohesion. Based on three subjects, their findings show that the intact left hemisphere has the greatest pronoun to antecedent ratio, the most links across propositional boundaries, the most links mediated by another cohesive item, longer spans of links in terms of propositions, and the most pronoun deletions (largely anaphoric reference). The evidence suggests that anaphoric reference is differentially controlled by the two hemispheres. An interesting negative finding of Lovett et al. is that a classification of pronouns into traditional parts of speech revealed no differences between the intact left and right hemispheres. These parts of speech (nominative, objective, possessive, relative, etc.) reflect a variety of semantic and grammatical relations. It would be hard to interpret such a difference if it were found. The lack of difference supports the notion that anaphoric reference is itself differentially processed by the two hemispheres, but that sentence processing involves a variety of subsystems that are distributed into both hemispheres. Given that the subjects of the study had one hemisphere removed shortly after birth and long before language develops, it is likely that the remaining neurological structures process language in ways that are not typical for normal children. Thus, a finding of hemispheric differences in the processing of anaphoric reference, but no differences when a variety of grammatical categories are included, provides evidence that the processing of anaphoric reference may be a relatively unitary phenomenon processed more typically in the dominant hemisphere, unlike more general syntactic processes involving both hemispheres.

A less biological cognitive approach to psychiatric language is suggested by Bellack, Morrison, and Mueser (1989). They note that social interaction unfolds rapidly, and so the cognitive processes must involve little planning. Rather, the language produced must be in relation to immediately preceding verbal and nonverbal events. To account for such behavior and the dysfunction in schizophrenia, Bellack, Morrison, and Mueser imply that speakers have readymade cognitive strategies that are called on when cues are presented in conversation. They note that schizophrenics are known to have deficits in a range of cognitive operations. The relation of such deficits to the specific problems in language can lead to an understanding of the processes underlying language use and help explain a range of deficits in terms of underlying processes.

There are a number of conceptual and methodological problems in studying the use of language in a cognitive and even biological context. There is a problem in conceptualizing the relation between cognitive and social processing. The language deficits of schizophrenics may be seen either as a cognitive problem in organizing thoughts or as a problem in expressing thoughts in a socially appropriate way. Rutter (1985) presents the problems in terms of the social processes. On the other hand, Bellack, Morrison, and Mueser (1989, p. 111) conclude that "it is virtually impossible to determine whether any speech anomaly is a manifestation of a linguistic problem or an underlying dysfunction in thought." In fact, a method of study is needed that permits examination of social and cognitive influence on language.

The work of Rochester and Martin (1977, 1979) combines both cognitive and social perspectives. They studied the language of their subjects in a variety of social situations that have different cognitive demands: an instructed interview, the recall of a narrative, and the description and interpretation of cartoons. A cognitive difficulty that contributes to atypical language may create a problem in social interaction. A difficulty in social interaction should prompt an investigation of an underlying cognitive processing defect. Carpenter (1987) properly cautions, however, against attributing causation to association in such circumstances. Rather, association can be used to form hypotheses that must then be tested by examining different kinds of data gathered under various conditions from different groups of subjects. An association in one part of the data can suggest a way of looking at other data to see if a common concept, perhaps of causation, is tenable. The description and use of data later in this chapter follows this pattern of association to hypotheses to examination of further data.

Another set of methodological problems has to do with the

classification of subjects. There is a wider problem of the value of case studies compared to group studies that is involved. If homogeneity cannot be established within a group, averaging over the group can eliminate atypical values on measures that are just the deficit at issue. This problem has been the focus of considerable recent debate as refered to in Chapter 3. The narrower issue for the language of psychiatric patients is set out by Halpern and McCartin-Clark (1984). In studying adult aphasics and schizophrenics, they argue that syndromes must be differentiated since different therapies may be involved. Although there may be an overlap of symptoms, it is still important to understand the underlying processing. The symptoms can then be interpreted in the context of other deficits or abilities. A particular linguistic deficit may indicate an organic, cognitive, or social locus of deficit depending on the other deficits that are present. It is the total picture of deficits and atypicalities that helps to group subjects appropriately and to create generalizations. Szatmari, Bremner, and Nagy (1989) make this point with respect to Asperger's syndrome. They note that although certain patients may have individual symptoms of Asperger's syndrome, they do not have "the entire constellation of clinical criteria."

The method in the following presentation of data is to start with the description of the functional linguistic atypicalities and to then consider other areas of processing that are part of the syndrome in question. In these studies there are a number of areas of uncertainty. The linguistic descriptions themselves represent a point in developing linguistic theory that is subject to revision and refinement. The selection of subjects is always dependent on complex clinical judgment and of the diagnostic criteria used. Like linguistic theory, diagnostic criteria can be improved on as further physiological evidence accumulates and theories of psychopathology advance. Nevertheless, the studies of language in psychiatric syndromes do seem to be replicable and clinically valid (see, for example, Bartolucci & Fine, 1987; Harvey,1983; Rund,1988; Rutter, 1985).

SCHIZOPHRENIA

The Issues

Schizophrenia is probably the psychiatric syndrome most studied in terms of language. Current theories and findings on schizophrenia are reviewed with an emphasis on language. The discussion includes the explication of thought disorder, the social and cognitive components of thought disorder, comparisons with other syndromes, information processing, and neuropsychological approaches.

The identification of thought disorder as the primary symptom of schizophrenia stems from the work of Kraeplin and Bleuler in the early part of the 20th century. Solovay, Shenton, and Holzman (1987, p. 13) note that thought disorder was "not intended to denote a unitary dimension or process; rather, it refers to any description, deficit or slippage in various aspects of thinking, such as concentration, attention, reasoning or distraction." They further identify Bleuler's concept of thought disorder as the primary symptom of schizophrenia, thus different in status from symptoms such as delusions and hallucinations that are taken to be accessory. A recent clinically oriented textbook account of schizophrenia lists the first-rank symptoms of schizophrenia as: auditory hallucinations, delusions of influence, and thought disorder (Birchwood, Hallett, & Preston, 1989). Thought disorders are further specified as: thought insertion ("the subject experiences thoughts which are *not his own*, intruding into his consciousness"), thought broadcast ("the individual believes his thoughts to be shared with others often over long distances"), audible thoughts ("the individual experiences his thoughts spoken out loud in his mind"), and thought withdrawal ("the individual experiences an abrupt cessation of all thoughts not due to activity or distractibility and believes that his thoughts have been removed from his mind by an alien force"). These symptoms rely heavily on the individual's report of his experiences. Solovay et al. (1987) ultimately characterize schizophrenic thought disorder in terms of fluid thinking, interpenetrations of one idea by another, unstable referents, and fragmented and elliptical communications.

As a number of researchers have pointed out (see Rochester & Martin, 1979 for a clear presentation), the relationship between thought disorder and language can be circular. Thought disorder is inferred from language, but it is the language that is described as disordered. If a speaker's language is described as disordered or loose, then it is concluded that this is the result of disordered thought. However, the presence of disordered thought is inferred from the linguistic evidence. This problem and an approach that attempts to limit the circularity of the concepts of language and thoughts is discussed below. First, though, schizophrenia itself is examined.

A broad approach to schizophrenia must include biological, psychological, and social systems. Carpenter (1987) suggests such an approach with two basic means of analyzing data. The analysis of function is accomplished by looking at the life story and results in the exploration of meaning. A second technique is that of correlation that explores mechanism by looking at form. These two explanatory methods use different data sources. The exploration of life story gives information concerning social and psychodynamic systems, and the exploration of correlation can give information about biological functioning. The two approaches have their strengths and weaknesses, and Carpenter's argument is that they must not be seen as mutually exclusive, but as complementary ways of studying schizophrenia. In accordance with this broad approach, Carpenter (1987, p. 3) sees schizophrenia as "an illness destroying the inner unity of mind and weakening the volition and drive that constitute our essential character" and in which "the patient's place in society erodes in an interactive process reflecting the incapacity to engage and sustain social bonds and society's reaction to the social and personal deviancy caused by the illness." There are thus psychological and social breakdowns which interact.

As a clinical syndrome, the individuals classed as schizophrenic must be sufficiently similar in signs and symptoms and perhaps in other elements of the disease model: onset, distribution, morbidity, course, and treatment response. However, the clinical boundaries are fuzzy, and the set of patients within the syndrome is thus heterogeneous. Carpenter therefore argues that the correlational approach is weakened. An additional contribution to the heterogeneity of the patients within the syndrome is the disjunctive nature of the definition of schizophrenia. Since there is a list of characteristics of schizophrenia, no set of which is necessary and sufficient for inclusion within the syndrome, patients with the same label of schizophrenia may not have any symptoms in common (see Birchwood et al., 1989, for one discussion of the problem).

Carpenter's (1987) approach is to look to models to provide direction for research. These models cannot be on one level of functioning (sociological, psychological, or biological), but must permit activity on one level to influence other levels—a reverberating system. The implications for schizophrenia are, according to Carpenter (1987, p. 5):

1. The study of schizophrenia must ascertain the nature of disordered function at multiple levels of human organization.
2. Interactions between these levels account for the manifestations of the disease.
3. When multiple levels simultaneously subserve an observed dysfunction, it is not a priori evident which is primary.

The approach to empirical data in the following study is initially correlational, but the use of functional linguistic theory provides information about the quality of social interactions. By relating the linguistic facts to information of other forms of cognitive processing, the cognitive processes that affect the social interactions can be indirectly explored. It is the detail of the linguistic theory that provides rich hypotheses about social interaction and cognitive processing. However, Carpenter's warning about attributing causation to one level or another must be heeded.

Language and Thought Disorder

The relation between language and thought in schizophrenia has been the subject of detailed arguments. These arguments will be reviewed with some of the relevant evidence. Rosenberg and Abbeduto (1982) summarize the early views of what they call schizophrenic language. They note the disjunctive criteria used to define schizophrenia and indicate that schizophrenic language participates in the disjunction. Only some patients labeled schizophrenic have schizophrenic language, and even in these patients such language is only intermittent. Furthermore, only production, and not comprehension, is affected. To increase the diagnostic and research difficulties, the characteristics of schizophrenic language, according to Rosenberg and Abbeduto (1982), are also found in other disorders and even in normals. This great uncertainty in the attribution of linguistic features to a syndrome suggests that a more detailed analysis of language is necessary. It is not easy to attain homogeneity in terms of diagnostic features of the speakers, so an analysis of language can point to commonalities in cognitive and social processing.

Chaika (1974) listed six features that, especially in combination, characterize the language of schizophrenics. These features are:

1. The inappropriate matching of semantic features to phonological strings, thus producing neologisms;
2. Paying attention to irrelevant semantic features;
3. Paying attention to irrelevant phonological features;
4. Not maintaining a topic;
5. Disruption in the ability to apply rules of syntax and discourse; and
6. Failure to detect errors in speech.

Chaika's approach focuses on the language inabilities of the schizophrenic, rather than on a difficulty in thought.

The debate about the locus of the disorder in schizophrenia followed immediately from Chaika (1974) and is briefly summarized in Rochester and Martin (1979). Some 10 years later the issues were raised again by Lanin-Kettering and Harrow (1985) and replied to by Chaika and Lambe (1985). Lanin-Kattering and Harrow (1985) present three substantive arguments against Chaika's overall approach to schizophrenic language. A fourth argument is one of simplicity of competing explanations and is not discussed here.

First, Lanin-Kettering and Harrow argue that regarding the problems of schizophrenics as a language disorder will slow research. They agree that thought is a theoretical construct and that language is the observable phenomenon. They claim that thought disorder as a construct within a set of interlocking relationships can be studied by a variety of methods. Consistent observations from different areas can validate the constructs of thought and of thought disorder.

Second, Lanin-Kettering and Harrow argue that the disorders in language are good clues to disorders in thought in schizophrenia. The evidence they present includes:

1. The co-occurrence of nonverbal problems such as object sorting with language problems,
2. The mixing of ideas, intermingling, and problems of ideational relevance,
3. The presence of strange nonlinguistic behavior such as delusions and posturing, and
4. The fact that delusions correlate with disordered speech.

Language, then, is not the only disorder, but offers a method of studying something more fundamental and pervasive in schizophrenia: thought disorder.

The third issue for Lanin-Kettering and Harrow is the relation between language and thought. They argue that language in use is based on thought, and at the level of semantics and discourse, language and thought cannot be separated. It is at this level that there is a disturbance in schizophrenic language. The real problem, they claim, is where to assign the disturbance in meaning and relevance, to thought or to language.

Chaika and Lambe (1985) use a restricted notion of language to argue against Lanin-Kettering and Harrow (1985). Chaika and Lambe firstly claim that the equation of language with thought is a fallacy. Evidence such as writer's block, aphasia, and mutism suggest that language and thought can be separated. Furthermore, there are cases of schizophrenia that do not exhibit language disorder. Even the argument that strange thoughts create both strange behaviors and strange language is questioned. Chaika and Lambe claim that the argument is circular since the strange language is itself one of the pieces of evidence for the concept of strange thoughts. Rather, they suggest that detailed analysis of language is needed to determine what the strangeness is in schizophrenic speech. This strangeness in speech can then be related to thoughts.

In terms of methodology, Chaika and Lambe disagree that it is possible to infer strange ideas and strange thinking from dysfunction on certain tasks. They claim that observing a difficulty in a task such as object sorting or the explanation of proverbs does not necessarily lead to an inference of disordered thought. Rather, there could be other sources of the difficulties.

Missing from much of Chaika and Lambe's approach is the use of language in context. Not only does language change (as Chaika and Lambe point out for the lexicon), but it changes when speakers agree to use it in new ways. This agreement depends on factors such as the social status of the speakers, the task at hand, and the situation (see, for example, Gregory & Carroll, 1978; Martin 1983b; Rochester & Martin, 1979). Any strangeness in schizophrenic speech derives from how it is used in context and what the typical use of language is in such contexts. Chaika and Lambe seem to reify language and then can compare the language of schizophrenics to a set of rules for normal language. Rather, the systems of language together account for language that is appropriate for given contexts. When studying the language of schizophrenics, the view of language must be broad. Schizophrenics do not function well in society largely because of language, and so it is the aspects of language that are needed for social interaction that must be studied. Therefore, the text-forming characteristics of language are important. If the speech produced does not fit in to its verbal and nonverbal context, then it will sound inappropriate or perhaps "strange" or "disordered."

Lanin-Kettering and Harrow infer disordered thought from what they view as disordered language. However, they do not consider a careful description of the characteristics of discourse to give some detail of disordered thought. Furthermore, thoughts themselves are interpreted as being reflected in language; for example, the intermingling in language reflecting disruption in thought. Language may reflect underlying processes, but these processes may not be directly identifiable in language. That is, concluding intermingling in thought from intermingling in speech assumes similar processes. On the other hand, the kinds of cognitive skills needed to produce language appropriate to the context may well be expected to serve other behaviors (perhaps eye tracking or object sorting). In these cases the evidence must be carefully considered, since there may be various intervening variables or intermediate processes. The work of Rochester and Martin is the closest in conception and detailed linguistic analyses to the empirical data reported here. Therefore, their work will be reviewed in some detail.

In his "sociolinguistic retrospective" of his work on schizophrenia, Martin (n.d.) sets out the relation between language and disruptions in sanity. He sees a disruption in sanity as the inability to share social reality. In turn, social reality is built up and displayed by cohesive discourse. People talk in order to build up and maintain a social reality. In social and, more particularly, verbal interaction individuals negotiate a common understanding of their environment and how they will share information. Each linguistic contribution to social interaction is in the context of the presumed or agreed reality up to that point. Language operates within the shared linguistic and nonlinguistic contexts. When language does not reflect what was taken to be shared, the speaker seems to be not in his social mind. Martin makes the point that it is not what a speaker says, but how it fits that matters. What a speaker says is to a large extent how it fits in. As Martin notes, hearers try to make sense of what is said. All hearers initially assume that their interlocutors are sane and can and do use their language to build and maintain social reality. Thus, when a degraded message is heard, the listener tries to fit it into the reality assumed to be shared up to that point. To state this linguistically, listeners assume that language has texture that relates it to the verbal and nonverbal context.

Lack of sanity is apparent when a speaker's language is uninterpretable. If a hearer cannot make sense of a speaker, then there is no shared reality. If the uninterpretability derives from an aphasia, then the hearer may attempt a nonverbal means of communication, which, depending on the type and severity of the verbal or cognitive impairment, may be successful in building a shared reality. Most schizophrenics do not have obvious impairments just in language or even in some very general area of cognitive processing. Rather, the schizophrenic seems to be using language to communicate, but the language is uninterpretable enough to thwart the usual attempt to build social reality with it.

Cohesion has a special role in creating social reality. Cohesion is the nonstructural part of the textual component of language (see Halliday, 1985), and it is the textual component that provides the resources to make language fit with its verbal and nonverbal context. Martin (n.d.) notes that lexical cohesion displays that the speaker is staying on the same topic, reference displays the continuing identity of participants, and conjunction shows the logical connections among clauses. All three kinds of cohesion are necessary to use language to create and sustain a shared reality and appear sane.

Rochester and Martin (1979) examined the speech of thought disorder and non-thought-disordered schizophrenics and nonpatient normal controls in three situations. The categorizing of thought disordered (TD) and nonthought disordered (NTD) was based on the judgments of two psychiatrists viewing videotapes of unstructured interviews and using a 4-point scale (Cancro, 1969). The three situations for gathering language samples were an unstructured interview, the retelling of a brief narrative, and the description and interpretation of 10 cartoon pictures. A 3-minute section of the unstructured interview was used for each subject. Thus, Rochester and Martin could study the language of the three groups of speakers and how they spoke in different situations.

In general, the schizophrenics used less cohesion than the nonpatient controls. More specifically, the thought-disordered schizophrenics used more lexical cohesion. Rochester and Martin (1977, 1979) also examined what they called retrieval categories that specify the location of the information necessary to interpret the cohesive item. They found that the thought disordered schizophrenics used the most exophoric reference in the noninterview situations. The thought-disordered speakers also used the most unclear reference. This difference was particularly strong in the narrative recall and the interview. The schizophrenic groups used the least amount of bridging—the reliance on the implicit verbal context. Thus, the nature of the social interaction in the various situations and the nature of the manipulation of information are associated with variation in the use of cohesion.

Harvey, Earle-Boyer, and Levinson (1988) have recently shown that the reference failures examined by Rochester and Martin are associated with more general information-processing difficulties. They show that digit-span performance with a distraction was negatively correlated to reference failures in schizophrenia, and that the severity of the thought disorder (judged clinically) was related to the susceptibility of distraction. Their work shows that the positive symptoms of thought disorder (pressure of speech, incoherence, derailment, etc.) are predicted by general serial recall ability rather than by the competence in reality monitoring. That is, some of the essential elements of schizophrenic language seem to be related to an aspect of information processing, distinct from the ability to determine whether some information was actually said or just thought about. The results suggest that the reference failures in schizophrenia that contribute to uninterpretable language may be associated with and even caused by information-processing difficulties that are evident in tasks quite different from spontaneous speech. In terms of Carpenter's (1987) approach there is then the possibility of an interaction between the ability to process language and the social effectiveness of the language produced. It is interesting to note that the effect of cognition is in terms of a basic processing ability rather than in a direct ability to distinguish reality from thoughts.

The schizophrenics' reliance on lexical cohesion found by Rochester and Martin has been replicated and extended by Manschreck, Maher, Hoover, and Ames (1985). In an investigation of nonschizophrenics and schizophrenics of various degrees of severity, they found that repetitions of three-word phrases varied with clinical severity measured by whether patients were hospitalized and the length of hospitalization. The schizophrenics repeated less common vocabulary rather than the most frequent words. However, the distance between repetitions did not discriminate the schizophrenics from the controls. Manschreck et al. (1985, p. 265) suggest that "in schizophrenic speech there is a breakdown in the mechanism that governs normal repetition patterns." The contribution of such repetition to social interaction and to the assessment of formal thought disorder must be explored functionally. In a model that includes both social and cognitive approaches to language, the use of repeated phrases is seen as an attempt to create cohesion and therefore texture. Repetition is a form of text creation; however, its overuse by schizophrenics may be an indicator of weakness in other text-creating devices, rather than just a deficit in a mechanism for repetition.

Bellack, Morrison, and Mueser (1989, p. 111) note that there are nonlinguistic factors that affect the communication of schizophrenics, but contend that disordered communication is a significant symptom on its own and not secondary to faulty reasoning or bizarre thinking. They state that "it is virtually impossible to determine whether any particular speech anomaly is a manifestation of a linguistic problem or an underlying dysfunction in thought." The difficulty in their approach (continuing from Rutter, 1985) is a dichotomy between thought and the language that is used to express thought to others. Since we have only language as the phenomenon that can be investigated directly, it is a reasonable object of inquiry. The concept of thought can be useful if it can be substantiated by other nonlinguistic data as was the issue in the Lanin-Kettering and Harrow and Chaika and Lambe controversy.

Comparative Studies

A series of studies has helped clarify the nature of schizophrenic language by comparing schizophrenics to other psychiatric groups. These studies look for commonalities between groups in order to understand the syndromes and their linguistic and cognitive underpinnings.

On the most general level, Halpern and McCartin-Clark (1984) compared 61 aphasics to 61 chronic schizophrenics. Both groups are difficult for hearers to interpret, but it is important to be able to differentiate the syndromes and to understand the deficits in the context of other deficits and abilities. They administered a large number of language tests that measured comprehension, production, and fluency. Of the tests that discriminated the schizophrenics from the aphasics, the schizophrenics were better on writing to dictation, syntax, naming, and fluency. The schizophrenics were poorer on relevance, showing little self-correction. Furthermore, schizophrenics made more errors, especially in naming and adequacy with increased periods of institutionalization. Although such a study does not suggest specific inadequate mechanisms underlying schizophrenic language, it does confirm the intact organization of most of a schizophrenic's language. The overlap in a listener's difficulty with schizophrenic and aphasic language does not indicate common underlying processes.

The comparison of schizophrenia and mania has been pursued in a number of ways. Harvey, Earle-Boyer, and Levinson (1986, 1988) have studied the relationship between distractibility, discourse failures, and cognitive deficits in schizophrenics and manics. Their measure of cognitive processing was serial recall, which other studies have correlated with clinical thought disorder. Distraction was introduced by having a male voice present distraction digits inbetween the target digits presented by a female voice. The distraction task affected the performance of both manics and schizophrenics. The information-processing performance of both groups was associated with the measures of discourse failure (ambiguous and unclear references as in Rochester & Martin, 1979). For the manics, recall performance predicts discourse failure suggesting a general information-processing deficit. In contrast, the schizophrenics' susceptibility to external distraction was most important in predicting this group's discourse failure. Thus, the surface-level similarity in cohesion failure seems to represent different underlying processing deficits, with the schizophrenics' deficit associated with auditory distraction in serial recall.

In the cross-temporal study of thought disorder in schizophrenics and manics, Harvey et al. (1988) again found differences underlying the performance of their two subject groups. In test-retest data over a period of four days they found that the cognitive defects of the manics on serial recall appeared to be a function of severity of positive thought disorder (pressure of speech, incoherence, derailment, etc.), whereas for schizophrenics it was distraction performance that contributed to the variance of positive thought disorder. To repeat, then, these studies suggest different mechanisms for manic and schizophrenic thought disorder. The results point to a locus for the cognitive impairment associated with an information-processing problem that contributes to language of schizophrenics that does not build a shared reality. Distractibility by verbal information is plausible in accounting for a schizophrenics' discourse. If language must be processed and negotiated in conversation or even in story recall (as in Rochester & Martin's narrative task), then that language may itself serve as a distraction that Harvey et al. (1988) show to contribute to severity of positive thought disorder. As positive thought disorder is defined by Harvey et al. (1988), language is the key component: pressure of speech, derailment, tangentiality, incoherence, illogicality. Thus, distraction for the schizophrenics is an important influence on the severity of a number of linguistic deficits. More precise differences in the processing of manics and schizophrenics must then await more precise assessment of the language variables. Instead of ratings on the above five (linguistic) signs of thought disorder, specific linguistic measures are needed.

Solovay et al. (1987) provide a detailed analysis of the thought disorder of manics and schizophrenics derived from responses to the Rorschach test. Twenty-three categories of thought disorder were scored. Some of these categories involve specific linguistic features, such as changes, perseverations, or neologisms. Other categories are inferences from the responses: flippant response, peculiar verbalizations and responses, idiosyncratic symbolism, confabulations, or contamination. Solovay et al. studied various ways of grouping the scores and arrived at characterizations of manic and schizophrenics thought disorder. The schizophrenic thought disorder is characterized as fluid thinking, interpenetrations of one idea by another, unstable verbal referents, and fragmented and elliptical communications. The thought disorder conveys "an impression of internal turmoil and bewilderment and may cause confusion in the listener as well" (Solovay et al., 1987, p. 20). The characteristics of manic thought disorder are "ideas loosely strung together and extravagantly combined and elaborated" (Solovay et al., 1987, p. 19). Both types of thought disorder show vagueness, perseveration, clangs, and inappropriate distance. Thought disorder is then seen as composed of a number of factors which only partly overlap in mania and schizophrenia. From the data presented by Solovay et al., it is not clear how important language itself is the determination of thought disorder. It is also important to distinguish the categories that infer thought disorder from linguistic data and those that rely on inferences of thought itself (e.g., confusion, fabulized combinations, confabulations, contamination).

Discourse analysis is used by Hoffman, Stopek, and

Andreasen (1986) to distinguish manics from schizophrenics. They wish to go beyond concepts such as loose associations to measures that permit inferences "regarding cognitive processes underlying speech production" (Hoffman et al., 1986, p. 831). Discourse hierarchies are built from statements and the dependency relations among them. Statements were defined as "any noninfinitive verb appearing in the text coupled with its (explicit or implicit) subject and complement" (Hoffman et al., 1986, p. 833). Subordination between statements was determined by truth values: "One statement was considered to presuppose or be subordinate to another if the first required the assumption of the truth of the second to be interpreted in context" (Hoffman et al., 1986, p. 833).

Manics and schizophrenics differed in the kinds of discourse structures they produced. The manics produced complex, well-formed messages in hierarchical substructures related by the assumption of truth among the statements. The schizophrenics produced smaller substructures. The manics had longer utterances and more nodes in the largest discourse trees. Hoffman et al. also correlated the size of the discourse trees to the number of deviances from a hierarchical structure. The manics showed a strong negative correlation on these two variables suggesting a deficiency in shifting from topic to topic. When the topics are relatively long, there are fewer shifts and less cases of deviance. However, for the schizophrenics the two scores are not significantly correlating, supporting a more general deficiency model for schizophrenic language. Hoffman et al. link these findings to other data showing that schizophrenics rely on extraneous cues such as phonetic similarities, word play, and affective factors in constructing discourse.

Hoffman et al. (1986) offer a valuable study in providing information about the semantic structure of schizophrenic and manic speech. The basis of the hierarchical structures is the truth-value relationship between statements. However, language is held together and made coherent by factors other than presupposition. The work of Sperber and Wilson (1986, and see 1987, for comments) proposes relevance as a general principle for the creation of appropriate language, and Halliday and Hasan (1976; Halliday, 1985) have developed the notion of text as a functional unifying factor for language in context. Thus, there are a number of measures more subtle than a dichotomy of true or false to show the relationship of one stretch of language to another. Ideally, these measures should be used in conjunction to build a portrait of deviant language and to permit the exploration of the underlying mechanisms.

Sociocognitive Approaches

Two recent approaches to schizophrenia have discussed the interaction of social and cognitive factors. Morrison and Bellack (1987) are primarily concerned with the social functioning of schizophrenics. They note that the deterioration in social relations is a diagnostic criterion and is present before and after acute stages of schizophrenia and when gross symptoms of psychosis such as hallucinations and delusions are controlled. Drawing on Nuechterlein and Dawson (1984), Morrison and Bellack suggest that schizophrenic symptoms are the product of vulnerability characteristics that derive from genetic influences interacting with the early physical and social environment. The vulnerability characteristics include:

1. "Reduced available information-processing capacity;"
2. "Autonomic hypersensitivity to adverse stimuli;" and
3. "Social competence and coping deficits."

The social skills of schizophrenics may not have developed normally or may have deteriorated as a result of institutionalization. Interactions in the family may also contribute to the social problems of schizophrenics and how they emerge. This combination of vulnerability factors and the social and biological interactions helps predict individual variation in schizophrenia and the variety of different episodic symptoms.

In terms of research, a balance of case studies and group studies are needed. Case studies allow the assessment of social abilities and other abilities, states, and deficits. Group studies are helpful in finding the general deficits in social ability that Morrison and Bellack note are so common in schizophrenics. The vulnerability characteristics suggest the kinds of variables that will be productive in detailing the mechanisms underlying schizophrenia. The model clearly indicates the need for studying the social interaction of schizophrenics, since that is a realm that suggests vulnerability for the disorder and is present at many phases and in many cases. Furthermore, the information-processing deficits should be studied and related to the social difficulties of schizophrenics.

A second account of the interaction of social and cognitive factors is presented by Rund (1988). Rund reviews cognitive theories of schizophrenia, including attention and information processing. He notes a connection among parental egocentricity in communication, anticipating information needs, and attentional disturbances in schizophrenics (see also, Rund, 1986). If there is not proper focusing on relevant stimuli, "the speech is characterized by a use of words and expressions that have not been made commonly known, monologues, use of words and expressions with idiosyncratic content, incomplete and interrupted sentences, irrelevant associations, perceptual misunderstandings, slips of the tongue, perseverations, tangential comments, etc." (Rund, 1988, p. 199). That is, a large number of specific symptoms in speech may be the result of both parental communication patterns and a cognitive deficit of attention in the speaker. Rund's analysis of empirical findings in the context of both social developmental factors and cognitive ones is support for the productivity of the approach.

Neuropsychological approaches

There are some recent neuropsychological approaches to schizophrenia that hypothesize models and mechanisms to explain thought disorder and language problems in schizophrenia. These approaches are powerful within their domains, but tend to exclude social interaction as influencing or being the product of language problems.

The model-theoretic approach establishes a formal model that then predicts further relationships and structures of objects that are being modeled. Matthysse (1987, p. 180) assumes that there are laws of thoughts that are "a set of necessary and sufficient conditions for thoughts to be well formed." Such laws are considered responsible for the ability of normal speakers to decide that certain thoughts of schizophrenics are not well formed. Matthysse then connects such a model of competence to an assembly of neurons as a model for a formal system of rules of thought. Several conclusions are drawn from the model-theoretic approach. First, a number of possible deficits rather than a single deficit is likely. Schizophrenics may have different deficits in the underlying model of the laws of thought, and it will be difficult to predict the deficit in individual cases. Second, the model predicts that the filtering out of inappropriately formed thoughts is not a normal process that is impaired in schizophrenic. Rather, the model assumes that only well-formed thoughts are produced. If there is a deficit in cerebral function then a filter is perhaps invoked accounting for the slow responses of schizophrenics.

A defect at the level of neurons would predict deficits in the rule systems represented by the neuronal assembly. It could then be expected according to Matthysse (1987, p. 182) that there would be performance problems "in other domains where normal competence can be described by formal rule systems." As Matthysse himself notes, syntax is such a domain, but the syntax of schizophrenic speakers is largely intact.

The model-theoretic approach of Matthysse (1987) is a powerful tool in relating behavior to neuropsychological structures, but has a number of serious limitations. First, thoughts are judged from language, and an appropriate formula must be determined to relate well- and ill-formed language to well- and ill-formed thought. If the syntax of schizophrenic speakers is not the indicator of ill-formed thought, then there must be some other level of organization of language that signals the presence of the ill-formed thought. Discovering and describing this level is a matter of better and more comprehensive models of language (as reviewed earlier). Furthermore, as studies such as Rochester and Martin (1979) show, the model of language has to include the situation of language use, so that the occurrence of disordered language, representing thought disorder in Matthysse's model, can be better predicted. If disturbances in language occur more frequently in some situations than others, then the model must include a component sensitive to the operative elements of the situations. In general, the model must clarify the relation between thought and language. As it stands, thought disorder is interpreted directly from disturbances in language, but the relevant analysis of language is not hypothesized. For example, what is the relation between the set of necessary and sufficient conditions for the production of well-formed thoughts and the set of necessary and sufficient conditions for the production of well-formed language in context (including, of course, discourse rules and appropriateness constraints)? Are these two sets of conditions identical or related in some other way, perhaps partially overlapping?

Firth and Done (1988) and Crosson and Hughes (1987) propose neuropsychological mechanisms identified closely with brain mechanisms to explain the nature of thought disorder in schizophrenia. Crosson and Hughes (1987) explicitly equate thought disorder with incoherent language output. They propose that schizophrenic language results from an impairment of an executive function responsible for coordinating simultaneous language processes. With lack of coordination, the language formulating mechanisms lose track of contextual referents. Alternatively, (a) it may be that a defect in attention leads to an inability to focus on the context when other language processes are engaged; or (b) a deficit early in the information-processing system results in poor storage of information in buffers, thus leading to a loss of context for later language production. Crosson and Hughes (1987) suggest that the defects in schizophrenic language can be related to the connections among various neurological structures rather than the structures in isolation. Their review of studies leads to connections of the limbic system, midbrain tegmentum, and globus pallidus to the nucleus accumbens and other structures related at one step removed from the nucleus accumbens.

Firth and Done (1988) suggest that the positive and negative symptoms of schizophrenia derive from different underlying psychological processes that are in turn related to different brain systems. The positive symptoms (hallucinations and delusions) are seen as the result of a failure in the internal monitoring of actions. The internal monitor normally indicates that an action is about to take place and its source is internal or external. If internally generated acts are not monitored, then the patient may experience himself "carrying out acts without awareness of a willed intention to perform such acts" (Firth & Done, 1988, p. 439). Auditory hallucinations are explained as "the result of the patient thinking or 'talking to himself,' but not recognizing the source of this stimulation" (Firth & Done, 1988, p. 440). Neurophysiologically, Firth and Done account for these spontaneous, self-generated acts in faulty connections between the prefontal cortex (which initiates intended self-generated acts) and the hyppocampus.

Negative symptoms (flattening of affect, poverty of speech, cognitive impairment) are associated with a defect in generating, rather than monitoring, self-generated action according to Firth and Done (1988). Studies from neurologically damaged patients suggest that the malfunction leading to the negative symptoms "lies somewhere in the pathways connecting the prefontal lobes and the striatum" (Firth & Done, 1988, p. 441). Although we cannot go into the detailed merits of the neurophysiological proposals, it is clear that detailed analyses of the language of schizophrenics will provide a clearer basis for the relating of the symptoms and psychological processes of schizophrenia to neurophysiological structures. Success in determining these structures can then be used to generate new hypotheses about the sets of symptoms and the language that is frequently used to identify them.

Summary

The linguistic and cognitive atypicalities in schizophrenia have been reviewed from a number of perspectives. Each theoretical perspective leads to different research strategies and different accounts of the atypicalities. The psychiatric approach defines schizophrenia in terms of signs and symptoms with an emphasis on thought disorder. Clinically useful groupings emerge, but given the circularity in the definitions of thought disorder and language disturbance and the operational vagueness of some of the symptoms, it is difficult to use the approach to examine underlying cognitive mechanisms or even specific deficits in social interaction. Categories such as thought disorder, delusional thinking, social withdrawal, or ambivalence do not present enough specificity to be related to mechanisms that may explain the processing difficulties or the social deficits found in patients.

Linguistic approaches to schizophrenia are also dependent on specific theoretical frameworks. Chaika's careful linguistic examinations of schizophrenia rely on a variety of linguistic variables including: neologisms, irrelevant semantic features, topic maintenance, syntax, and discourse rules. Illuminating as these categories can sometimes be in describing schizophrenic language, they do not represent a theoretically motivated view of language that accounts in a unified way for either the cognitive processing of language or the social impairments resulting from the peculiar language often produced by schizophrenics.

The work of Rochester and Martin, on the other hand, is grounded in a functional theory of language that attempts to account for the communicative effect of each atypicality found in the language of schizophrenics. Their work is an advance toward explaining the social impairments of the speakers and why some speakers sound as if they have disordered thoughts. However, Rochester and Martin do not emphasize the cognitive processing difficulties that may underlie at least some of the typical language of schizophrenics.

At this point neuropsychological theories can be added to studies of specific linguistic deficits. The function linguistic theory can help explain the socially bizarre language of schizophrenics and neuropsychological theories, and even neurophysiological approaches can suggest processing defects and neurological systems that are involved in the output of such language. Although the link between neurophysiology and language in schizophrenia is not well developed, the use of functional linguistic theories in such work can supply specific data about the linguistic atypicalities that matter in social interaction.

METHODOLOGY

The language of schizophrenics is evident to different extents depending on context (Rochester & Martin, 1979). This variation is an important consideration in gathering data. The task of all speakers is to contribute language to situations in a way that is relevant and appropriate. Rochester and Martin (1979) found that in the interview situation thought disordered schizophrenics used more unclear references (additioning and ambiguous references) than in other situations. Halpern and McCartin-Clark (1984) similarly found that the schizophrenics in their study did worse in nonstructured situations compared to structured verbal tasks such as naming. Informal interviews are ecologically valid in that they are typically used for diagnostic purposes (Spitzer, Endicott, & Robins, 1978). Although a psychiatric interview is not a typical use of language in the culture, there are a number of reasons for assuming its representativeness. Topics such as family, school, and hobbies found in the interviews are everyday topics that arise outside psychiatric settings. The relationship of professional or service provider to the client is also common. Although the specific functional tenor may be undetermined or underdetermined (what is the interviewer really trying to accomplish?), speakers should be able to adjust to such a situation and may have some experience in doing so (in meeting people for the first time, phatic communication).

Conversation, however, is not static but is negotiated by the speakers. The interviews, then, must be seen as evolving interaction that is sustained by both speakers. Unlike recall tasks or other highly structured verbal tasks, the language of an interview is the product of the speaker's ability and desire to communicate in socially appropriate ways. The overall setting is predetermined, and the conversational partner is given, but the patient is still responsible for shaping and sustaining the interaction. The language used in such circumstances reflects many of the features of day-to-day interaction in real contexts.

The approach in the following studies is to closely analyze the language of schizophrenics in interviews. The analysis of cohesion provides a theoretical basis for knowing how language should be used (e.g., unclear references are not desirable) and for predicting how specific uses of language will fail to be interpreted or will require an atypical method of interpretation. Different types of schizophrenic speakers can be compared and, they can be compared to speakers who are not schizophrenic. Such comparative studies point to underlying similarities and differences among the groups of speakers and to the relevance of other symptoms within each syndrome. Quantitative comparisons, even on small numbers of speakers, are useful in exploring differences in kind and differences of degree in language. The use of a relatively large number of detailed language variables provides a rich data source for investigating the kinds of relationships existing in the language of various speakers. It is the detailed analysis of language that offers an escape from the confounding of language and thought. Lanin-Kettering and Harrow (1985, p. 3) claim that it is "hard to see how intermingling can be a consequence of only the disordered use of words and sentences independent of thought." At least one difficulty with such a claim is that it does not recognize the levels of language (such as cohesion and other elements of discourse) that contribute to the identification of intermingling. The linguistic indicators of concepts such as thought disorder and intermingling must be determined in order to provide the basis for associations with other levels of functioning (see Chaika & Lambe, 1985, for some detailed comments on the issue).

STUDY

The conversations that formed the data for the following analyses were gathered for a study of the language of psychiatric patients (Bartolucci & Fine, 1987). Nineteen subjects were engaged in a 10-minute conversation by the clinician in charge of the cases as part of the clinical interaction. The subjects were familiar with both the interviewer and the office where the conversation took place. The interviewer asked open ended questions and the subjects seemed reasonably comfortable. The audio tape recorder was in view and subjects had given consent to the recording. The criteria for selecting subjects were: (a) diagnosis of schizophrenia, mania, or depression according to the Research Diagnostic Criteria (Spitzer, Endicott, & Robins, 1978). A patient with Korsakoff syndrome was also included and is part of a separate study. (b) Ability to cooperate; that is, reasonable amount of language production and no extreme agitation. (c) English as a native language.

The main study compares 15 subjects for whom full linguistic data and IQ data were available. This group consists of 8 schizophrenics (6 acute, 2 chronic), 3 manics, and 4 cases of depression. A case study is presented of the Korsakoff syndrome and a matched control. In addition, a longitudinal study is presented for one schizophrenic case, one manic case, and the Korsakoff syndrome.

RESULTS

The language of a number of schizophrenic subjects has been analyzed from both social and cognitive points of view. In particular, the language will be considered as it relates to concepts of thought disorders. A number of studies have pointed out the asocial effects and perhaps the social causes of schizophrenic language (e.g., Bellack, Morrison, & Mueser, 1989; Rund, 1988). To study the specifically social use of language, a measure of the construction of text in cooperation with the interlocutor has been developed. The index of self-referencing compares the number of anaphoric links that have antecedents in the speaker's own earlier speech compared to the number of anaphoric links to the interlocutor's speech. The number of words spoken by each speaker is used to control for the relative voluability of the two speakers.

The index is constructed as follows:

$$\frac{L-S}{L-O} \times \frac{W-O}{W-S}$$

where $L - S$ is the number of endophoric links to the subject's own language, $L - O$ is the number of endophoric links to the other speaker's language, $W - O$ is the number of words spoken by the other speaker, and $W - S$ is the number of words spoken by the subject. The higher the index, the more the speaker is drawing on his own earlier language as a source for semantic continuity. The index is sensitive to social interaction since it takes into consideration that conversation is mutually constructed by the parties involved and that the speakers must fit the meaning of the current contribution into the meaning that has been mutually constructed up to that point. The index of self-referencing was calculated for the 10-minute informal interviews.

The index was correlated with verbal IQ as measured by the comprehension, similarities, and vocabulary subtests of the WAIS (Wechsler, 1944), $r = .60$, $t = 3.1215$, $df = 17$, $p < .01$ (two-tailed). In fact, the comprehension subscale was not correlated with the index, rather, it was the explanation of verbal material in the vocabulary and similarities subtests that were related to the index of self-referencing. The better explanations of verbal concepts were associated with conversational cohesion that tended to be based on the speaker's own language. There were no significant correlations of the index with nonverbal subtests of the WAIS (block design and picture arrangement) nor with recall of verbal material (Babcock story recall; see Rapaport, Gill, & Schafer, 1968). Thus, the processing and construction of social interaction signaled by cohesion is unassociated with measures of nonverbal processing and even not associated with memory for structured verbal information. Rather, the presentation of verbal information to an interlocutor (the tasks in the verbal subscales of the WAIS) is associated with the semantic unity built up in a speaker's own language. If there is a peculiarity in the language of the psychiatric patients, it is in not constructing cohesive links within their own speech. Such an ability contributes to the social interaction and is associated with general verbal-processing skills rather than with more general cognitive skills or with specific verbal memory skills.

The finding of an emphasis on within-speaker continuity in conversation being associated to intact-verbal processing is consistent with other studies. Lovett, Dennis, and Newman (1986) report that hemidecorticates with intact left hemispheres tended to put stories into dialogue form more than those with intact right hemispheres. The speakers with intact left hemispheres also used pronouns more frequently and more frequently placed pronouns in the dialogue segments of their stories. This evidence suggests that left-hemisphere functioning contributes both to the use of endophoric reference and to the construction of dialogue forms. The use of cohesion by the psychiatric speakers suggests this same relationship of left hemisphere processing (the index of self-referencing was not associated with performance subscores) with cohesion and dialogue construction.

The index of self-referencing was compared for the eight schizophrenic patients and the eight nonschizophrenic patients. Although the level of self-referencing was higher for the schizophrenics (2.23 compared to 1.87), the difference was not significant ($t = .79$, $df = 14$, $p > .1$). Although there is a relation between general verbal organization and the continuity of a speaker's own semantic information, there is not a specific relation to the diagnosis of schizophrenia. Crosson and Hughes (1987) suggest that some schizophrenics compensate for the random release of language segments. This random release due to a dysfunction in inhibitory circuits leads to incoherent language. The data on self-referencing indicate that the mechanism does not relate specifically to how information is continued in interaction. The schizophrenics show no difference compared to other psychiatric patients on which information is successfully extended in dialogue. How information is continued in interactions by schizophrenics is related to general verbal processing rather than a particular mechanism of inhibition. Further evidence for this conclusion is that a judgment of thought disorder was not correlated with the index of self-referencing (Spearman rho $= -.27$, $f = -1.01$, $df = 13$, $p > .1$). Whatever the factors that contribute to clinical judgments of thought disorder, they are not specifically related to the choice of which information is successfully continued in conversation.

Firth and Done (1988) propose that positive symptoms of schizophrenia result from a failure in the internal monitoring factions that leads to an inability to distinguish the source of acts as either self-generated or elicited by external stimuli. The monitoring of the source of information in conversation would seem to be a plausible process that could be affected by a confusion between internal and external stimuli. The data on self-referencing do not support such an hypothesis. Neither the diagnostic category of schizophrenia nor the clinical judgment of presence and severity of thought disorder are significantly related to self-referencing.

If the level of self-referencing is not related to clinically rated thought disorder, what kind of presentation of information does interfere with communication? Rochester and Martin (1977, 1979) showed in some detail that failures in cohesion contribute to unclear language that is labeled as thought disordered. In particular, unclear endophoric reference was at a higher level in the language of schizophrenic speakers whose language is considered thought disordered. What Rochester and Martin have done is to specify linguistic factors that contribute to the assessment of thought disorder. The finding of unclear reference in the language of schizophrenics was replicated by Bartolucci and Fine (1987). This paper also demonstrated that it is the violation of the listener's expectation of appropriate reference rather than the absolute amount of unclear reference that is associated with schizophrenic language. Thus, the failure to give interpretable references to the hearer is a noticeably disrupting aspect of schizophrenic language that is not directly related to a number of other aspects of the presentation of information and the cognitive processes related to these organizations of information. The disruptions in language are noticeable, because they impede the interpretation of the speaker's meaning in context. This disruption of meaning is then often used to infer clinical states such as thought disorder, intermingling, loose associations, derailment. The specification of unclear reference as contributing to the judgment of thought disorder not only provides a reliable indicator, but help explains why schizophrenic speech suggests labels such as thought disorder and derailment.

The failures in reference are linguistically failures to signal continuity of participants. The speaker is simultaneously signaling the continuity of some participant in the discourse and not providing the listener the means to create that continuity. Suggestions of the social process of providing information to listeners are found in a number of studies of schizophrenia. Rutter (1985) and Bellack, Morrison, and Mueser (1989) attribute the apparently disordered communication of schizophrenics to the social processes needed to present information in a way that is compatible with the information needs of the listener. Halpern and McCartin-Clark (1984) show that schizophrenics are poor in maintaining relevance, and Hoffman, Stopek, and Andreasen

(1986) note that schizophrenics rely on clues such as phonetic similarities, word play, and affect rather than on the semantic continuity in language. The disruptions of referential chains may also contribute to the smaller discourse hierarchies found by Hoffman et al. (1986). If participants are not successfully continued from one statement to another, then the subordination relationships based on truth values will not be created. Although a specific cognitive underpinning to cohesive weakness is not clearly established, its relative independence from other verbal cognitive processes suggests a rather separate cognitive process, perhaps related to abilities in the processing of social information. The relationship of cohesive weakness to thought disorder and to the diagnosis of schizophrenia then suggests the social component of these categories: Thought disorder is specified when a listener cannot interpret the speaker according to the expected conventions for using language in context.

Lexical cohesion signals to the hearer that the same lexical items are relevant to the current stretch of language as were used in some prior stretch. The use of lexical cohesion in this study is limited to lexical items based on the same root. Thus, synonyms, subordinates, and superordinates are not considered. These classes of lexical cohesion tend to be infrequent and difficult to identify. Lexical items based on the same root may involve changes in derivational and inflectional morphology (e.g., drive, drives, driver, drive-in), and even without such changes they may not convey identity of reference (e.g., "My driveway deteriorated in three years. Any driveway put in by an amateur is like that." where the two instances of *driveway* do not have an identity of reference). In investigating the repetition of lexical roots, the text-forming nature of the repetition must be kept in mind. These repetitions contribute to the message that the stretches of language are relevant to each other as the language is formulated in the overall verbal situation. Lexical repetition, as other kinds of cohesion, displays the relevance of the current stretch of language to the verbal context. Speech that studiously avoids lexical repetition in favor of reference or perhaps lexical synonyms would suggest that the speaker is avoiding the established terminology, and so sets himself apart from the conversational flow, even if identity of reference is signaled by other means. Although it is not clear in other studies, the analysis of lexical repetition here includes just lexical items from open classes, since repetition of items from closed grammatical classes such as articles, prepositions, and auxiliary verbs adds little to the cohesiveness of text.

Lexical repetition is analyzed for the eight schizophrenics (two chronic and six acute), three manics, and four depressed patients described in Bartolucci and Fine (1987). The case of Korsakoff psychosis is investigated separately. The frequency of lexical repetition as a percentage of all the words spoken by the subjects is presented in Table 4-1. The individual data points as well as means are given. Although there is a spread of values in the use of lexical repetition, there is a tendency for the chronic schizophrenics to use relatively more lexical repetition than the acute schizophrenics. The less frequent use of lexical repetition by the acute schizophrenics may indicate reliance on other kinds of cohesion. This hypothesis can be examined with the data from Table 4-2. Table 4-2 presents lexical repetition as a percentage of successful endophoric cohesion of nominal groups (lexical repetition and reference—substitution and ellipsis are almost never used and have been excluded from these analyses). The acute schizophrenics rely considerably more on lexical repetition than on reference compared to other psychiatric patients. The chronic schizophrenics, in particular, use reference to signal the continuity of participants.

Thus, when lexical repetition is seen as one way of constructing coherent text, the acute schizophrenics show the most reliance on it. The formation of relevant, interpretable contributions to conversations (i.e., text) is taken as necessary for successful social interaction. It is how different groups of speakers try to attain this goal that is interesting. In a picture description task performed by schizophrenics, Manschreck et al. (1985) found that there was a positive relation between phrase

Table 4-1. Repeated lexical items as a percentage of all words spoken in psychiatric syndromes

	Schizophrenics			
	Acute	*Chronic*	*Manics*	*Depressed*
	14	29	20	20
	12	18	14	20
	14		13	18
	20			19
	28			
	10			
means:	16	24	16	19

Table 4-2. Lexical repetition as a percentage of successful endophoric cohesion of nominal groups (lexical repetition and reference) in psychiatric syndromes

	Schizophrenics			
	Acute	*Chronic*	*Manics*	*Depressed*
	90	66	77	68
	56	55	53	62
	85		73	68
	82			69
	80			
	70			
means:	77	61	68	67

repetitions (two and three words at a time) and formal thought disorder and a positive relation between length of hospitalization and the repetition of longer phrases. This study apparently did not distinguish open and closed class words so that much repetition may be of frequently occurring closed class words. Manschreck et al. partially control for this factor by considering word frequency. Their findings support in part the findings on lexical repetition. They found that inpatients repeated less common words (and therefore likely to be open class words that create cohesion) than outpatients. Manschreck et al. suggest that in schizophrenic speech there is "a breakdown in the mechanism that governs normal repetition patterns" and consider a short-term memory deficit as a cause.

Rochester and Martin (1979) also found especially high levels of lexical cohesion in the interviews of their thought-disordered subjects compared to non-thought-disordered schizophrenics; the nonpatient controls were in the middle. The levels of lexical cohesion cannot be directly compared across the studies because of differences in methods of tabulation, but the relationships among the groups seems consistent: the more disorganized the speaker (inpatient, acute, thought disordered), the more the reliance on lexical cohesion. Rochester and Martin (1979) suggest that the reliance of thought-disordered schizophrenics on lexical cohesion reflects a dependence on lexical items as "foci for discourse topics." The neuropsychological approach of Crosson and Hughes (1987) to schizophrenic language would suggest that lexical cohesion is an easy way to attempt to create cohesion if there is impairment in mechanisms that keep track of contextual referents or in attention that is needed to focus on context. Similarly, if there is a dysfunction in the buffers that maintain context, lexical cohesion rather than reference would be a relatively easy way to create cohesion. Crosson and Hughes (1987, p. 616) suggest that some schizophrenics can compensate for deficits in controlling language "by using a very basic set of internal contextual referents which are inappropriately repeated in numerous circumstances giving the appearance of idiosyncratic and personalized thinking." For such a proposal to succeed, the variation in the amount of lexical cohesion used in interviews compared to narratives reported by Rochester and Martin (1979), and the variation along the chronic–acute dimension reported above would have to be integrated into the neuropsychological approach. Carpenter (1987) argues that this integrated approach is just what is needed. The detailed linguistic analyses suggest the kinds of neuropsychological mechanisms involved in schizophrenia and can be the basis for further cognitive investigations involving both verbal and nonverbal processes.

From the listener's perspective, rather than the cognitive processing perspective, a reliance on lexical repetition at the expense of other kinds of cohesion can account for some of the clinically described characteristics of schizophrenic speech. Rochester and Martin (1979) suggest that an emphasis on lexical repetition has to do with the topics presented by schizophrenics. The lexical items help retain the impression of the same topic even if the continuity of participants is occasionally interrupted by unclear endophoric reference. The repetition of lexical roots may also contribute to the impression that schizophrenic language is inappropriately built on irrelevant phonological or semantic features of prior language. The neuropsychological proposals will ultimately have to be related to the effect on communication. This relationship can be mediated by a functional linguistic theory that suggests the cognitive processing needed to achieve typical interpretable language in a variety of situations.

Summary

The investigation of a number of characteristics of the language of schizophrenics demonstrates the complex relationship among language and social and cognitive processes. In conversation, a speaker must display continuity from prior language to the current contribution. The appropriate extension from the speaker's own prior language is related to general verbal ability, but not to specific factors underlying schizophrenia. On the other hand, unclear attempts to extend meaning from prior language reliably characterize language as schizophrenic. Another characteristic of the language of schizophrenics, a reliance on repeated lexical items, suggests both relationships to cognitive mechanisms and a factor underlying some clinical concepts in the diagnosis of schizophrenia.

SCHIZOPHRENIA IN RELATION TO MANIA AND DEPRESSION

Introduction

Although schizophrenics are the most noticeable group, other groups of psychiatric patients also may use language atypically. In any case, it is useful to compare schizophrenics to other psychiatric patients in order to check the specificity of the language characteristics attributed to schizophrenics. In a parallel way, comparisons with other psychiatric groups can be a check on the hypothesized social and cognitive processes associated with schizophrenia.

There is reason to believe that depressed patients may have communication difficulty in some way resembling that of schizophrenics. Asarnow, Goldstein, and Ben-Meir (1988) found that the family interactions of half their sample of depressed children were deviant in the same way as the interactions of families of children with schizophrenic spectrum disorders. However, for depressed children, parental communication patterns were not associated with the severity of the impairment, or with cognitive functioning measured by the WISC-R (Wechsler, 1974). These specific findings thus show no relation between a history of exposure to unusual communicative patterns and cognitive processing for the depressed children. In children with schizophrenic spectrum disorders, there is a subset that does show a relation between severe impairment and poor cognitive functioning and families with particularly deviant communication.

There is also a comparison to be made between the language used by manics and the language used by schizophrenics. Rosenberg and Abbeduto (1982) note that "schizophrenic language" is found in manics. Hoffman et al. (1986) have studied the language of these two groups of speakers using discourse analysis. They found that manics produce longer utterances than the schizophrenics—a finding not surprising since pressure of speech is a criterion of mania (e.g., Feighner et al., 1972). The manics, though, unlike the schizophrenics, shift from one discourse structure to another. Some of the variables characterizing schizophrenic language are examined in the language of manic and depressed speakers.

Results

Reference and lexical cohesion are compared for the group of patients. Unclear endophoric references are characteristic of some schizophrenic speech in interviews. Table 4-3 presents unclear reference (ambiguous or requiring the addition of information) as a percentage of all types of endophoric and exophoric reference. The schizophrenic group shows more such unclear reference than the manic or depressed groups. Furthermore, the acute schizophrenics have more unclear references than the chronic schizophrenics. The results, although calculated slightly differently than Bartolucci and Fine (1987), show the same elevated level of unclear reference only in the schizophrenic group. The high level of unclear reference in one manic speaker may point to a difficulty in diagnosis (see the discussion in Hoffman et al., 1986, on high manic schizophrenics). The unclear reference which contributes to the interference in communication is specific to the schizophrenics. The levels of implicit verbal reference (bridging, Table 4-4) and reference to the nonverbal speech situation (exophora, Table 4-5) do not show differences among the groups. This similarity among the groups supports the conclusion that it is the unclear references rather than some overall change in referencing strategy that contribute to the difficulty in interpreting schizophrenics.

The use of repetition of lexical items is presented in Table 4-1 and Table 4-2. Again, the manic and depressed speakers resemble each other and generally resemble the schizophrenic speakers. If there is an effect of atypical communication in the families of depressed patients or in the way manics and schizophrenics shift from one discourse hierarchy to another, it is not clearly found in the patterning of repetition.

To study the relation of cognitive processing and communi-

Table 4-3. Unclear reference as a percentage of all types of anaphoric and exophoric reference

Schizophrenics			
Acute	*Chronic*	*Manics*	*Depressed*
21.1	4.8	1.2	0.8
6.1	7.4	4.4	3.6
9.7		14.0	2.8
5.3			2.6
10.0			
14.9			

Table 4-4. Implicit verbal reference (bridging) as a percentage of all types of anaphoric and exophoric reference

Schizophrenics			
Acute	*Chronic*	*Manics*	*Depressed*
0	1.4	0.6	1.0
2.5	1.2	2.8	0.6
0		1.8	0.9
4.8			3.0
2.0			
3.2			

Table 4-5. Exophoric reference as a percentage of all types of anaphoric and endophoric reference

Schizophrenics			
Manics	*Depressed*	*Acute*	*Chronic*
68.4	55.4	66.1	57.1
51.1	31.5	36.6	40.7
78.7		51.5	60.0
68.6			55.1
52.2			
59.1			

cation difficulties in the families of schizophrenics as suggested by the relationship found by Asarnow et al. (1988), the specific linguistic variables at risk in schizophrenic language and disruptive of the communication process must be investigated. The results presented suggest that the locus of language difficulties associated with schizophrenia is fairly specific and characterizes schizophrenic language as unlike that of mania and depression despite reasons for suspecting overlap either in the etiology of the communication difficulty or in the reported characteristics of the language. Rochester and Martin (1979) found that unclear reference is important in characterizing the language of schizophrenics and a nonpatient population. The presented results (as well as Bartolucci & Fine, 1987) suggest that it is those linguistic variables that specifically hamper communication that also distinguish the language of schizophrenics from the language of other psychiatric patients. The linguistic variables are explored further in the longitudinal case studies.

ALCOHOL AMNESTIC DISORDER

Introduction

Alcohol Amnestic Disorder (Korsakoff's syndrome) is a psychiatric disorder associated with prolonged and heavy use of alcohol. It is characterized by major memory impairments (American Psychiatric Association, 1987). This syndrome provides an opportunity to study language use and particularly cohesion when there is a set of specific cognitive impairments and a clear organic etiology. Given a cognitive deficit, the question of what functional areas of language are affected can be posed. An extensive study of Korsakoff's syndrome is not presented, rather, the issue is how cohesion works when there are certain cognitive deficits and how the cognitive deficits are associated with social uses of language in conversation.

Unlike schizophrenics, patients with Korsakoff's syndrome are not known or identified by a specific impairment in verbal communication. Rather, there is a definite cognitive impairment in memory. This impairment may lead to the use of imaginary events to fill in the blanks in memory (confabulation). However, these confabulations do not impair interaction, and their plausibility can make them hard to detect. Despite no clear impairment in verbal interaction, the presence of a substantial cognitive impairment that effects some verbal functioning presents the possibility that the use of cohesion may also be affected. If such an effect is found, then associations can be made between elements of cognitive functioning and cohesion as an aspect of language processing.

Methodology

The methodology in this study of alcohol amnestic disorder is as follows. A case study is presented with the emphasis on the analysis of cohesion from an unstructed interview. The situation is the same as that used in the analysis of the language of schizophrenics. In addition, the study is longitudinal over a period of one month. The subject was interviewed twice, four weeks apart, so that the analysis can consider the speaker as her own control. As a further control, a subject matched for age, sex, education, and occupation was interviewed. In order to assess the cognitive deficits, a number of verbal and nonverbal standardized tests were administered. Since verbal processing is specifically relevant, a number of tests of verbal discourse processing were adapted and presented to the Korsakoff subject. Results from all these tests provide information about cognitive processing that can then be related to the use of cohesion by the Korsakoff subject.

The specific cognitive tests are as follows. The results from these tests are presented and discussed as they are relevant to the findings on the use of cohesion.

Wechsler Adult Intelligence Scale (WAIS, Wechsler, 1944). Seven subtests from the WAIS were administered to the subject and control to obtain verbal and performance scores. The subtests used are verbal: comprehension, similarities, vocabulary; performance: digit symbol, picture completion, block design, picture arrangement.

Benton Visual Retention Test (Benton, 1963). This test assesses visual retention and perception by asking subjects to reproduce an abstract line drawing presented for 10 seconds. A score is determined by scaling the number of correct and incorrect figures reproduced according to IQ. A score three points below the score predicted by the IQ score suggests an acquired cognitive impairment. A strong tendency for errors to occurs in a single visual field may indicate a specific problem in the contralateral hemisphere.

Babcock Test (see Rapaport et al., 1968). The Babcock Test assesses the recall of auditory narrative material. A four-sentence story is read to the subject and a recall is requested both immediately and after 10 minutes. After the first recall, the story is read again and followed by a 10-minute delay during which the subject works on arithmetic problems. The story is divided into units, and the number correctly recalled is scored.

The Korsakoff subject was a 52-year-old woman at the time of testing. She was brought to the Emergency Department of a General Hospital, because she was found wandering in the streets in the early hours of the morning. At admission she was disoriented and frightened. Her confusional state subsided, but she showed an inability to recall recent information, although she was otherwise appropriate in her behavior. She remembered details of her personal past. However, she often confabulated about the immediate past. For example, she told an interviewer that a child's voice in the next room belonged to her granddaughter who was visiting her. The visit actually took place a day earlier. The confabulations decreased over six weeks, but her memory of recent events did not improve. Two months after discharge, her deficit persisted apparently unchanged. Her history, gathered from relatives and friends, revealed long-lasting alcohol abuse. The subject had been employed as a hospital technician. The control subject was a female 55 years old at the time of testing. She worked as a secretary in a government health agency.

Results

At the first testing of the Korsakoff subject there was an almost complete loss of short-term verbal memory. On the Babcock test (see Table 4-6) the subject remembered no information on the immediate recall and only scored 1 on the delayed recall. These scores can be compared to 11 and 19 for the control, and a normal range of 24 to 30 for the two recalls combined. At the time of this first test the subject had a verbal IQ of 84, a performance IQ of 79, and a full-scale IQ of 81 (see Table 4-7). Thus, although the memory impairment is close to absolute, general verbal and nonverbal functioning is in the normal range.

The Benton Visual Retention Test shows a considerable deficit in nonverbal processing. The results are presented in Table 4-8. The consistent elevation of errors in the right visual

Table 4-6. Results on Babcock Test for Korsakoff and Control

		Korsakoff	
	Control	*First Testing*	*Second Testing*
Immediate recall	11	0	4
Delayed recall (10 minutes)	19	1	4

Table 4-7. Results on WAIS IQ scales for Korsakoff and Control

		Korsakoff	
	Control	*First Testing*	*Second Testing*
Verbal	120	84	86
Performance	134	79	95
Full Scale	127	81	89

field strongly suggests a specific left-hemisphere deficit. The overall impairment in visual retention shows some improvement from the first test to the second test four weeks later.

Language Analyses

Given these general abilities and deficits of the Korsakoff, the focus will return to the use of cohesion in unstructured conversations. The clinical impression is that the Korsakoff's language is not impaired or difficult to interpret. However, a close examination of cohesion reveals how the Korsakoff's language is constructed to fit into verbal interactions and reveals associations with some of the cognitive deficits.

Unclear. Unclear reference is a characteristic of schizophrenic language in interviews. However, the Korsakoff very rarely used ambiguous reference or required the hearer to add information in order to interpret her speech. In fact, the presence of only one unclear reference requiring the hearer to add information (a

Table 4-8. Results on Benton Visual Retention Test for Korsakoff and Control

		Korsakoff	
	Control	*First Testing*	*Second Testing*
Correct	7	1	2
(expected correct)	7	5	5
Errors	4	20	13
(expected errors)	3	7	7
	Errors as percentage of total errors		
Omissions	0	19	9
Distortions	12	19	9
Perseverations	12	3	9
Rotations	25	11	18
Misplacements	0	0	9
Size errors	0	3	0
Left errors	25	16	14
Right errors	25	30	32

proportion of references of 0.4%) is much below the level of the control (3%) and below the level reported for controls by Rochester and Martin (1979) of 4%. In this first interview the Korsakoff speaks minimally and can apparently keep track of the number and identity of the participants she is speaking about. In the second interview, in a state of clinical improvement, the rate of unclear reference in fact increases to 4%.

As well as considering additioning and ambiguous references as unclear, Rochester and Martin (1979) suggest that there is a continuum from implicit verbal references (bridging) to the unclear references requiring additioning. Bridging and additioning can be seen respectively as successful, and unsuccessful attempts to create implicit verbal cohesion. Table 4-9 presents the data on bridging and additioning in two ways: the sum of these two categories as a percentage of all endophoric reference, and the ratio of additioning to bridging. In the first interview, the Korsakoff rarely attempts to use inference. Such a low level of inference helps explain the low level of unclear reference. The speaker rarely attempts to use inference and therefore rarely fails. In the second interview the Korsakoff more frequently uses verbal inference and also occasionally fails to accomplish this inferencing.

The ratio of additioning to bridging helps to illuminate the processes involved. The Korsakoff in the first interview uses little inference but uses more bridging than additioning. However, in the second interview there is about as much bridging as additioning. The control uses more bridging than additioning. In the first interview, then, the low level of inferencing helps account for the low level of unclear reference. In the second interview, when there is more inferencing, the Korsakoff fails to make the inferential links clear about as often as she succeeds in making them clear. Using more verbal inference is probably an indication of the improved social

Table 4-9. Additioning and bridging as a percentage of all endophoric reference and as a ratio of each other

		Korsakoff	
	Control	*First Testing*	*Second Testing*
Additioning & bridging as percentage of endophoric reference	17	4	11
Ratio Additioning: bridging	1:3	1:3	1:1

functioning reported clinically for the Korsakoff. Verbal inference signals to the hearer that speaker and hearer share a social and verbal space and so do not have to communicate explicitly at every point where there is a choice between explicit and implicit signals. However, the relatively great amount of failure to create clear inferential links suggests a processing defect. This processing defect is marked in the first interview by the very low frequency of inferencing and is not disruptive in the second interview, because the overall rate of unclear referencing is still in the normal range. Thus, the speech of the Korsakoff is not markedly difficult to interpret and is socially functional. Nevertheless, there is some indication of a difficulty in the processing of verbal material that implicates verbal memory. This difficulty, reflected in spontaneous conversation, parallels the findings for narrative recall on the Babcock test. The almost complete loss of memory for verbal material at the time of the first testing corresponds to few attempts at inferencing in spontaneous language. The speaker may have very little ability to keep track of the identity of participants in the discourse. The later partially successful attempts at constructing verbal inference for the hearer parallel a limited recovery of memory function as seen in the Babcock results.

Lexical Cohesion and Conjunction. Cohesion is achieved not only by reference, but frequently also by lexical repetition and conjunction. Lexical cohesion (the repetition of the same content word root) comprises about one-third of the cohesive ties in the Korsakoff's two interviews and in the interview of the control (see Table 4-10). However, in terms of the number of words spoken, the Korsakoff initially repeats content words more frequently than she does when she has improved clinically. The increased use of repetition in terms of the number of words spoken suggests the verbal memory impairment evident on other measures. Reusing the same content words may be an efficient way to create cohesion without risk of being unclear and without the need for more complex processing of verbal material.

At the first testing when the Korsakoff is more disorganized there is an elevated use of conjunction as well as lexical cohesion. The Korsakoff uses more conjunction in relation to other forms of cohesion and in relation to the number of words spoken. This increased use of cohesion is not related to pressure of speech that could be hypothesized to create conjoined series of statements loosely connected by conjunctions. In fact, the second interview with less conjunctions was

Table 4-10. Use of lexical cohesion and conjunction by Korsakoff and control

		Korsakoff	
	Control	*First Testing*	*Second Testing*
Lexical cohesion as percentage of all cohesion	35	34	32
Lexical cohesion per 100 words	13	20	14
Conjunction as percentage of all cohesion	19	28	18
Conjunction per 100 words	7	17	8

spoken by the Korsakoff slightly faster (3.8 words per seconds) than the first interview (3.6 words per second). The appropriate use of conjunctions is evident in the following excerpt from the Korsakoff's second interview (note the use of "and but," "and," "but"):

> and but I feel that he's going through a lot now and I want to take it off his back because. he's a sergeant of detectives on the police force he's doing very well but there's only so far you can go in this world.

As with lexical cohesion, conjunction makes limited demands on cognitive processing. Conjunction can be used to link stretches of language of various lengths, and the specificity of the semantic link can be varied from unmarked to marked.

Self-Referencing. In conversation, endophoric conjunction can be built on the speaker's own language or the interlocutor's language. As described for schizophrenic language, the index of self-referencing measures the balance of cohesive links to the speaker and interlocutor, taking into account the relative volubility of the two speakers. The values for the Korsakoff's first interview, second interview, and control are, respectively 1.58, 2.06, and 3.49. These results are generally congruent with the results from schizophrenic language. With improvement, the Korsakoff draws relatively more from her own speech than from the interviewer's speech. Atypically, this increase in the index of self-referencing is not associated with an increase in verbal IQ. This finding will be discussed in relation to the discourse tests.

The structure of nominal groups with nouns as heads are indicators of the complexity of the semantic resources used. In the Korsakoff's first interview, there is very little information in nominal groups except for the head itself. In only a few nominal groups is the head accompanied by anything more than a deictic or numerative. The nominal groups, "the front concrete" and "a little part of the concrete," for example, convey more information than the Korsakoff's typical nominal groups such as "a mail," "three weeks," "check-ups," "doctor," "a bunch of questions," "thirteen years," "some duplicates." In the second interview, the Korsakoff places considerable information into nominal groups including cohesion to earlier nominal groups. Examples of these more extended nominal groups are: "a sergeant of detectives on the police force," "a bit of concrete that was sticking up in the driveway," "a very hard worker," "this business of getting by in the world," "a big bouquet of flowers," "a medical term that I don't understand." The control speaker not only uses such extended nominal groups, but also links the nominal groups by cohesion. This use of extended nominal groups and cohesion is illustrated in the following conversation with the control subject.

I: . . . Jan told me umm you have a lot of umm idiomatic expressions that you occasionally use umm words that rhyme with each other

Control: hm hm you're thinking of rhymings

I: right

Control: that I always use I used to hear it a lot when my parents were alive and I was very small because . . . they were both from London and they were both born in the east end of London and I think that this is where most of this rhyming slang came from.

In the control's last turn the nominal group "the east end of London" includes the lexical repetition "London," and the nominal group "most of this rhyming slang" includes lexical repetition of "rhyming" and "slang" as well as the endophoric reference link signaled by "this."

In terms of the amount of information packed into nominal groups, the Korsakoff initially uses quite reduced nominal groups that a month later are more expanded. The use of cohesion in more complex nominal groups follows the same pattern. There is very limited use of cohesion in complex nominal groups initially, somewhat more in the second interview, but still very restricted compared to the control. The Korsakoff does not place much information into any one nominal group, and in nominal groups that do have more information than a head noun, there is rarely a cohesive link. These facts suggest that the keeping track of cohesive information and building cohesive links is a cognitive load in addition to the construction of complex nominal groups that the Korsakoff finds very difficult.

Discourse Tests. Detailed analyses of cohesion illuminate the processing of language at one level of text formation. An organization of verbal material at a higher level is the structuring of verbal material into well-formed stories or narratives. The sequence of information in narratives follows typical patterns, and users of a language seem to use these patterns to organize information and to assist in recall. At the time of the Korsakoff's second interview, a number of tests of the subject's ability to use narrative discourse structure were made.

The first discourse test was modeled on Stein and Glenn (1979). The purpose was to study the effect of the organization of narrative material on the Korsakoff's amnestic syndrome and to study the effect of different kinds of interaction on the Korsakoff's recall. The aim was to learn more about the particular abilities and deficits in the cognitive processing of verbal material.

A passage from Stein and Glenn (1979, p. 79), "The Tiger's Whisker," was read to the subject.

> Once there was a woman who needed a tiger's whisker. She was afraid of tigers but she needed a whisker to make a medicine for her husband who had gotten very sick. She thought and thought about how to get a tiger's whisker. She decided to use a trick. She knew that tigers love food and music. She thought that if she brought food to a lonely tiger and played some soft music the tiger would be nice to her and she could get the whisker. So she did just that. She went to a tiger's cave where a lonely tiger lived. She put a bowl of food in front of the opening to the cave and then she sang some soft music. The tiger came out and ate the food. Then he walked over to the lady. He thanked her for the delicious food and the lovely music. The lady cut off one of his whiskers and ran down hill very quickly. The tiger felt lonely and sad again.

After a 20-second delay during which the subject counted, 3 content-free questions were asked (e.g., "Could you tell me the one thing that happened in the story that was the most important thing to remember?"). These content-free questions asked for information from the story, but did not give any specific semantic clue about the information requested. After the content-free questions there was a 10-minute intervening nonverbal task and a request for a recall of the story. After the recall, the subject was asked a series of 13 "why" questions about the story. The questions were randomly ordered in terms of the sequence in the story of the expected answers.

Compared to the grade 5 and even the grade 1 students studied by Stein and Glenn (1979), the Korsakoff showed very poor recall of the test story in response to content-free probes. Grade 5 students respond with a mean of two statements for each content-free question, but the Korsakoff replied to only the first question and gave a rather vague answer: "The lady . . . did some work there . . . but she played a big role in it." The control subject gave one statement for each question, apparently regarding that to be the requirement of the situation.

In contrast to the poor recall in response to content-free questions, the Korsakoff answered the "why" content questions well. Table 4-11 provides the accuracy and error scores for the Korsakoff, control, and Stein and Glenn (1979) student groups. Errors are scored only if the answer "clearly contradicted the original story information." The categories of information given by the Korsakoff roughly follow the pattern of the control and students with internal responses given most frequently.

After a 10-minute delay, the Korsakoff was asked to tell the story of "Tigers's Whisker." Her recall contains the basic structure of the story with three full and one incomplete statements. In comparison to the response to the content-free questions, the delayed recall was quite improved. These results can be compared to the recalls of the verbal material in the Babcock test. The Korsakoff recalled almost no material in the immediate recall condition of the Babcock, but she did recall in the delayed condition her own incorrect response from the immediate recall condition. It was hypothesized that the social

Table 4-11. Accuracy of answers to content questions for Korsakoff, control and student groups

	Errors	*Unanswered*	*% Correct*
Korsakoff	8	8	84
Control	0	0	100
Students			
Grade 5	2	4	94
Grade 1	12	7	81

interaction or the attempted organization and expression of information in the immediate recall condition aided later recall. This hypothesis is supported by the second discourse test using the Stein and Glenn story material: The interaction and expression of information of the content-questions seems to have aided the following recall of the story.

The results of the Stein and Glenn discourse test indicate that the Korsakoff has a major impairment in the recall of connected text. However, interaction during which another speaker supplies semantic cues enables the Korsakoff to retrieve some information. The subject retrieves roughly the same kinds of information (as measured by story grammar categories) as other speakers. These two findings on the difference between noncontent questions and content questions and the use of story structure suggest that the Korsakoff has an impairment in memory, but can exploit semantic cues or structure to aid in recall.

To further test the Korsakoff's memory for verbal material, a discourse test based on Stein and Nezworski (1978) was developed. A story was read by the subject for the explicit purpose of remembering the story for later recall. In order to test the subject's ability to organize information without the burden of recalling information, the story was divided into 12 statements with each statement typed on a separate slip of paper. The subject was asked to unscramble the slips to reconstruct the story.

As with the recall of other stories, the Korsakoff's unprompted recall of the story was very impoverished. She recalled and added inferences in an order consistent with a well-formed story. The Korsakoff omitted information, but did not distort the order of information. In sorting the statements on slips of paper, the subject largely depended on story grammar categories. The two statements in each story grammar category were placed next to each other for four of the six categories. Furthermore, errors in ordering were made in the categories (internal responses, reactions) the children remembered least. These results indicate that the Korsakoff can use abstract story structures when the burden of memory for propositional information is removed.

In general, the discourse tests suggest that the Korsakoff can exploit clues or semantic structures when they are available, either through interaction or as well-learned abstract structures. This ability of the Korsakoff can be related to the building of cohesion links in conversation. The index of self-referencing suggests that with clinical improvement, the Korsakoff more frequently builds cohesive links from her own language. In the first interview, she depends more on the language of the interviewer to provide the basis for her cohesive links. The shift to using more links to her own language in the second interview suggests that as her condition improved, she was less dependent on external information to form cohesion, a process requiring verbal memory skills. Thus, there is a congruence in the abilities identified by discourse memory tests and as found in spontaneous conversation: The deficit in memory underlies both the use of cohesion in conversation and the poor recall of discourse.

Summary

The case study of a Korsakoff amnestic syndrome shows cohesion as a means of relating language to various components of cognitive processing. The defect in verbal memory is related in complex ways to cohesion. In a state of greater disorganization, the subject's use of cohesion was adequate. However, closer examination reveals that the kind of cohesion that would develop into unclear messages is underused, reducing the likelihood of cohesion failures. With some improvement in mental state, there is a change in the balance of cohesive devices used. This change, in turn, is associated with the surfacing of some cohesive failures. Thus, there is not a simple relationship between the interpretability of the cohesion in spontaneous speech and the underlying cognitive processes. Evidence from verbal and nonverbal tests indicates a deficit in verbal memory that is nonetheless sensitive to how the subject tries to retrieve information. The Korsakoff subject's memory is aided by verbal cues and by well-learned abstract structures. These felicitating factors may also play a role in the organization of spontaneous language, as revealed in the analysis of cohesion.

The Korsakoff's spontaneous language exploits her intact cognitive abilities. The use of lexical repetition and the avoidance of implicit verbal reference are ways that cohesion reveals the deficits found on other measures of cognitive functioning. Cohesion helps to fill in some of the details of the cognitive deficit that is clearly manifested in a severe verbal memory problem and that leads to the clinically described confabulations.

LONGITUDINAL STUDIES

Introduction

The analyses so far have regarded psychiatric syndromes and the associated uses of language as discrete, static entities. The syndromes have been compared to each other. However, individuals change over time, and the psychiatric state may change. This time dimension allows the study of the variability of the use of cohesion and the relationship between that variability and the clinical state of the speaker. The perspective of clinical state is important, since it is an informed judgment of the speaker's ability to function normally in typical social circumstances. The judgment is based on comparisons with many individuals who exhibit similar symptoms and have followed a similar course. Cohesive relations show the relevance of language to other stretches of language and to the nonverbal situation. These connections have been shown to contribute to the interpretability of the speaker and to be indicative of the cognitive process needed to participate in conversation. The issue to be dealt with is how the use of cohesion by a single speaker may change over time. The technique is to use each speaker as his or her own control. Thus, various idiosyncratic factors of the speakers will be constant, and the differences in language use can be taken as reflecting changes in the processing and social abilities of the speaker. One specific issue is whether certain relationships of language and cognitive processing are independent of clinical change. Thus, longitudinal analyses can provide basic information about the use of cohesion and the cognitive and social processes underlying cohesion. The language of a manic and an acute schizophrenic speaker is analyzed. In addition, the longitudinal data of the Korsakoff subject will be referred to. Each speaker was interviewed twice by the same clinician. The characteristics of the speakers are listed in Table 4-12.

Results

As with the cross-sectional data reported above, the longitudinal data reveal a positive relationship between the index of self-referencing and verbal IQ, but not performance IQ. Table

Table 4-12. Characteristics of patients studied longitudinally

Age	*Sex*	*Diagnosis*	*Clinical change*	*Period between tests (weeks)*
49	F	Schizophrenia	deterioration	4
20	M	Manic	improvement	2
51	F	Korsakoff-Wernicke	improvement	4

4-13 presents the relevant longitudinal data. With changes in psychiatric state and verbal IQ, the index of self-referencing is nevertheless related to verbal IQ. The evidence suggests that the general verbal ability measured by verbal IQ subtests also underlies an aspect of interactional patterning. As with the group data, the higher the verbal ability, the more the cohesion to a speaker's own language rather than to the interviewer. This relationship in the longitudinal data combined with the same relationship in the cross-sectional data points to a consistent relationship between cognitive processing and the language of interaction. The various abilities that contribute to effective answers on the verbal IQ subtests are also contributing in different ways to conversation. In the verbal IQ subtests there is little interaction between tester and subject. The tester presents information for comprehension and explanation but there is no opportunity for dialogue. In particular, there is little opportunity for the subject to create a variety of cohesive links to either his own or the interviewer's prior language. In addition, the scoring of the verbal IQ subtests is unlikely to be affected, even indirectly, by changes in the index of self-referencing. The verbal IQ scores and the index of self-referencing thus do not seem to be directly related to each other. Rather, the positive relation of these variables is attributed to the cognitive processing involved. This cognitive processing perhaps has an indirect effect on the social interactions of the speaker.

The aspects of cohesion that have a direct impact on the interpretability of the speakers (additioning and ambiguous references) are not related to the cognitive measures associated with self-referencing. There is a distinction between an aspect of cohesion that is positively related to verbal IQ and thus certain cognitive processes, that is, the index of self-referencing, and an aspect of cohesion that impairs interpretability (additioning and ambiguity), but is not related to these same cognitive processes. This distinction is stable across different diagnoses and across time when there is change in the psychiatric and cognitive

Table 4-13. Longitudinal results for IQ and index of self-referencing

	Clinical Change	*Performance-IQ*	*Verbal-IQ*	*Index of self-referencing*
Schizophrenic				
1st test		95	84	2.83
2nd test	deterioration	89	79	1.43
Manic				
1st test		53	53	.35
2nd test	improvement	55	79	2.02
Korsakoff				
1st test		79	84	.35
2nd test	improvement	95	86	1.68

states of the speakers. Table 4-14 presents the data for cohesive weakness in these longitudinal cases. The use of unclear cohesion is a good indicator of the uninterpretability of a speaker, but it is only one measure of how language can be atypically constructed for interaction.

A speaker links nominal groups by reference (anaphora) or may use nominal groups to refer to information not in the verbal context, but present in the nonverbal situation (exophora). However, some nominal groups may not set up any phoric links at all. These nominal groups (e.g., "a boy," "a ball" in "A boy saw a ball") do not in themselves contribute to cohesion, with the exception of a possible lexical link (to be discussed separately). A large proportion of nonphoric nominal groups or a shift over time to more nonphoric nominal groups indicates less cohesive language and probably a shifting of topics. The use of nonphoric nominal groups over time is given in Table 4-15. Only the manic

Table 4-14. Cohesive weakness (additioning and ambiguity combined) as a percentage of all phoric nominal groups over time

	Clinical change	*Additioning and ambiguous reference*
Schizophrenic		
1st test		17
2nd test	deterioration	11
Manic		
1st test		9
2nd test	improvement	4
Korsakoff		
1st test		0.4
2nd test	improvement	4

shows any substantial change in the use of nonphoric nominal groups. He uses relatively few such groups with improvement in clinical state. This change may well be a factor contributing to a judgment of better clinical state. In the following example the manic uses a number of nominal groups, but all of them are either anaphoric or exophoric.

Manic: Yes. they (the voices) haven't come back . . . now that I feel good I feel good inside they're not like they're not even close yes that's when I was feeling really bad.

Nonphoric nominal groups may be either specific or generic (the whole of a class of participants). Generic nominal groups may neutralize the definite-indefinite distinction and number (Martin, forthcoming). Martin compares "the true hot deserts" and "cool deserts" to show that generic entities can be introduced in either a definite or indefinite nominal group. Either the singular "a book" or the plural "books" can be generic in a sentence such as "A book/books would be regarded as a sign of culture in this room." The explanation given by Martin for the possible neutralization of distinctions in generics is that generics depend less on context than specific nominal groups. To interpret a generic nominal group, the hearer need only be aware of the language systems themselves, whereas the use of a specific nominal group makes a claim about the relevance of some subset of the total class of objects to the particular verbal context and/or nonverbal situation. The percentage of nonphoric nominal groups that are generic is presented in Table 4-16. The rate of nonphoric generic nominal groups moves, over time, in

Table 4-15. Nonphoric nominal groups as a percentage of all nominal groups over time

	Clinical change	*Nonphoric nominal groups*
Schizophrenic		
1st test		21
2nd test	deterioration	21
Manic		
1st test		25
2nd test	improvement	17
Korsakoff		
1st test		22
2nd test	improvement	23

the direction of clinical change. Rochester and Martin (1979) found that for interviews, thought-disordered schizophrenics and normal controls had relatively high levels of generic reference, and that nonthought disordered schizophrenics had lower levels. They attribute this pattern to the nonthought disordered speakers trying to avoid stressful or difficult verbal operations. This explanation is supported for the current longitudinal data when the rates and directions of change for generic nominal groups are compared to the rates and directions of change for attempts at implicit referencing. Table 4-17 presents the attempts at implicit verbal referencing (bridging and additioning) as a percentage of all endophoric references. As with generic referencing, the attempts at implicit referencing move in the direction of the clinical changes. A speaker judged clinically to be improved attempts more implicit verbal references. This argument assumes that the schizophrenic and manic patients are nonthought disordered in terms of Rochester and Martin's subject groups, an assumption confirmed by independent ratings of only two on the 4-point thought-disordered index used by Rochester and Martin. Thus, both generic references and attempts at implicit verbal referencing are related to the avoidance of difficult referring patterns. Using subjects as their own control helps to demonstrate how the linguistic variables are related to the clinically judged ability to function in socially appropriate ways. Despite different diagnoses, severity of initial state, and different clinical course, the relationship of generic references and implicit references to clinical state is constant. Rochester and Martin's proposed underlying mechanism of avoidance of problematic referencing patterns is thus supported by the longitudinal data on diverse speakers.

Lexical cohesion is one cohesive technique that may be used when more difficult kinds of cohesion are either not attempted or fail. Rochester and Martin (1979) report that thought-disordered schizophrenics rely on lexical cohesion in interviews more than the other groups of speakers. For the subjects studied longitudinally (see Table 4-18), there is no clear trend for lexical cohesion to be associated with better functioning. In general, the schizophrenic and manic rely on lexical cohesion the most, and the manic uses less lexical cohesion with clinical improvement. Although suggestive of the Rochester and Martin pattern, the data are not consistent.

Although conjunction is not a link from one nominal group to another, it serves to create cohesion by linking clauses and units

Table 4-16. Generic nominal groups as a percentage of nonphoric nominal groups, over time

	Clinical change	*Generic nominal groups*
Schizophrenic		
1st test		34
2nd test	deterioration	4
Manic		
1st test		29
2nd test	improvement	33
Korsakoff		
1st test		14
2nd test	improvement	23

Table 4-17. Additioning and bridging (implicit verbal reference) as a percentage of all endophoric reference, over time

	Clinical change	*Additioning and bridging*
Schizophrenic		
1st test		23
2nd test	deterioration	15
Manic		
1st test		5
2nd test	improvement	16
Korsakoff		
1st test		4
2nd test	improvement	11

below the rank of clause. Different levels in the use of conjunction are not directly related to the interpretability of the speaker. The examination of conjunction in the longitudinal data nevertheless reveals a process of change. The rate of conjunction is presented in Table 4-19. The data reveal that the typical level of conjunction is about seven instances for every 100 words. Variations from this frequency are associated with more impaired states. This kind of patterning is in contrast to the patterning of the reference variables. The various measures of referencing show disparate initial levels of use, probably relating to different syndromes and degrees of severity. The referencing variables have also been shown to distinguish the syndromes and be explanatory of the difficulties in interpreting some speakers. The use of conjunction, however, does not have such salience in terms of diagnostics or interpretability, but can

Table 4-18. Lexical cohesion as a percentage of successful explicit endophoric cohesion, over time

	Clinical change	*Lexical cohesion*
Schizophrenic		
1st test		80
2nd test	deterioration	74
Manic		
1st test		77
2nd test	improvement	67
Korsakoff		
1st test		65
2nd test	improvement	65

still be considered an aspect of cohesion that contributes to the particular ways that speakers construct text.

Conclusions

The longitudinal data demonstrate a number of relations among cohesion, cognitive processes, and clinical state. The longitudinal methodology confirmed the result from cross-sectional data that verbal IQ and the index of self-referencing are related. The construction of text in conversation involves extending meaning from the language used earlier. This continuity of meaning from speaker and interlocutor is typically in favor of the speaker's own earlier language. The continuity of the speaker's own language apparently creates textness that the hearer can

Table 4-19. Conjunction per 100 words, over time

	Clinical change	*Conjunction per 100 words*
Schizophrenic		
1st test		7.2
2nd test	deterioration	3.8
Manic		
1st test		4.6
2nd test	improvement	7.1
Korsakoff		
1st test		17.0
2nd test	improvement	7.6
Control		6.9

process and interpret. From the speaker's perspective, the ability to sustain links to one's own language derives from general verbal processes also underlying verbal IQ. Such a relationship found both in cross-sectional and longitudinal data suggests an important role for cohesion in understanding cognitive processes and social interaction. A measure such as the index of self-referencing is both reflective of certain cognitive abilities and an indication of how speakers construct text in cooperation with another speaker. More generally, a functional view of language can thus relate the socially relevant abilities of speakers to specific kinds of cognitive processing.

The longitudinal data also help distinguish the issues of the interpretability of language and the typicality of language patterning. Atypical use of cohesion, for example, conjunction, may not be directly related to the interpretability of the speaker, but nevertheless may indicate a change in clinical state. Similarly, changes in the index of self-referencing do not seem to be directly associated with interpretability. Thus, the data on cohesive weakness, which helps to explain why some speakers, especially thought-disordered schizophrenics, are difficult to interpret, reflect just the aspect of cohesion that is directly noticeable in interaction. Other aspects of cohesion are also used with certain frequencies and contribute to the interactive construction of text. However, departures from the typical frequencies do not directly affect interpretability. It is possible, though, that such quantitative atypicalities do contribute to a particular style of communication that may sound "odd" or "peculiar" without being unusually difficult to interpret.

CONCLUSIONS

This chapter has examined cohesion in psychiatric subjects. These cases involve clear difficulty in social or cognitive functioning that are relateable to the use of cohesion. The approach of using speakers with clinically defined syndromes provides a description of functioning that is valid in comparison to other speakers both normal and psychiatrically classified. The disturbances in contributing to the building of text are not of one kind. Different atypicalities in the use of cohesion are associated with different diagnoses and severity of the psychiatric conditions. Cohesion involves a number of separate components which are related in different ways to success or failure in social interaction. Unclear cohesion is a manifest example of how cohesion can impede the interpretability of a speaker. However, other uses of cohesion may indicate more subtly that a speaker is not constructing interaction in the usual way. Such measures of cohesion nevertheless help characterize a speaker's interactions and help relate the interactions to characteristics of the psychiatric syndromes.

In relating cohesion to cognitive processes, a number of both cohesive measures and cognitive measures are needed. Since cohesion itself creates a number of different relations in language, it is reasonable to expect that the various kinds of cohesion are related to a number of different cognitive measures. The data show that factors such as verbal memory, verbal IQ, distractibility, and perhaps the tracking of information are related to components of cohesion in various subjects. The longitudinal studies demonstrate a consistency in the relationship between cohesion and cognitive measures and also show how the measures of cohesion can reflect changes in the clinically determined level of functioning. Cohesion can indicate some of the underlying cognitive and social characteristics that vary with changes in clinical state. As in comparative studies of different subjects, some of the changes in cohesion may not be in obvious and undesirable linguistic measures. Cohesion may sometimes account for noticeable difficulties in interpretability and sometimes help locate and explain more subtle social or cognitive processes.

5

DEVELOPMENT: INTERACTION OF SPEAKERS

INTRODUCTION

The previous three chapters have looked in some detail at the language of speakers with psychiatrically specified problems. These speakers have clear difficulty in communicating in typical social situations. The following chapters examine the development of the use of language and specifically of cohesion. These two sets of data are linked by the fact that there is a less than complete fit of the language with the social norms for communication. Language must fit with and build interaction according to the social patterning of the speech community. Examining the language of children is a way of showing the use of cohesion to interact appropriately. For both children and psychiatric subjects the issue is where in the linguistic system is the lack of fit or the development. More specifically it is the parts of language that are responsible for the creation of text that are of interest. Since text is language operative in situations, the study of cohesion specifies the links of relationships that speakers encode between language and context—verbal and nonverbal.

Phoricity as one part of cohesion involves the use and presumption of verbal and nonverbal information. In particular, phoricity in nominal groups signals how participants are reidentified as conversation proceeds. Conjunction operates slightly differently in that it signals the relations between clauses. For both conjunction and phoricity, as well as other types of cohesion, the linking of language to context is typical, given aspects of the context involved. Some of these aspects of contexts include turn-taking and nonlinguistic factors such as the social relationships between speakers and the specific task. The developmental approach in the following chapters is designed to examine the process of young speakers learning to construct text, taking into account a range of other relevant factors.

The study of both psychiatric syndromes and language development has important applied implications. Social interaction is the goal of communication and is constructed by language. If such social interaction is not attained, then the speaker will not be recognized as a full member of the community. The goal of the functional study is to provide the details of "not meaning the way the members of the community typically mean." The typical use of language circumscribes what it takes to mean typically in the community. Consequently, a description of atypicalities is (a) a good description of developmental processes if those atypicalities follow a course towards the typical with increasing age; and (b) an account of the failures to fully enter a community. The elements of language that are not used typically reveal something of more basic social and cognitive processes underlying language.

Rather than focusing on the individual in relation to typical forms of communication, Chapter 7 compares two groups of children from different social classes. The objective is to try to identify differences in the social communication that the two groups of children are learning. The results show few differences between the two groups, although there are clear differences in the language produced on different tasks. The patterns of communication being learned by the two groups are very similar.

In examining how reality is built in conversation, language must be related to nonlinguistic factors. This chapter presents some of these nonlinguistic factors that relate to cohesion. The relationships may be in both directions: extralinguistic factors influencing the use of cohesion, and cohesion helping to realize or encode nonlinguistic facts. Four kinds of nonlinguistic factors are examined: (a) turn-taking, (b) the social status of the interlocutor, (c) the number and kind of participants in the conversation, and (d) the distance of cohesive links. As theories of language become increasingly broad these factors may be incorporated into linguistics. For example, Halliday's work on speech function (Halliday, 1984; Ventola, 1988) is an attempt to use a broad semiotic approach to linguistics to link the upper levels of linguistic theory to how speakers influence each other's turns. Sinclair and Coulthard (1975) provide a method of conversational analysis in terms of exchange structure, but without explicit systematic relation to grammatical functions. The work of Berry and Butler, reviewed in Butler (1985), and Fawcett, van de Mije, and van Wissen (1988), has linked grammatical and semantic levels to conversational analysis. The social status of speakers is quite relevant to linguistic choices, but is itself outside language. Similarly, the length of cohesive links, although involving language, is not part of a linguistic system of entry conditions and options. The length of cohesive links may have to do with the processing abilities of the mind in the context of a conversation. Since the factors considered in this chapter may not be strictly linguistic, the description and explanation is not in terms of how different parts of the linguistic system fit together, but in terms of how cohesion is used in the context of nonlinguistic factors, which nevertheless play a role in conversation. The values of these nonlinguistic factors must then derive from notions of social order or organization of conversation.

METHOD

The data in this chapter and the following chapter are based on conversations of 5-, 7-, and 9-year-olds. Students from 5 to 9 were chosen so that the early years of formal education were covered. During this period children are learning to interact in structural settings outside the family.

The data was gathered from two elementary schools in Toronto, Canada. In all, 13 classrooms were used. Six students—3 males, 3 females—were selected randomly from each class. For each age level, eight conversations were recorded: four were dialogues between one of the target children and a friend selected by that student. The other four conversations involved pairs of target children with their classroom teacher (the teacher dialogues). There were thus 24 conversations involving 36 students and 12 teachers. The 5-year-old group was aged 5:1 to 6:3 with a mean of 5:6 (males 5:7, females 5:5). The 7-year-old group was aged 7:3 to 8:4 with a mean of 7:9 (males 7:7, females 7:10). The 9-year-old group ranged in age from 8:4 to 10:3 with a mean of 9:5 (males 9:2, females 9:8).

The conversations were recorded in small rooms within the schools. The recorder was not hidden, and the microphone was attached to the back of an extra chair to avoid a formal recording atmosphere. The same recorders had been given to the teachers for classroom use a month earlier to accustom students to them. Each conversation lasted 5 minutes, and a transcription in standard orthography was prepared by pairs of transcribers. The cohesion, intonation, and conversational analyses were then added to the transcripts.

TURN-TAKING

The analysis of the conversations is based on the relatively linear and nonsemantic proposals of Sacks, Schegloff, and Jefferson (1974). The *turn* is defined as an interactional unit: a stretch of language spoken by one speaker. It is bounded by the speech of another speaker or by the beginning or end of the conversation. The interactional unit of the turn arises from the need to have only one participant speaking at a time (in most conversations) and the subsequent need to order and distribute turns among speakers. The study of cohesion will then be with respect to this very basic linear relationship among turns. The set of turns is given in Table 5-1. The turns represent sets of dependencies among utterances. The sequences Question–Answer–Confirmation, Imperative–Response, and Statement–Come-back were defined. The Question and Imperative turns were coded by listening to tape-recordings of the conversations and following a transcript. The conversational status of a turn could be determined by intonation, syntax, or by paralinguistic features. What is important is how the turn is interpreted in terms of conversational organization. If a turn sounds like a question, then the addressee will have to treat it as such. The addressee's turn will be expected to be relevant to the question turn.

The second-pair partners (Answer, Response, Come-back) are defined by their position in conversation immediately following

Table 5-1. Turns coded for conversational analysis

First-pair partners (1st)	Second-pair partners (2nd)
Question (Q)	Answer (A)
Imperative (I)	Response (R)
Statement (S)	Come-back (B)
Third turn (3rd)	
Confirmation (C)	
Other - turns not in conversational sets.	

the corresponding first-pair partners of the set. Second-pair partners may not always be semantically appropriate to the first-pair partners, but are nevertheless interpreted as relevant to the first-pair partners. If the second turn (or the third turn in the case of a confirmation) starts another set of turns, then the turn is coded as part of both sets. Typically these double-coded turns are AQ (Answer–Question) and CQ (Confirmation–Question). Like the second-pair partners, the confirmation (C) turn is defined by its location in sequence. It is the turn after an answer turn that is spoken by the speaker of the preceding question turn. The confirmation turn is the slot available for the questioner to acknowledge the answer to the original question. Turns not part of these conversational sets were coded as "other." These other turns do not have the same constraints as turns in the conversational sets.

The turns are grouped (see Table 5-1) according to how they are used to guide conversations. Question and Imperative turns are grouped as first-pair partners (1st) and represent local control of the conversation. They specify the nature of the following turn as dependent on the current turn. Answers and Responses are second-pair partners (2nd) and are dependent in terms of conversational organization. The speaker of a second-pair partner has the role of reacting to the prior speaker. Turns that are double coded serve in more than one conversational set. There are two important combinations: 2nd + 1st and 3rd + 1st. Turns that are 2nd + 1st include: answer–question, answer–imperative, response–question and response–imperative. These 2nd + 1st turns represent a changeover in the control of conversation. The speaker of the second turn fills a slot set up by the speaker of the prior turn but then also specifies the turn type for the original speaker. The third turn becomes a second-pair partner in a conversational set started and controlled by the second speaker. In the following excerpt, the first turn is a question that constrains the second turn. The second turn is thus a second-pair partner. This second turn is not only an answer but also includes a question that starts another conversational set constraining the third turn by the speaker to the second speaker.

1: Do you like playing ... I mean like at recess.
2: Yes ... what kinda game do you play at recess.

The second type of combined turn that is found frequently is the 3rd + 1st turn. These turns are both a confirmation to an answer and either ask a question or issue an imperative. These turns complete a question-answer-confirmation sequence and begin a new sequence starting with Question or Imperative. Unlike the 2nd + 1st sequence, 3rd + 1st sequences leave the control of the conversation with the same speaker. The original answerer is then in the position of answering the second question. The first and third turns below are spoken by the same speaker and both ask questions of the second speaker. The control of the conversation remains with the first speaker.

1: Do you think that there're going to be guinea pigs on the farm when we get there what do you think we'll find on the farm.
2: Horses.
3: Good have you ever been to a farm.

Turn-taking and the sequential conversational sets that turns form provide a framework for understanding how cohesion is used in conversation.

The use of referential cohesion and conjunction are examined below in terms of the turn-taking structure of conversation. The first issue is how frequently anaphoric reference is used to create cohesion relative to other types of cohesion. Table 5-2 presents anaphoric reference as a percentage of all types of cohesion by age and by the type of turn, in which the reference item is used. There is a greater proportion of reference in second-pair partners compared to first-pair partners. These second-pair partners are conversationally dependent on the prior turn and also set up anaphoric links more frequently than do first-pair partners. Anaphoric reference establishes a link to an antecedent that is required for the interpretation of the anaphoric item. This link must be reestablished by the hearer in order to interpret the utterance. The link is also usually a link of identity of meaning, unlike conjunction or lexical cohesion.

The use of such anaphoric reference in second-pair partners establishes clearly that the speaker is continuing to speak about the same entities, be they mentioned in the first-pair partner or earlier in the conversation. Second-pair partners, more than first-pair partners, are tightly connected semantically to earlier stretches of language. Both the conversational dependence of following a first-pair partner and a comparative preference for anaphoric reference signal the speaker's continuity of the conversation in terms of what has happened so far.

A closer examination of Table 5-2 shows how speakers treat the turns that belong to two conversational sets. In turns that change the locus of control from one speaker to another (2nd + 1st), teachers (T) use a relatively high proportion of anaphoric reference. In contrast, students use a relatively low proportion of anaphoric reference in these changes of control turns. The students' use of anaphoric reference is similar to their use of it in first-pair partners, whereas the teachers' use of anaphoric reference is similar to their use in second-pair partners. The quantitative distribution of reference suggests that students regard the turnover of control turns differently from their teachers. For the students, the 2nd + 1st turn is similar to first-pair partners that start a conversational set, but for the teachers, it is similar to a turn that is dependent on a prior turn. The teachers use the specific anaphoric reference to signal that the new conversational set starting with the 2nd + 1st turn is heard as connected to the prior stretches of language. The 5-year-olds use few 2nd + 1st turns, and so the 26% of cohesion that is anaphoric in these turns is based on relatively few instances compared to the older students. The older students, on the other hand, establish less of an identity of reference with prior stretches of language. In the following excerpt, the second turn is a 2nd + 1st turn in which the control of conversation is changed from the first speaker to the second speaker. In this

Table 5-2. Anaphoric reference as a percentage of all cohesion by age and by type of turn

	TYPE OF TURN			
Age	*1st*	*2nd*	*3rd + 1st*	*2nd + 1st*
5	12	20	17	26
7	5	16	4	5
9	15	22	12	10
T	12	20	20	18

(n = 856)

second turn there is no anaphoric reference, although there is lexical cohesion (*game*, *play*, *recess*) and exophoric reference (*you*).

1: Do you like playing . . . I mean like at recess.
2: Yes . . . what kinda game do you play at recess.

The 2nd + 1st turn for older students is less connected to earlier language by identity of reference and more by cohesion such as conjunction and lexical repetition. It is likely, then, that the older students less frequently make their 2nd + 1st turns about the same entities that have been discussed. Rather, their use of lexical and conjunctive cohesion signals a continuation in the same topic or field but with some drift, or at least indeterminateness, in the identity of entities. One can suggest that for older students the 2nd + 1st turns are looking forward and are similar to first-pair partners rather than oriented backwards.

The shift in balance from one type of cohesion to another can be revealing about how speakers are using the turn-taking system. Both the turn-taking system and cohesion have a role in relating one stretch of language to another. The turn-taking system establishes the local linear dependence of one turn on another, whereas cohesion creates continuity both within and across speakers and turns. The functional effects of the turn-taking and cohesion systems should thus be related. The quantitative data suggest that the greater dependence of second-pair partners in the turn-taking system is related to greater specificity of a continuing entity in the conversation. The two systems are jointly displaying the connectedness of the current stretch of language to an earlier stretch of language. Furthermore, the independence of the two systems permits variation in how their use is interrelated by different speakers. Although the two organizations in language have the same general function of connecting language together for the speaker and hearer, the organizations are nevertheless independent and exploited differently by various speakers under different conversational conditions.

Reference (Phoricity)

Anaphoric reference sets up cohesive links between one stretch of language and another. Exophoric reference, in contrast, directs the hearer to the nonlinguistic situation to determine the meaning of the reference items. Exophora will be examined as a proportion of all cohesive links and as a proportion of referential links both anaphoric and exophoric. Table 5-3 presents exophora as a percentage of all cohesion. Students use exophora less in second-pair partners than in first-pair partners. The conversational constraint of the second-pair partner is associated with less direct connection to the nonlinguistic situation and correspondingly more connection through cohesion to the verbal context. The teachers seem to use cohesion differently and do not show a variation in their use of exophora in different types of turns. The teachers are in control of the dialogues and, it is argued, do not have the same constraint to answer a question as students do. That is, a second-pair partner spoken by a teacher is not as constrained as a second-pair partner spoken by a student. Further evidence for this view comes from the use of exophora in turns that do not belong to conversational sets. In these turns the students' rate of exophora is 30% of all reference compared to 19% in second pair partners. For teachers, the rate in the unconstrained turns is 29%, compared to 34% in second-pair partners. The use of exophora in turns not part of conversational sets by students is more frequent than its use in second-pair partners, thus supporting the hypothesis that it is the conversational constraint imposed on the second-pair partners that is associated with the lower use of exophora. Again, for the teachers this constraint is not as strong as it is for the students, and there is less difference between turns that are not constrained and those that are strongly constrained by a prior turn.

The analysis of exophora has shown a sensitivity to the conversational control in conversation and to the identity of the speaker. Teachers use language differently, possibly because of the difference in relative social status in a conversation. The

Table 5-3. Exophoric as a percentage of all cohesion by age and by type of turn

	TYPE OF TURN			
Age	*1st*	*2nd*	*3rd + 1st*	*2nd + 1st*
5	34	23	26	33
7	42	21	34	29
9	23	13	26	29
T	35	34	24	32

(*n* = 1123)

constraints from the turn-taking structure of conversation do not apply absolutely, but rather are conditioned by the relations of the speakers involved. Teachers do not have the same responsibility to answer a question from young students in an informal nondidactic setting as students have to answer teachers. This difference in constraint is also evident in the cohesion system. Different kinds of meaning relationships are expressed when there is conversational constraint (relatively less exophora reference) compared to when there is not. This difference in conversational constraint can be a product of the relative social statuses of the speakers and of the turn-taking organization in conversation.

So far exophora has been analyzed as a proportion of all the cohesion used by the speakers. However, exophora is an option in the reference system. As an option in the reference system, exophora directs the hearer to find information in the nonverbal environment in order to be able to interpret the current message. This pointing to the nonverbal environment is in contrast to other reference signals to the verbal (anaphora, cataphora, comparative) environment. Taken in the context of other options in the reference system, exophora is one specific instruction to the hearer and one specific way that the speaker chooses to create links to information that is needed in the interpretation of language. The use of exophora as part of the reference system can be studied quantitatively by computing exophoric reference as a percentage of all the options in the reference system. These data are presented in Table 5-4 for first-pair partners and all other conversational turns by age. As seen for exophora in relation to all other types of cohesion, more exophora is used in turns that begin conversational sets of utterances than in other turns. Largely this use of exophora is the use of first- and second-person pronouns identifying the speaker and addressee. The first turn of a conversationally dependent set of turns is used to establish the conversational relationship. The speaker must establish that the intended hearer is listening and that the speaker will be taking the floor (often to speak about himself or herself).

Of the groups of speakers, it is only the youngest (the 5-year-olds) that do not show a substantially greater use of exophoric reference in first-pair partners. These speakers seem not to have integrated the relationship between exophoric reference and the value of conversational turns. The use of exophora by the older students and the teachers shows an

Table 5-4. Exophora as a percentage of reference options (anaphora, exophora, cataphora, comparative), by major type of turn, by age

	TYPE OF TURN	
Age	*1st pair partner*	*Other turns*
5	69	73
7	88	61
9	67	40
T	58	49
	(n = 1604)	

adjustment to this type of turn. These speakers differentially use exophora to establish the speaker–addressee relationship in first-pair partners. They combine exophora to the nonverbal environment with the turn beginning a conversationally constrained set of turns. The 5-year-olds do not demonstrate that the use of exophora and the turn-taking organization of conversation can be nonrandomly related to achieve specific effects in communication. More than the development of use of any particular system, the advanced stages of language development may be in learning how to use linguistic systems so that the value of one option is systematically related to the value of options in other systems.

Conjunction

Conjunction as a cohesive device instructs the hearer to interpret what follows, in a given way, as related to what has gone before. Unlike reference, a stretch of language with conjunction is not uninterpretable without a link to some other stretch of language. The conjunctive link specifies how two stretches of language are to be interpreted in relationship to each other, but each stretch remains interpretable on its own. In "John saw the car and he went out to look at it," the second clause is linked by conjunction to the first clause. If the reference items *he* and *it* are replaced by full nominal groups, then the second clause is entirely interpretable ("John went out to look at the vehicle"). On the other hand, "He went out to look at it" is not interpretable without a verbal context that provides antecedents for the anaphoric references.

As with referential cohesion, the data on conjunction are first presented in relation to other types of cohesion, and then the subtypes of conjunction are analyzed. The use of conjunction as a percentage of all cohesion is given in Table 5-5 for each major type of turn and by age. There is an increase of 50% or more in the use of conjunction in second-pair partners compared to first-pair partners. Thus, in turns that are second-pair partners, there is a relatively greater use of cohesive signals to the hearer to interpret a following stretch of language in relation to a preceding stretch of language. The following teacher and 5-year-old segment demonstrates how a long question turn (a first-pair partner) can have no conjunctive links but have exophoric links (*you*), anaphoric links (*there*), and lexical repetition (*animals* is repeated from an earlier turn). In contrast, the short answer has two cohesive links both of which are conjunctive (*only*—adversative conjunction, *and*—additive conjunction).

T: Why didn't you go there? Have you any are there any animals are there animals at grandpa's farm?
S: Only squirrels and frogs.

In considering turns that are both a third member of a conversational set (a confirmation) and the first-pair partners in the next conversational set (3rd + 1st), Table 5-5 shows that the rates of conjunction for the 7- and 9-year-olds and the teachers are considerably closer to the rates for first-pair partners rather than to the rates for conjunction in second-pair partners. The higher rate of conjunction associated in all groups of speakers with the dependent nature of second pair partners is used by the 5-year-olds in the third- combined with first-pair partners turns. The older students and the teachers encode conjunction in the third- plus first-pair partner turns as similar to first-pair partner turns that are independent of prior turns but constraining of the following turn. The 5-year-olds, in contrast, treat the same

Table 5-5. Conjunction as a percentage of all cohesion by type of turn by age

	TYPE OF TURN				
Age	*1st*	*2nd*	*2nd + 1st*	*3rd + 1st*	*Other*
5	11	19	11	19	13
7	12	18	15	12	9
9	12	19	8	5	4
T	6	15	3	7	7
				(*n* = 865)	

combined turns as constrained by the prior turn. It seems that, for the 5-year-olds, the confirming nature of the turn is significant in constructing the conjunctive links, but for the older speakers it is the status of the turn as a first-pair partner that is reflected in the use of conjunction.

These turns that are both the third member of a prior conversational set and the first-pair partners in a new conversational set have the function of continuing the control of conversation. In the light of this conversational function, the older students and teachers are using conjunction in such turns as they would to constrain a following turn, whereas the youngest group of students uses conjunction as if the turn were not about to constrain a following turn. The more developed relation between turn-taking and conjunction is thus to treat the continuation of control turn (3rd + 1st) as looking forward in the conversation to the next conversational set. This finding is similar to the data on anaphoric reference that suggested that, for the older students, turns that change the locus of conversational control (second-pair partners combined with first-pair partners) also look forward in the conversational organization by having a distribution of reference similar to first-pair partners rather than second-pair partners. The dependent turns have relatively high amounts of conjunction indicating that information is being added in various ways to already existing information. In the forward-looking, constraining turns, there is relatively less of this conjunction compared to other types of cohesion. These constraining turns have more of a tendency to use reference and lexical cohesion, that is, cohesion that links individual pieces of information rather than clauses that have to be interpreted in relation to each other.

To test further the function of turns that are in conversational sets, the turns were divided into those that belong to conversational sets (first-pair partners, second-pair partners, third-pair partners) and those turns not part of conversational sets and so only loosely bound in conversational structure (see Table 5-6). The general pattern is that conjunction is a cohesive device used more in turns that are bound by conversational organization to other turns. As indicated above, the important aspect of the conversational organization for older speakers is the dependence of a turn on a preceding turn. There thus seems to be a congruence in the function of conversational organization and conjunctive cohesion. Turns conversationally dependent on prior turns and interpreted by the hearer in terms of the prior turn (the turn following a question is always interpreted as being in response to that question) use cohesion that relatively increases the necessity for the hearer to interpret what is said in relation to earlier language.

To this point, conjunction has been presented in relation to other forms of cohesion. Conjunction is itself a subsystem with the types of conjunction (additive, temporal, adversative, causal) contrasting with each other. If a conjunctive link is to be built, then the speaker may choose to present the link in a number of ways (see Martin, 1983a, for a detailed analysis of the systems of conjunction). The most frequent types of conjunction are additive, temporal, and causal, which will be dealt with in that order.

Additive conjunction is the unmarked type of conjunction and simply directs the hearer to interpret what follows as connected to what precedes. The first question is whether speakers use such unmarked conjunction differentially according to the turn-taking organization of conversation. Table 5-7 presents the distribution of additive conjunction into each major type of turn for each age group. The table shows into which turns additive conjunction is placed as a percentage of all the use of additive conjunction for that age group. The 5-year-olds are unlike the older students in having a substantial amount of additive conjunction in turns not part of conversational sets and less in second pair partners (answers to questions). It is in these turns not part of conversational sets that the 5- and 7-year-olds have more additive conjunction in relation to other types of conjunction (see Table 5-8). For turns that are not part of conversational sets, the 5-year-olds have both relatively more unmarked additive conjunction compared to their other conversational turns and relatively more unmarked additive conjunction compared to other types of conjunction and the rate of additive conjunction used by the 9-year-olds. The 5-year-olds then have turns that are not part of conversational sets and these turns have unmarked additive conjunction.

To generalize, the youngest group produces talk that is least constrained in conversational organization and within those turns uses conjunction with the least amount of semantic

Table 5-6. Conjunction as a percentage of all cohesion in turns within and outside conversational sets of turns

Within Conversational Sets (1st, 2nd, or 3rd)	*Outside Conversational Sets*
12	8
	(n = 965)

Table 5-7. Additive conjunction in major types of turns as a percentage of additive conjunction in all turns for each group of speakers

	TYPE OF TURN					
Age	1st	2nd	3rd	3rd + 1st	2nd + 1st	Other
5	8	39	5	3	—	39
7	6	66	2	4	11	8
9	6	58	13	2	2	11
T	10	8	11	68	3	—
						(n = 594)

Table 5-8. Additive conjunction as a percentage of all conjunction by type of turn, by age

	TYPE OF TURN					
Age	1st	2nd	3rd	3rd + 1st	2nd + 1st	Other
5	74	57	43	56	—	68
7	64	71	50	38	73	72
9	75	65	74	80	50	51
T	46	71	78	60	100	—
						(n = 594)

specificity. In turns for which there is conversational constraint, the 5-year-olds are similar to the older students (at least in types of turns with 50 or more conjunctive relations). The 5-year-olds thus have the least amount of dependence in their language both in terms of conversational constraint and in terms of specificity of conjunctive relations when these two kinds of organization overlap. It is the co-occurrence of high rates of the two types of nondependence that distinguishes the 5-year-olds.

Temporal and causal conjunction occur much less frequently than the unmarked additive conjunction. Table 5-9 presents temporal conjunction as a percentage of all conjunction by type of turn and by age. In the three most frequent types of turns, second-pair partners (answers), other (turns not in conversational sets) and 3rd + 1st turns (confirmations combined with question), there are few differences among the groups. Overall there is an increase in the use of temporal conjunction with age in the unconstrained turns (other). These turns are relatively free from conversational constraint both from a prior turn and in influencing a following turn. In considering the additive and temporal conjunction together, there is a development away from unmarked additive conjunction and to temporal conjunction in the unconstrained turns. Thus when the influence of conversational organization is weak, older children increasingly prefer temporal relations. In turns that are more constrained conversationally, the use of temporal conjunction decreases with age, especially for: (a) third turns combined with first-pair partners, and (b) second-pair partners combined with first-pair partners. Although the rate of temporal conjunction is similar for all speakers when different types of turns are pooled together, there is a complementary relation between conversational constraint and using temporal conjunction. When there is relatively greater conversational constraint, relatively less marking of conjunctive relations as temporal takes place with increasing age. The speakers are developing the reciprocal relations of two kinds of specificity (of conversational organization and semantic relations of conjunction).

There is little use of causal conjunction compared to additive and temporal conjunction. Table 5-10 presents causal conjunction as a percentage of all conjunction for each type of turn by age. In comparison to additive and temporal conjunction there is little variation among the speaker groups in use of causal conjunction in turns not part of conversational sets ("other" in Table 5-10). If there is a relation between conversational organization and conjunction, it exists only for part of the conjunction system: the most frequently used options. Of course, with little use of some options it could be expected that floor effects lead to little variability. However, such floor effects and lack of variability can be interpreted functionally. Infrequently used options are not related to other organizations of conversation and do not show developmental changes as students grow older. Growth in ability to use language seems to take place in systems and options that occur frequently and thus frequently carry a functional load (see similar arguments in Fine, Bartolucci, & Szatmari, 1989).

The turn-taking organization of conversation realizes functions of control in the dialogue. The talk of speakers is made

Table 5-9. Temporal conjunction as a percentage of all conjunction by type of turn, by age

	TYPE OF TURN						
Age	*1st*	*2nd*	*3rd*	*3rd + 1st*	*2nd + 1st*	*Other*	*All Turns*
5	11	14	14	33	33	13	14
7	29	13	17	31	–	17	15
9	–	10	13	20	13	26	13
T	46	–	–	21	–	–	20
							(n = 143)

Table 5-10. Causal conjunction as a percentage of all conjunction by type of turn, by age

	TYPE OF TURN						
Age	1st	2nd	3rd	3rd + 1st	2nd + 1st	Other	All Turns
5	5	18	43	–	33	11	16
7	–	10	17	–	18	–	10
9	6	17	3	–	38	11	14
T	–	–	11	14	–	50	12
							(*n* = 129)

interpretable in the context by the talk of other speakers. Cohesion also signals how language is to be interpreted. These two forms of organization are related by the probabilities of using an option from one system simultaneously with an option from another system. The actual ordering of the system and therefore any possible temporal ordering of the selection of options is not the subject of this study. Rather, the interrelationship of the different organizations is at issue.

SPEAKER STATUS

The analysis of conversational turn-taking and cohesion concerned two interrelated organizations of language. Cohesion sets up a link between one stretch of language and another so that the antecedent of the cohesive item (antecedent will be used loosely to include the prior information of a conjunctive link) can be studied, as well as the location of the cohesive item itself. In the conversations studied, there are three possible speakers of the antecedent of a cohesive item: the speaker of the cohesive item, another student in the conversation, or the teacher (in the dialogues with teachers). In the teacher's talk, the link may be to an antecedent in the teacher's earlier language or to a student's language. Identifying the speaker of the antecedent information enables the study of cohesion to be related to the social roles of the speakers in a conversation. Turn-taking structure accounts for the turn-by-turn relations among speakers, whereas the identity of a speaker as student or teacher is a more permanent and pervasive element of social relationship. Furthermore, the study of the speaker of the antecedent of cohesive links shows how a speaker draws on his or her own speech, compared to the speech of another participant in the conversation. The analysis of the speaker of the antecedents to cohesive links will include reference, conjunction, and lexical cohesion.

REFERENCE (PHORICITY)

Referential cohesion signals the hearer to use some information found elsewhere to interpret the current cohesive item. Determining the antecedent for the referential link indicates to which other speaker the current speaker directs the hearer. Typical (or typical probabilities) of reference to one speaker or another suggest ways that the hearer should expect to understand the speaker. From the speaker's perspective, the distribution of antecedents in prior speech may indicate how that speaker is monitoring the language of the conversation and building links to it.

For the three groups of students, there is a strong pattern to build referential links to the speaker's own language. There is little linking to the teacher's language and an intermediate level of linking to the student interlocutor (see Table 5-11). The overall pattern, then, is for speakers to use demonstrative reference largely to connect one stretch of language to an earlier stretch of their own language. This pattern becomes stronger with age as more links are built to the student's own earlier language and fewer links are built to the other student in the conversation.

The choice of demonstrative reference is just one of the available options in the endophoric reference subsystem. The location of the antecedent for demonstrative reference can be studied in relation to antecedent location for all kinds of reference. Table 5-12 presents the data. This table shows that there

Table 5-11. Location of antecedents of demonstrative reference as percentage of all antecedents of demonstrative reference by age

	LOCATION OF ANTECEDENT		
Age	*Student's own Language*	*Other Student's Language*	*Teacher's Language*
5	54	33	14
7	67	27	6
9	76	21	2
T	–	52	48

is a decrease with age in the use of demonstrative reference in relation to other kinds of reference linked to both the student's and to the interlocutor's language. Demonstrative reference is specific reference but does not give much information about the antecedent. *This* and *that* encode, respectively, the features 'near' and 'not near' and *the* as a demonstrative reference item is even less specific about the identity of the antecedent (see Halliday, 1985, p. 290f). Use of demonstrative reference decreases with age, regardless of the location of the antecedent, as other more specific types of reference are used. More specific reference is needed as the conversations become more elaborate and more entities are introduced that could be antecedents for demonstrative reference. Evidence for the greater possible confusion of antecedents is that the number of full clauses per utterance increases with age: 5-year-olds: .64 full clauses per utterances; 7-year-olds: .86; 9-year-olds: 1.1. As shown in Table 5-12, for each age the highest rate of demonstrative reference is in links to the other student, followed by links to the student's own language. That is, there is a lower rate of linking to self compared to other kinds of reference. The more specific kinds of endophoric reference tend to be used for links to the student's own language. For reference, there is a tendency not to use the less specific demonstrative reference for links to the speaker's own language and moreso for links to the teacher's language. The specificity of a referential link is sensitive to the speaker whose language is being linked to. For the most socially remote interlocutor (the teacher), students use the least amount of relatively unspecific demonstrative reference and therefore more relatively specific reference. The relation between the speaker of antecedent information and the semantic specificity of cohesive items is explored further when considering conjunction.

Personal reference gives more information than demonstrative reference to guide the search for the appropriate antecedent.

Table 5-12. Location of antecedents of demonstrative reference as percentage of antecedents of all reference for the given location, by age

	LOCATION OF ANTECEDENT		
Age	*Student's own Language*	*Other Student's Language*	*Teacher's Language*
5	44	53	22
7	30	44	21
9	21	33	11
T	–	48	37
		(*n* = 368)	

Table 5-13 shows that, indeed, relative to demonstrative reference, personal reference is favored as a way of linking to the teacher. Although it requires corroboration by further data, it can at least be speculated that students consider speech connected to a teacher's speech to require the most specific type of reference.

Conjunction

Conjunction also links one stretch of language to another. The link of conjunction is usually more local than that for reference, connecting adjacent pieces of language. The prior piece of language, here loosely called the antecedent, is related to the following stretch of language. Since the link is of adjacent stretches of language, we would expect that links to the speaker's own language would predominate. Table 5-14 in fact shows that for additive conjunction (representing 70% of all conjunction) the linking is overwhelmingly to the speaker's own prior language, and becomes moreso with the older groups of students. Despite the availability of teacher talk, students rarely link their language by additive conjunction to what the teachers say, even compared to links to the student interlocutor. As with other types of cohesion, there is a developmental trend for older students to link more to their own language. Conversation involves connecting together the language of the speakers, but additive conjunction, the unmarked use of conjunction, is used to link a speaker's language to that speaker's own language.

The use of additive conjunction can be compared to the use of other types of conjunction. Additive conjunction merely indicates that the prior and the later stretches of language should be interpreted with respect to each other. The other types

Table 5-13. Location of antecedent of personal reference as a percentage of antecedents of all reference for the given location, by age

	LOCATION OF ANTECEDENT		
Age	*Student's own Language*	*Other Student's Language*	*Teacher's Language*
5	52	42	78
7	58	48	71
9	66	64	83
T	–	42	52
		$n = 635$	

Table 5-14. Location of antecedent stretches of language for additive conjunction as a percentage of all antecedents of additive conjunction by age

	LOCATION OF ANTECEDENT		
Age	*Student's own Language*	*Other Student's Language*	*Teacher's Language*
5	76	19	5
7	90	8	1
9	95	4	1
T	–	18	80

$n = 606$

of cohesion specify the semantic relationship between the two stretches of language. Table 5-15 compares additive conjunction to the more marked forms of conjunction by presenting additive conjunction as a percentage of all conjunction for links to each class of speaker. There is a decrease in the use of additive conjunction in relation to other types of conjunction in linking to the language of the other student in the conversation. However, there is little variation in the principal use of additive conjunction, linking to the student's own language. If there is any trend, it is for additive conjunction to be used more frequently with age than other types of conjunction to link to the speaker's own language. The more marked and varied types of conjunction are used increasingly to link to the speech of the other student in the conversation. This pattern seems to be found also in the conjunctive links to the teachers. In general, more marked conjunctive forms are used by older students to link to their interlocutors.

The teachers use conjunction somewhat differently than the students. The teachers are similar to the youngest students in having much additive conjunction (71% of all conjunction) in

Table 5-15. Additive conjunction as a percentage of all types of conjunction for the given location of linked information, by age

	LOCATION OF LINKED INFORMATION		
Age	*Student's own Language*	*Other Student's Language*	*Teacher's Language*
5	63	73	32
7	71	59	10
9	68	60	15
T	–	71	54

$n = 606$

links to student language. This result is an indication that the teachers are creating links to student language similar to the way students make links and tend to continue the semantic relations of student speech without adding specific semantic information. However, in considering the links within the teachers' own language, there is the lowest level (54%) of using additive conjunctive compared to other types of conjunction. Students use additive conjunction within their own turns at the rates 63%, 71%, and 68%. Teachers are thus introducing a large proportion of marked semantic relations within their own speech for the students to interpret.

The greatest change in levels of use of additive conjunction is also found in the speech of the teachers. They use additive conjunction in 54% of their conjunctive links to themselves and 71% in links to students. This difference may reflect an adjustment in how to continue student speech but a presumption that students can interpret the teacher speech with its more frequent marked conjunctive relations.

In summary, the use of conjunctive semantic relations is sensitive to age and to the speaker of language being linked to. There are more differentiate conjunctive links to other speakers with increased age. Teachers, on the other hand, have more marked relations linking within their speech but comparatively little marked relations when linking to students' speech. This patterning suggests an aspect of teachers' register when speaking to students: an adjustment of the rate of unmarked and marked conjunctive relations depending on the language being linked to. A similar adjustment takes place in the language of the students. For the students, however, it is the identity of the speaker of the prior language as self or other student that is associated with variation in the use of conjunction. With age, students adjust the use of conjunction in linking to the interlocutor. Thus the nonlinguistic factor that is associated with the use of marked and unmarked conjunction can be either the age of the speaker or the identity of the interlocutor whose language is being linked to. These findings can be compared to the use of reference to link to the language of the speakers in a conversation. In the reference system, the least specific type, demonstrative reference, is used less frequently to link to both the student's own language and to the teacher. In contrast, for conjunction the least specific type, additive conjunction, is used less frequently to link to the teacher's language.

Perhaps a broad notion of amount of specificity is needed to generalize about how the semantic information in cohesive signals is used in relation to such nonlinguistic factors as the age and status of the participants in a conversation. Tentatively, the use of specificity in the reference system seems associated with the social remoteness of the speakers: The teacher is linked to by the more specific type of reference. For the conjunction system, the more specific semantic options are selected for linking to the teacher, whereas for the reference system, the more specific option is selected for linking to both the teacher and relatively often the other student in the conversation. For these two systems, the semantic relationships of cohesion are consistently reflecting elements of differential social interaction.

Temporal conjunction sets up a specific conjunctive link that gives the relationship in time of the two stretches of language. The distribution of these temporal conjunctions in terms of the speaker of the prior information is given in Table 5-16. The teachers use temporal conjunction overwhelmingly to link to their own earlier language, similar to their use of causal conjunction and in contrast to additive conjunction. For the students, as well as the teachers, temporal conjunction draws mainly (82% to 93%) on the speaker's own language and seems to develop with age to link more to the student's own language.

Temporal conjunction can be seen as one of the options in the conjunction system that links to each of the speakers in the conversation. Table 5-17 presents temporal conjunction as a percentage of all types of conjunction linking back to the different speakers. The 5- and 7-year-olds use a higher rate of temporal conjunction when linking their language to the teacher compared to when linking to a peer. This effect, as will be seen, is similar for causal conjunction. For both these types of marked conjunction, there are more specific links to the teacher. As was noted earlier, teachers use more specific links to their own

Table 5-16. Location of antecedent stretches of language for temporal conjunction as a percentage of all antecedents of temporal conjunction, by age

	LOCATION OF ANTECEDENT INFORMATION		
Age	*Student's own Language*	*Other's Student's Language*	*Teacher's Language*
5	82	8	10
7	88	3	9
9	93	7	–
T	–	5	95
		n = 138	

Table 5-17. Temporal conjunction as a percentage of all types of conjunction, for the given location of linked information, by age

	LOCATION OF LINKED INFORMATION		
Age	*Student's own Language*	*Other Student's Language*	*Teacher's Language*
5	15	7	14
7	15	13	30
9	13	20	–
T	–	6	22
		$n = 138$	

language and this use of specificity is followed by the younger students in their linking to teacher language. There may thus be an extension of the teacher's pattern of conjunction into the student's use of language.

Like temporal conjunction, causal conjunction is a marked type of conjunction and specifies a causal connection between the two stretches of language. As the following analysis shows, the use of causal conjunction is similar to temporal conjunction in relation to the speaker of the language being connected to. Table 5-18 presents causal conjunction as it is linked to the speech of various speakers. Most of the student causal conjunction is linked to the speaker himself or herself and the teachers' use of causal conjunction is also predominantly linked to the teachers' own talk. Causal conjunction in general is thus used mainly to relate two stretches of one speaker's language rather than to link the language of different speakers.

Given this tendency to use causal conjunction to extend the speaker's own language, the relationship to other types of conjunction can be studied. Table 5-19 presents causal conjunction as a percentage of all types of conjunction for links

Table 5-18. Location of antecedents stretches of language for causal conjunction as a percentage of all antecedents of causal conjunction, by age

	LOCATION OF ANTECEDENT INFORMATION		
Age	*Student's own Language*	*Other Student's Language*	*Teacher's Language*
5	68	9	24
7	77	–	23
9	74	4	22
T	–	14	86
		$n = 127$	

to each interlocutor. The rate of using causal conjunction in opposition to other types of conjunction is greater for links to the teachers' language. The rate, furthermore, increases with age from 39% for the 5-year-olds to 50% and 78% for the 7- and 9-year-olds, respectively. Questions concerning causality from the teacher increase in frequency and are often responded to with answers that include causal conjunction. There is not a general developmental increase in the expression of causality, but an increase in interaction with a speaker who demands the expression of causality and provides language that can be linked to causally.

Although students increase the amount of causal cohesion used in linking to teachers, the rate of using causal conjunction is similar for students linking to their own language (15%, 9%, 11%) and for linking to the language of the student interlocutor (10%, 0%, 13%). These rates are also similar to teachers' use of causality in linking to the language of the students (12% of all types of conjunction). The variability in the links formed by causal conjunction stems clearly from the teachers' use of language that results in causal connections being built by the students and these causal connections becoming more frequent in the language of older children.

This pattern of the expression of causal conjunction can be compared to the use of the unmarked additive conjunction. There is a much greater use of causal conjunction compared to additive conjunction in linking to the language of the teachers. There is developmental variation for both additive and causal conjunction in the links to teacher language. This variation is proportionately greatest for linking to teachers compared to the variability in linking to the student language. From Table 5-15 and Table 5-19, the range in additive conjunction is 22% (10%

Table 5-19. Causal conjunction as a percentage of all types of conjunction, for the given location of linked information, by age

	LOCATION OF ANTECEDENT INFORMATION		
Age	*Student's own Language*	*Other Student's Language*	*Teacher's Language*
5	15	10	39
7	9	–	50
9	11	13	78
T	–	12	12
		n = 127	

- 32%) and a factor of 3, and the range for causal conjunction is 39% (39% - 78%) and a factor of 2. The variability, and therefore the functional load carried by the variability, is found in some parts of the linguistic system in relation to some aspects of the nonlinguistic context. If there are speakers who do not use language in accordance with the expectation of other participants in the conversation, the atypicality of the language use and the atypicality of meanings expressed may be in relation to specific elements outside of language. Language is not just a selection of structural or semantic elements, but selections in verbal and nonverbal contexts. Those contexts may have features (the current example is teacher language) and statistical properties that are associated with typical uses of language determined probabilistically. Speakers who have different probabilities of using certain linguistic options may sound unusual in the contexts and functionally may be expressing unusual meanings given the contexts.

Lexical

For the sake of completeness, a short discussion of the use of lexical repetition and how it links to the language of various speakers follows. The location of the prior lexical element was identified for each case of lexical repetition of nonfunction words. The distribution of these prior lexical items is given in Table 5-20. There is little variation by age. The variation by speaker of the prior lexical item reflects the different amounts spoken by the speakers. The teachers link their language slightly more to their own speech (64%) than do students (53% - 57%).

Table 5-20. Location of prior lexical item of lexical repetition, as a percentage of all locations of prior lexical items, by age

	LOCATION OF PRIOR LEXICAL ITEM		
Age	*Student's own Language*	*Other's Student's Language*	*Teacher's Language*
5	53	31	17
7	57	32	11
9	54	36	10
T	–	37	64
		n = 2381	

DIALOGUE TYPE

The analyses of cohesive links have dealt with the nonlinguistic factors of turn-taking organization and the speaker of the language being linked to. A third nonlinguistic variable is the number and identity of the participants in the conversation. The teacher dialogues (TD) involve two students and their classroom teacher whereas the dialogues (D) involved only two students. The two kinds of dialogues differ, then, in two ways (a) the number of participants, and (b) the presence or absence of a teacher. The analysis of cohesion and situation starts with reference followed by conjunction.

Reference (Phoricity)

Earlier analyses have shown that personal reference as a more specific type of referring than demonstrative reference is used more by older students and when more specificity in identifying antecedents is useful. A similar value for personal reference compared to demonstrative reference emerges from the study of the two kinds of dialogue. Table 5-21 presents personal and demonstrative reference as percentages of all endophoric reference in the two dialogues, by age. The teacher dialogues have more personal reference and less demonstrative reference than the dialogues for each age group. The three-way teacher dialogues may require more specific reference to avoid ambiguity with three participants contributing to the conversation. The relatively low use of personal reference by the teachers (48%) may be due to their social role and directing function: Students should closely monitor what a teacher is saying and the links to antecedent noun phrases, so the more specific personal reference is used relatively less frequently.

The difference between personal and demonstrative reference has to do with the subsystems of personals and demonstratives. Since there are more semantic/structural realizations for personal reference (e.g., sex: he, she, it; number: singular, plural; case: they, them) in English, there are more contrasts available (see Fawcett, 1988, for a thorough account of the complexity of the system of personals). The relative number of contrasts in the subsystems relates to the use of those systems in different situations. The analysis shows how there can be a renewal of

Table 5-21. Demonstrative and personal reference as a percentage of all endophoric reference in dialogue (D) and teacher dialogues (TD), by age

SPEAKERS	*5*	*7*	*9*	*Teachers*
Demonstrative reference				
D	49	39	28	–
TD	31	25	19	42
Personal reference				
D	47	53	65	–
TD	66	61	66	48
			$n = 385$	

connection between abstract linguistic systems and how they are exploited in various circumstances. The probability of deciding to use one option from a system is dependent on the characteristics of the nonverbal situation. One of these characteristics can be the number of participants and therefore the number of linguistic entities introduced and the potential misunderstanding that may result. Choosing to use the personal reference subsystem rather than demonstrative reference opens up more options with a corresponding greater potential for discriminating among the linguistic entities introduced.

As well as anaphoric links within the text, exophoric links in the two kinds of dialogues suggest how the nonlinguistic differences in the conversations help shape how meaning is presented. The use of exophora is presented as a percentage of all cohesion in Table 5-22.

Exophora gives the hearer the instruction to find information outside the text in order to interpret the text. Table 5-22 indicates that to establish the interpretation of speech, the hearer in a teacher dialogue must make fewer connections outside of language and relatively more connections within language. In absolute frequency, the teacher dialogues have only 40 to 51 percent of the exophoric items of the student-only dialogues. A three-way conversation perhaps necessitates proportionately greater signaling of the connection of one piece of language to another. In addition, the presence of the teacher

Table 5-22. Exophora as a percentage of all cohesion in dialogues (D) and teacher dialogues (TD), by age

SPEAKERS	*5*	*7*	*9*	*T*
D	30	32	20	–
TD	22	19	12	25
			$n = 1546$	

may reduce the amount of situationally shared information and so lead to a lower level of exophora.

Conjunction

The analysis of conjunction in the two types of dialogues shows little variation. Table 5-23 presents the use of the unmarked additive conjunction and the more marked causal and temporal conjunction. There is consistently more causal conjunction in the teacher dialogues compared to the student-only dialogues. This increased use of causal conjunction is not just a matter of imitating the patterning of the teachers, since the teachers have the relatively low rate of 12% causal conjunction. Rather, the interaction of teacher and student is reflected in a change in the students' use of conjunction.

An examination of the use of temporal conjunction shows that the increase of causal conjunction in teacher dialogues is not part of a general use of more marked conjunction in these conversations. The effect of the teachers' participation in the dialogues was restricted to causals within the cohesion system.

For all types of conjunction, the youngest speakers (5-year-olds) show the least amount of variation from one type of dialogue to the other. Thus an element of development is the sensitivity to the nonverbal aspects of the context and the variation in the use of linguistic options.

LENGTH OF COHESIVE LINKS

Cohesion has been analyzed in relation to the turn-taking structure of conversation, the speaker of the stretch of language

Table 5-23. Major types of conjunction as a percentage of all conjunction in dialogues (D) and teacher dialogues, by age

SPEAKER	*5*	*7*	*9*	*T*
Additive				
D	64	60	70	—
TD	56	73	59	55
Causal				
D	15	8	8	—
TD	18	11	20	12
Temporal				
D	14	18	12	—
TD	15	13	13	20
			n = 493	

that the cohesive item is linking to, and with regard to the number of speakers in the conversation. Another factor that is not derived from linguistic systems is the length of the cohesive links. Since the focus of the study was on interaction, the length of cohesive links was measured in turns. The measure is thus concerned with how many turnovers of the floor have taken place between the antecedent information and the cohesive item. A distance of zero indicates that antecedent information (for all types of cohesion) and cohesive item are found in the same turn. A distance of 1 indicates that the antecedent information is in the turn of the immediately preceding interlocutor, and so on. Table 5-24 presents frequency of each link length as a percentage of all cohesive links.

Among the students, the main shift with age is from a distance of 1 (the immediately preceding turn of the interlocutor) to a distance of zero (the speaker's own current turn). In comparing the overall range of shorter cohesive links, the student groups are about equal in their use of cohesive links up to a distance of two turns. For all links to the current turn and the two prior turns the percentages are 73%, 76%, and 77% for the 5-, 7-, and 9-year-olds, respectively. That is, for these ages there is no evidence of generally longer cohesive links with increasing age.

A comparison of the students to the teachers shows that the teachers have relatively few cohesive links to the current turn (distance zero), but more links of two turns in length (usually to the teacher's own language) and more longer links of three to four turns. Teachers, then, are using cohesion to link their own nearby utterances together and are using cohesion less than the students to create links within the current utterance.

Table 5-24 shows that only about 8% of cohesion links back

Table 5-24. Percentage of cohesive links of various lengths, by age

AGE *Lengths of Cohesive Links (in Turns)*	*5*	*7*	*9*	*T*
0	32	44	48	25
1	30	24	19	26
2	11	8	10	17
3-6	11	9	10	14
7-10	3	4	4	4
11 +	5	3	4	5
			$n = 5224$	

seven turns or more. Across speaker turns there seems to be a limit to the length of cohesive links. There may be processing limits that have to do with the number of turnovers of the floor in conversation, as well as more traditional constraints in terms of time or number of words.

The teachers and the students seem to be using cohesion as a nonstructural text-forming device differently. The teachers use cohesion to link to their own language in a noncurrent turn and also at a moderate distance of three to six turns. In contrast, the students use cohesion increasingly with age and at levels higher than the teachers to link to the current turn. Cohesive links operate in the context of the turn-taking organization of language. As well as exploiting a rather tight conversational structure of question-answer-confirmation/question, teachers also bind a conversation together by relatively high levels of cohesion that link their language to turns of one and three turns' distance. The teachers use cohesion to link about equally to their own current turn and to the adjacent student turn, whereas the older students tend to create links within one turn considerably more than to an adjacent peer turn.

From the hearer's perspective, the patterning of lengths of cohesive links suggests slightly different interpretation strategies. In listening to a fellow student, the hearer should expect cohesion to link to the current speaker's earlier talk. In listening to a teacher, the hearer can expect the teacher talk to be interpretable in relation to the listener's and the teacher's talk in about equal proportions. The connections between the teacher and the student are encoded for the local environment of the current or immediately prior turn. These differences are not likely to be related to intelligibility. Rather, the variation encodes how interlocutors share information and the presumptions that speakers make about each other's state of knowledge and ability to interpret and built text from incoming messages.

CONCLUSION

This chapter has studied the developmental of cohesion in the context of other aspects of conversation. What develops in school-aged children is the use of language appropriate to context. The investigation shows several aspects of the relation to context. There can be a reinforcing relation between cohesion and turn-taking. Second-pair partners in conversational sets (mainly answers to questions) are closely tied to the first-pair partners in terms of turn-taking and also in terms of relatively high levels of anaphoric reference. In terms of development, there appears to be a learning of value of options in cohesion being combined with certain turn-taking options. The relationship between the two sets of options also reflects differences in social roles. Teachers and students make typically different simultaneous choices from turn-taking and cohesion. The examination of the use of exophora also shows on adjustment according to the type of conversational turn. However, the youngest group of speakers shows less of this adjustment. One aspect of language development, then, is greater variability and variability according to conversational context. Older speakers relate the functions of options from one system to the functions of options from another system in the organization of language in use. Similar developmental relationships hold between conjunction and turn-taking. There are two general points to be made: (a) the functions of cohesion in creating text relate in specific nonarbitrary ways to other aspects of organizations in the use of language, and (b) children are still learning these relationships during the early years of formal schooling.

Cohesion is also found to relate to characteristics of the speakers and to the overall structure of the conversation. The use of the reference subsystem is adjusted by the students to take into account the teacher's special role. Similarly, causal conjunction is increased by the older students only in links to teachers. In comparing conversations with teachers to conversations without teachers present, there is more variation in the use of conjunction by the older students. Again, the increased variation in relation to an aspect of the context is itself an indicator of development.

The development of the use of cohesion (or any functionally based component of language) must be seen in two perspectives. First, language is sensitive to the context of its use. This may be a truism, but it requires a study of the functional bases for the variation. Furthermore, the development of language can reveal the dimensions of language and context that are related, and how the functions are combined. The second perspective is of cohesion realizing differences in meaning typically found in various contexts. Some of these contexts may be the local context of turn-taking structures, or more global considerations of social status or conversational setting. Each set of contexts defined in some manner has typical meanings associated with it, as revealed by differences in the use of cohesion. Speakers learn to approximate the expected meanings of the community as they grow older. Language development is not just learning to use the right linguistic tools, or even the right amount of those linguistic tools. Rather, it is the more fundamental use of the functions of language in the contexts that are expected for them. These contexts include both other functions of language and extralinguistic factors. The linguist has the phenomena of linguistic realizations to account for, but these realizations are only the end of the process of language use and derive from more basic contextual and functional foundations of language.

6

DEVELOPMENT: INTERACTION OF LANGUAGE SYSTEMS

INTRODUCTION

This chapter examines cohesion in the light of two interrelated functional systems: theme-rheme and given-new. First these two systems are outlined and then data are presented from the study of children's language that show how the different language systems work together. The data come from a study of 5-, 7-, and 9-year-olds and their teachers. This developmental perspective will be useful for examining the growth of language functions and how the relationship among language functions may change. The intention is not to present the data as a study of language development per se, but rather to use the developmental dimension to learn about how language works.

Thematic Structure

In the domain of the major clause in English, there is an organization of elements into a thematic structure consisting of theme and rheme. The system is realized as a sequence of elements; the theme is first, followed by the rheme. Although the identity of theme and rheme is in terms of order, the essential definition is functional (Halliday, 1985). That is, the theme has a function in language that is different from the rheme. Halliday (1985, pp. 38-39) glosses the theme as "the starting-point for the message; it is what the clause is going to be about. . . that with which the clause is concerned. . . so part of the meaning of any clause lies in which element is chosen as its Theme." The unmarked option for theme is determined by the mood system. In a declarative, the subject is the unmarked option for theme, in a wh- interrogative it is the wh- item ("Where did he go?") and in a yes-no interrogative it is the finite verbal element ("Did he go?") The unmarked option is chosen unless there is a good reason not to choose it; the marked options for theme involve foregrounding of some element, usually for emphasis.

Certain adjuncts may be placed first in the clause and still permit thematization of some other element. Discourse adjuncts (e.g., however) and model adjuncts (e.g., perhaps) may be followed by thematization of another sentence element. Sentences (1) through (4) show that the use of these types of adjuncts does not preclude what Halliday (1967) called thematization in the cognitive area of meaning, or what he later calls the topical theme (Halliday, 1985). It is these topical themes that are taken as the marked and unmarked themes in the following study. The topical themes carry major information in the ideational component of language and it is how this information is mapped onto the given-new system and is dealt with by cohesion that is of interest. The study follows Halliday (1985, p. 61) in interpreting what is thematic as being up to "the first element that has some representational function in the clause (the 'topical' Theme)." Discourse and modal adjuncts are thus not taken as theme marked when they occur in first position in a clause.

(1) However John ate the pie yesterday.
(2) However, yesterday John ate the pie.
(3) Perhaps John ate the pie yesterday.
(4) Perhaps yesterday John ate the pie.

Information Structure

As well as an organization of thematic structure consisting of theme and rheme, there is an organization of information into given and new. This organization has as its domain the information unit with an obligatory new and an optional given function. The realization of the information unit is the pitch contour which extends over the tone group. Within the tone group, one foot carries the main pitch movement or tonic prominence. The sentence element that take the tonic prominence carries the information focus. Usually, the foot with the tonic prominence is the culmination of the new information. In: "I saw the man with the big HAT," the tonic prominence would normally be on *hat*. (Capitals are used here and elsewhere to indicate tonic prominence.) *Hat* therefore would be the culmination of the new information. In this case, as in many unmarked cases, there is indeterminacy concerning the left-most boundary of the new. The above sentence could be in answer to several questions corresponding to different amounts of new material:

What man did you see?
new = the man with the big hat
What was the man you saw wearing?
new = the big hat
What did you see?
new = the man with the big hat
What did you do?
new = saw the man with the big hat
What happened?
new = I saw the man with the big hat.

Typically, the new is the "last functional element of clause structure in the information unit" (Halliday, 1985, p. 275)—in the above example, "the man with the big hat."

The speaker uses the given-new organization to create a relationship between speaker, hearer, and the situation they are in. Halliday (1985, p. 277) gives the meaning of given and new as "information that is presented by the speaker as recoverable (Given) or not recoverable (New) to the listener." The given may have been previously mentioned or available in the nonlinguistic environment (such as *I* or *you* to refer to the speakers themselves). More generally, the given is presented to the hearer as something that should be known and is presumed by the speaker to be shared with the hearer. The hearer should interpret what is coded as given as if it were shared, even if it is in fact not known to the hearer. That is, the hearer must recognize that there is a meaning in encoding information as given: This information is to be taken as shared whether or not it is initially known to the hearer. The speaker does not expect the hearer to question the given part of the message, even if is unknown to the hearer (see the experimental evidence summarized in Clark & Clark, 1977, suggesting that people do follow such a strategy). Information coded as new, on the other hand, signals the hearer to regard it as new and to be attended to. Again, the information itself may not be new but the speaker is using linguistic resources to say to the hearer that the speaker wants the information regarded as new.

To generalize about the use of given-new organization, the hearer must interpret the speaker's decision of what to code as given and what to code as new. If the distribution of given and new in the message matches the hearer's knowledge state, then the hearer can interpret the speaker as being cooperative and will add the new information to his existing knowledge state. If there is not a match between the given and new in the message and the hearer's knowledge state, then the hearer usually assumes that the speaker is being cooperative and the hearer must trust the speaker and follow along with the conversation. It may be the case that the speaker is deliberately manipulating the relationship between the distribution of given and new information and the known information states of the speakers to attain a certain effect. Take the following constructed example:

A: I realize that we inconvenienced you yesterday.
John and I were both held up in traffic.
B: You were late for YOUR appointment.

The facts of the situation are clear to both A and B. Certainly A is aware that he was late for his appointment, having just tried to excuse it and apologize for it. Nevertheless, B places the tonic prominence on *your* to signal it as new information. What is new in this case is that speaker B is signaling to A that A should realize that it was his (A's) appointment that was missed, thus suggesting perhaps some responsibility for the lateness, or that A was the party that would suffer in B's opinion. A speaker can thus use the distribution of given and new to make a point about what the hearer should known. The hearer should then interpret the message and be abused, reprimanded, informed, insulted, informed, and so on, depending on the relationship between speaker and hearer.

The interpretation of given and new is thus not an absolute linguistically based instruction but is, rather, dependent on the wider linguistic and nonlinguistic situation, including the (assumed) knowledge states of speaker and hearer. The distribution of given and new can be manipulated independent of word order, and thus independent of the theme-rheme system. Although in declarative clauses the tonic prominence and thus the new falls on the last sentence element in the unmarked clause, the tonic prominence can be placed on any accented syllable, and in very marked cases even on unaccented syllables. When the information focus is moved away from its unmarked location, the scope of the new is determinate and there may be given information following the new information. In the sentence: "John SOLD the book to Mary," the speaker marks *sold* as new information. This sentence can only be an answer to "How did Mary get the book from John?" or in response to a statement or implication that John presented the book to Mary. The information (the book to Mary) after the marked information focus (*sold*) is coded as given. The tonic prominence and thus information focus may be placed on an element that has been moved out of its unmarked order in the clause and placed at the beginning (e.g., "YESTERDAY, John sold the book to Mary," or "To MARY, John sold the book"). Again, the effect of this marked information focus is to code the remainder of the clause as given.

As can be seen from the last examples, the distribution of given and new information is mapped onto the theme-rheme structure of the clause. The following discussion just deals with declarative mood, but similar arguments and examples can be presented for yes-no and wh- interrogatives and for imperatives. See Halliday (1967, 1985) for further details of these cases. In the unmarked case, the information focus will fall on the last element of the rheme. Thus there will be a theme that is given, given information in the rheme (before the information focus), and new information in the rheme. In the marked case, there will be new information either in the rheme (*sold* in: John SOLD the book to Mary) or in the theme (*yesterday* in : YESTERDAY, John sold the book to Mary), and old information either in the theme or rheme. To summarize, the marked given-new structures are used only when there is some communicative reason not to use the unmarked. There may, in fact, be degrees of markedness extending up to the unacceptable. The more marked a clause is, the fewer contexts it can be reasonably used in, since the special reasons for each departure from the unmarked would all have to be present (see Fine, Bartolucci, & Szatmari, 1989).

There is a relationship between the use of cohesion and the use of the given-new and theme-rheme organizations. Cohesion creates text and texture by signaling that one stretch of language is related to some other, usually earlier, stretch of language. Since cohesion is usually connecting backwards in text, it will usually be concerned with information that is shared by speaker and listener. For this reason, we would expect cohesive items to be found relatively frequently in the given part of the clause. However, as has been outlined, the coding of information as given and new is not solely dependent on the knowledge state of the speakers. The placement of cohesion into different parts of the clause is thus part of the overall strategy of presenting information that the hearer can interpret in the verbal and nonverbal context. Davies (1989) presents a study of the interaction of cohesion and the placement of the tonic prominence that partially realizes the given-new structure. He had subjects orally read a passage and found that the placement of the tonic prominence was a function of knowing the context and therefore knowing what should be treated as given and new. Furthermore, knowledge of cohesion (for example, lexical repetition) is used to determine the assignment of given and new in the clause. Specifically, if a lexical item at the end of a tone group is recognized by the reader as given information, then the reader placed the tonic prominence earlier in the clause. The reader, knowing the functional values of tonic prominence and cohesion, placed the tonic prominence signaling information as new on a word other than a cohesive item, which signals information as given.

STUDY

The data to be examined for cohesion and the given-new, theme-rheme structure come from 24 5-minute conversations from 5-, 7-, and 9-year-old monolingual speakers of English. At each age level there are 12 subjects, 6 male and 6 female. Half the conversations are between a student and a friend that the student selected (the dialogues – D). The other conversations had one student from the original pair, with a new partner from his or her classroom and included the classroom teacher (the teacher dialogues—TD). The tonic prominence was marked on transcripts of the conversations, including the language of the teachers. Each cohesive item was also coded for type (as will be shown in the results) and for its location with respect to the theme-rheme, given-new systems. Thus each cohesive item was coded as being in the new unmarked (NU) part of the clause, the new marked (NM), the old theme (LT), the old rheme (LR), or a stretch of language without enough structure to be analyzed into given-new and theme-rheme. In all, 6,875 cohesive items were coded. For further details of the sample and coding see Fine (1978). The following analysis first deals within various forms of reference and anaphora, then deals with conjunction, briefly reports on lexical cohesion, and finally considers cohesion and the use of given-new and theme-rheme in the context of the turn-taking organization of conversation.

REFERENCE (PHORICITY)

Exophora

The reference system as presented in Halliday and Hasan (1976), Halliday (1985), Rochester and Martin (1979), and Fine, Bartolucci, and Szatmari (1989) involves a number of successive distinctions. One important distinction in terms of frequency and the difference involved in processing is between endophoric references and exophoric references. Exophoric references (such as *I*, *you*, *mine*, *we*) require that information from outside the verbal environment be used to interpret the language. The speaker is assuming shared knowledge about the physical world. Of the 1,507 instances of exophora in the data, 79% fall within the given part of the clause and 18% within the new part of the clause. This bias toward the given part of the clause reflects a semantic congruence between the feature of "given" in the given-new system and the value of exophora. In these conversations, the exophora was largely the speech roles of *I*, *you*, *my*, *your*, and so on, that are coded as available to the hearer in the given-new system and as available in the physical situation of the conversation.

The distribution of exophora in the given and new parts of the clause can be compared to the distribution of anaphora (see

Table 6-1). Anaphora is more likely than exophora to be found in the new parts of clauses but the overall bias toward the given parts of the clause still remains. The greater rate of placing anaphora in the new part of the clause suggests that the speakers are saying something newsworthy about what has been coded as known to the hearer from linguistic rather than nonlinguistic sources. The exophora placed in the new is chiefly a matter of saying something about one of the participants in the conversation (*I*, *you*), whereas anaphoric reference can include anyone or anything that has been previously mentioned or is presumed to have been mentioned. Thus a natural semantic limitation on the range of information that exophora can encode has an effect on the probabilities of the association of exophora with the options from the given-new system.

A more detailed analysis of exophora can be obtained by further breaking down the categories of given and new. If a cohesive item is found in the new part of a clause it is marked as new 34% of the time. This can then be compared to lexical cohesion by repetition of the same lexical item. Lexical repetition is a frequent type of cohesion (2,382 instances, or 35% of the cohesion in the data) that sets up not a referring relationship between cohesive item and antecedent but rather merely signals that there is continuity in lexical choice and likely in the identity of the items as well. For lexical repetition, 39% of the items are in the new and 53% are coded as given in the clause. That is, for lexical repetition the split of 39-53 into new and given, respectively, is less extreme than the split of 18-79 for exophora. For exophora to be coded as new is much more unusual than for lexical repetition to be coded as new.

New information may be encoded as marked or unmarked. For exophora the new is marked 34% of the time, whereas lexical repetition is marked as new only 20% of the time. There is further evidence of the relationship between marked new and exophora when the data are considered developmentally. Table 6-2 presents the rate of marked new exophora as a percentage of all the exophora coded by the given-new system as new.

Table 6-1. Percentage of exophora and anaphora in the given and new parts of the clause

	Given	*New*	
Exophora	79	18	(*n* = 1507)
Anaphora	69	25	(*n* = 1092)

Developmentally the marking of new increases, indicating, it is suggested, greater need for the marking of exophoric cohesion when it is receiving the unusual encoding of new information. There is thus a direct relationship between the likelihood of being coded as given information and the likelihood of being in the marked new. If a cohesive item has a strong tendency to be coded as given information, then when it is coded as new information it has a greater probability of being marked as new. The marking, as it were, draws attention to the unusual status of the cohesive item as part of the new information. There is thus a sensitivity of the probability of occurrence of an option from one system with the occurrence of an option from another system. Furthermore there seem to be reasonable explanations in terms of the functions of the systems for the probabilistic relationship of the options from the two systems.

Demonstrative

Two kinds of endophoric reference are frequent in the data: demonstrative reference and personal reference. Demonstrative reference has a specifying function that directs the hearer to look for some specific information in the verbal environment. The demonstrative *the* is the unmarked demonstrative and merely signals the hearer that the hearer knows the information. *This* and *that* add the information that what is needed is 'near' or 'remote' from the speaker's perspective (Halliday, 1985, pp. 290-294).

As can be seen from Table 6-3, the rate of demonstrative endophoric reference drops distinctly with age. The older students but not the teachers are using less of this somewhat nonspecific form of reference that only gives minimal semantic and structural clues about the antecedent information. The

Table 6-2. Exophoric cohesion coded as marked new as a percentage of all exophora coded as new, by age

	Age of Speaker			
	5	*7*	*9*	*Teacher*
Exophora coded as marked new	27	28	43	41
				n = 99

teachers do rely on demonstrative reference at a rate similar to the most elevated level for the students. This may be an indication of the teachers accommodating their language to the perceived needs of the students.

A closer look at the use of demonstratives shows how this type of cohesion is coded by the given-new and thematic systems. Table 6-4 presents demonstratives in selected parts of the clause as a percentage of all demonstratives. With age, there seems to be a movement of demonstrative reference toward the later part of the clause as well as diminishing use of demonstrative reference. The former result may well be a product of the longer clauses and hence longer rhemes used by the older students. Nevertheless, the results can also be interpreted as indicating that the semantic value of the rheme is compatible with the signal of demonstrative reference, "to find the antecedent earlier in the text." In fact, 30% to 40% of all demonstrative reference is found in the unmarked new part of the clause, that is, within the rheme. There thus seems to be a strong role for demonstrative reference in sustaining the presence of information accessible to speaker and hearer even when new information is being presented. The increasing rates of demonstrative reference in the rheme also suggest that through the course of the clause there is an interplay of given and new information such that each part of the clause has resources for introducing new information and for signaling information that has previously been introduced.

A special case of the interplay of demonstrative reference with the thematic structure of the clause is the use of such reference in the unmarked theme which is coded as given by the information system. In this case, both the thematic structure and the cohesive item encode a similar message of "this information is available to you, the hearer." Table 6-5 presents demonstrative reference as a percentage of all endophoric reference in the unmarked themes of clauses. Although the number of data points is small, the teachers show the most redundancy in using

Table 6-3. Demonstrative reference as a percentage of all endophoric reference, by age

	5	7	9	*Teacher*
Percentage demonstrative reference	40	30	24	42
				n = 382

Table 6-4. Demonstrative reference in selected parts of the clause as a percentage of all demonstrative reference, by age

	Thematic part of clause	
Age	*Theme*	*Rheme*
5	26	61
7	34	54
9	24	74
T	21	74
		n = 349

this double encoding of presumably shared information. Teacher talk may use this redundancy to ensure that the social reality that is being built up between teacher and student is, in fact, shared.

Personal

Personal reference, like demonstrative reference specifies the antecedent for the cohesive item. Unlike demonstratives, personals specify all of gender (*he*, *she*), number (*he*, *they*), and possessive (*he*, *his*). That is, personal reference provides more clues about the antecedent information than does demonstrative reference (see Halliday, 1985, pp. 290-294).

For all speakers, personal reference makes up 76% of reference in unmarked themes (given) and 68% of reference in the given part of rhemes. This dominance of personal reference in the given part of clauses indicates a coding of the continuity of information about people and things. Once established, entities are sustained by personal reference and the coding of that information by the thematic structure as given. This bias for encoding personal reference as given is not found for demonstrative reference for which the rate in the given parts of

Table 6-5. Demonstrative reference as a percentage of all endophoric reference in unmarked themes, by age

	5	*7*	*9*	*Teacher*
Percentage demonstrative reference	21	24	11	39
				n = 66

clauses is 20% (theme) and 27% (rheme) (see Table 6-6). The increased specificity of the personals compared to demonstrative reference may have a role in the bias for using personals in given parts of the clause. The specificity of personals contributes to easier identification of antecedent information compared to demonstratives. Because there is the possibility of relatively easier linking to the antecedent information, the speaker can more dependably code personal reference as given with confidence that the hearer will be able to make the appropriate link to the necessary information. The frequencies of use of one system—the reference system—are thus related by the functions of the options in that system to the functional value of the given-new system. The systems are related functionally and this functional relationship is expressed through the probabilities of the realizations of the two systems. To look at the data another way, the probabilities relating the realizations from two different systems are not merely interesting or informative about the patterns of language, but have clear functional motivations.

The relationship between personal reference and the location in the clause can also be examined developmentally. There are two approaches to the relationship: (a) the decision to use personal reference instead of some other kind of reference; and (b) the decision of how to encode the personal reference in the clause. Table 6-7 presents the use of personal reference as a percentage of all kinds of reference according to the encoding in the clause and by age. There is a slight trend for the personals to be encoded more in the new parts of clauses with increasing age. The youngest speakers do this the least and the other students are similar to each other. As in a number of analyses, the teacher speech falls in between the ends of the developmental pattern. Placing more personals in the new part of the clause may be a technique for being more secure in the

Table 6-6. Personal and demonstrative reference as a percentage of all reference, by part of clause

	Given		*New*		*No*
	Theme	*Rheme*	*Unmarked*	*Marked*	*Thematic Structure*
Personal reference	76	68	24	39	12
Demonstrative reference	20	27	59	36	58
					n = 1045

Table 6-7. Personal reference as a percentage of all reference by given-new encoding in clause, by age

	Part of clause	
Age	*Given*	*New*
5	72	19
7	70	34
9	80	32
T	60	25
		(n = 663)

signaling of continuity of information when the information structure of the clause codes the information as new.

The second perspective for looking at personal reference developmentally is to consider how personal reference is encoded in the clause rather than seeing it in the context of the other options of the reference system. Table 6-8 shows the parts of the clause into which speakers place the personal reference that they are using. If there are any developmental patterns, and it is not clear that there are, there seems to be a preference with age to place the personal reference in the new rather than the given part of the clause and to place personal reference in the rheme rather than the theme. The functional effect of these shifts is to exploit the specific referring nature of personal reference to ensure the hearer is connecting stretches of language to what is known and what has gone before.

In discussing demonstrative reference, it was noted that the teachers double encode given information by using demonstrative reference in the unmarked (given) themes of clauses. This double encoding is considerably more frequent for personal reference. Since the personal reference system has more options available (for gender, number, etc.) than the demonstrative

Table 6-8. Distribution of personal reference into parts of the clause as a percentage of all personal reference, by functional system, by age

	Given-new system		*Theme-rheme system*	
Age	*Given*	*New*	*Theme*	*Rheme*
5	90	8	54	44
7	83	15	40	58
9	86	14	47	51
T	86	12	21	79
	n = 663		n = 663	

reference system, it can be used to sustain longer chains and perhaps at a greater distance. Given the choice to use either personal or demonstrative reference, speakers place 37% of the personal reference in given themes and only 17% of the demonstrative reference in given themes. That is, the greater specificity of personal reference makes it effective in establishing the starting point of the message, when that starting point is encoded by the information system of the clause as given.

Cataphora

Anaphoric reference is thus used by the speaker in nonarbitrary ways with respect to the organization of the clause in terms of theme-rheme and given-new. The pattern of intersections of options from the systems indicate that the functions of the systems help explain the patterns and frequencies observed in the data. There are two other types of cohesion that, while not being anaphoric reference, are closely related. Cataphoric cohesion points forward in the text and directs the hearer to wait for the information necessary. Some cataphora is referential (e.g., *this* in: This is how to build a snowman: Pick a cold, dry day . . .) and other cataphora is conjunctive (e.g., *first* in: Then when we came to the school um first we all went to the store and we bought some popsicles. . . .) Although cataphora is relatively infrequent (52 cases out of over 6,800 instances of cohesion in the corpus), it is generally (70% of the time) coded as new information. This finding supports the glosses proposed for the given-new system and again shows how the given-new system and cohesion work together to present messages to the hearer. The 30% probability of finding cataphoric cohesion in the given part of the clause indicates that there is still a reasonable probability that a tension will be set up between the cohesion and the part of the clause in which it is encoded. This tension can be exploited by the speaker for various purposes.

Substitution

The second type of cohesion related to anaphoric reference is substitution. Substitution links linguistic items by using a grammatical signal. The signal is grammatical because it comes from a closed set of choices. The nominal substitute is *one* as in: "Do we have paper clips? No, do you want one?" Substitution is anaphoric in that it directs the hearer to an earlier stretch of language for its interpretation. However, it merely provides the information that a certain category of unit (nominal, verbal, clause) is to be found and interpreted at the given location. As with cataphoric cohesion, the frequency of substitution is relatively low: 46 in the corpus. Of these instances, 47% occur in the given parts of clauses and 10% in the new. The remainder occur in stretches with no given-new structure, mainly clausal substitutes of *so* and *not*. Unlike personal and demonstrative anaphoric references, substitution makes no use of semantic distinctions such as number or gender in creating the cohesion. The interpretation of the substitution item is fully determined by the class of the substitution (nominal, verbal, clausal), and so the link to the antecedent should be unimpeded by a coding of the substitute item as new. When there is a possibility of coding the item as given or new, speakers overwhelmingly choose given.

Conjunction

Conjunction creates cohesion somewhat differently than reference. Reference instructs the hearer to some other stretch of language for the information necessary to interpret the current item. Conjunction instructs the hearer to interpret what follows in a certain way, given what has preceded. The different subcategories of conjunction further specify the kind of semantic connection between the two stretches of language (see Martin, 1983a). The least marked type of conjunction is additive conjunction (mainly *and*), which merely establishes that there is a conjunctive relation. The following analysis will be based on the paradigmatic relationship among the subcategories of conjunction. With the subcategories viewed as members of a paradigmatic set, the proportion of each subcategory as a part of all the uses of conjunction becomes a useful measure. In analyzing texts, such a proportion indicates the semantic relationship that the speaker typically expresses and the meaning that the hearer must typically interpret. Overall, conjunction is placed into the new part of the clause twice as frequently as into the given part of the clause. This distribution is due to the relative ease of developing the unmarked new part of the clause. For this study, the first sentence element (see

Butler, 1985, for elaborations on the technical use of the term) in declarative clauses without marked themes was taken as given. Subsequent sentence elements up until the last sentence element could be coded as new so that there was a greater possibility of an extended stretch of language being coded as new.

As noted, additive conjunction is the unmarked choice from the conjunction system. Distinct from the other options that will be discussed, it does not signal a specific relationship between the two stretches of language being connected, only that a relationship exists. Additive conjunction is used if there is no good reason to use another type of conjunction. Table 6-9 shows additive conjunction as a percentage of all conjunction by age and by part of the clause. Additive conjunction, relatively more than other subcategories of conjunction, is placed in the given part of the rheme with increasing age. This result may in part be a consequence of the move away from utterances that do not encode conjunction within the given-new and theme-rheme systems of the clause. In the 5-year-olds' language, 90% of the conjunction occurs in such sections of the clause. As the figures for all parts of the clause combined (the "total" column) show, there is no clear pattern in the data away from additive conjunction with increased age. Rather, there are variations depending on the information status of the part of the clause in which the conjunctive item is functioning. This interaction of factors will be returned to when considering other types of conjunction.

The results for additive conjunction can also be considered just in terms of the given-new system. When the data are recalculated as the use of additive cohesion placed in the given and new parts of the clause, Table 6-10 is obtained. Additive

Table 6-9. Additive conjunction as a percentage of all conjunction by part of clause, by age

	Given		*New*		
Age	*Theme*	*Rheme*	*Unmarked*	*Marked*	*Total*
5	25	24	64	16	60
7	100	33	89	7	67
9	100	63	82	23	65
T	100	29	46	33	55

n = 606

Table 6-10. Additive conjunction in the given-new system as a percentage of all additive conjunction, by age

Age	*Given*	*New*
5	3	7
7	9	17
9	6	24
T	8	15

conjunction is specifically being used in the parts of clauses coded as new. Since there is very little conjunction in the marked new sections of clauses (only 3% of all the additive conjunction and less than that for the 5- and 7-year-olds), the increase in additive conjunction is found in clauses of unmarked word order and intonation focus. It is these more or less typical clauses that are being expanded by using the unmarked additive cohesion in the new rheme.

Temporal conjunctions are the next most frequent type of conjunction after the unmarked additive conjunctions. Table 6-11 presents additive conjunction as a percentage of all conjunction by part of clause and by age. This table shows a decrease in the use of temporal conjunctions in the unmarked new and the given part of the rheme. Table 6-12 specifically extracts and recalculates the data for theme and rheme. With increased age, there is a preference for temporal conjunction rather than other types of conjunction (although the relatively small number of data points should be noticed). Temporals are used more for marked themes and less for information in the rheme. Developmentally, then, conjunctions become a more important device for drawing attention to the temporal orientation of the clause. Temporal relations are being singled out by the older students and perhaps being upgraded from being coded as given or unmarked new to the special role of marked new in the clause.

The overall developmental pattern for conjunction becomes clearer by comparing additive and temporal conjunction in the new sections of the clause. Table 6-13 presents the data. Temporal conjunctions increase in the marked new but decrease in frequency compared to other conjunctions in the unmarked new. Additive conjunction increases in frequency in the unmarked new but not clearly so in the marked new. The interaction of the given-new system with the choices in conjunction seems to be as follows: Additive conjunction is used

Table 6-11. **Temporal conjunction as a percentage of all conjunction by part of clause, by age**

	Given		New		
Age	*Theme*	*Rheme*	*Unmarked*	*Marked*	*Total*
5	0	65	29	42	14
7	0	33	11	67	15
9	0	19	6	60	13
T	0	57	31	50	20
				n = 143	

Table 6-12. **Temporal conjunction as a percentage of all conjunction, for theme and rheme, by age**

Age	*Theme*	*Rheme*
5	42	48
7	67	20
9	60	10
T	50	44
		n = 87

increasingly with age to extend the new information when that information is not being highlighted. When information is being highlighted as new information, then it is increasingly temporal relations from one stretch of language to another that are coded as new. Older students draw the hearer's attention to the temporal relations rather than to simple additive relations. Temporal relations and additive relations seem to serve different functions in the development of conversation. Temporal relations develop to signal relationships that the speaker wants to point out as unexpected for the hearer and additive conjunction is used to extend the usual load of new information.

Not only is temporal conjunction being used by the older students to mark new information, but the older students are changing the general use of these temporals. Table 6-14 presents temporal conjunction in the given and new parts of clauses as a percentage of all temporal conjunction, that is, the distribution of temporal conjunction into different parts of the clause. Although the number of data points is relatively small, there seems to be a distinct movement of temporal conjunction into the new part of the clause and away from the given part. Although there is not a strong movement with age away from simple additive conjunction, a closer look at temporal conjunction has shown that the use of temporal conjunction is

Table 6-13. Additive and temporal conjunction as a percentage of all conjunction in the new part of the clause, by age

	Unmarked New		*Marked New*	
	Additive	*Temporal*	*Additive*	*Temporal*
5	64	29	16	42
7	89	11	7	67
9	82	6	23	60
T	46	31	33	50
				(*n* = 206)

Table 6-14. Temporal conjunction in the given and new parts of the clause as a percentage of all temporal conjunction, by age

Age	*Given*	*New*
5	27	30
7	20	38
9	7	55
T	33	42
		n = 87

developing with age to signal the parts of the clause as a message that the hearer should especially attend to.

After additive conjunction and temporal conjunction, the third most frequent type of conjunction in the date is causal conjunction. There are relatively few cases of causal conjunction, and 86% of them fall in stretches of language with no given-new theme-rheme structure. There is perhaps a decrease in the use of causal conjunction in the marked new. If this pattern were established with more data, then it could be concluded that temporal and causal conjunction develop complementary roles in the development of language. Temporal conjunction is increasing, upgraded into new and marked new parts of clauses, and causal conjunction is moved away from the highlighted new parts of clauses.

Lexical

Lexical cohesion comprises 35% of the cohesive ties in the conversations analyzed. As can be seen from Table 6-15, the use of the same lexical root (i.e., without regard to any derivational or inflectional morphology) dominates the category of lexical

Table 6-15. Lexical root cohesion as a percentage of all lexical cohesion, by part of clause, by age

	Given		*New*	
Age	*Theme*	*Rheme*	*Unmarked*	*Marked*
5	86	98	94	100
7	84	93	93	80
9	92	93	92	91
T	88	94	93	95
				n = 2382

cohesion. There are no developmental patterns in the data. As Yang (1989) has found, it may be the overlapping of chains of lexical items that signals a difference in the quality of a message. Overall, 53% of the lexical root cohesion is found in the given parts of the clause, and 39% in the new parts of the clause. Thus lexical root cohesion is largely used to establish the continuity of the message in combination with the given part of the clause that also signals that the information should be familiar to the hearer. There is a slight developmental pattern to place more lexical root cohesion into the new part of the clause and within the new part into the marked new (see Table 6-16). Although lexical root cohesion is chiefly used in the given part of the clause there is a tendency for the older students to place it in the new part of the clause. As with other forms of cohesion, we see the development of more elaborated stretches of new information that are tied to previous language by various types of cohesion.

The most frequent types of cohesion have now been analyzed in detail with respect to their encoding by the given-new and theme-rheme systems. The various types of cohesion are now compared to each other as they are used in the new part of the clause. It is by examining the marked and unmarked coding of new information that the role of marking in the information

Table 6-16. Lexical root cohesion in the new parts of the clause as a percentage of all lexical root cohesion, by age

		NEW	
Age	*Marked*	*Unmarked*	*Total*
5	4	31	35
7	7	35	42
9	12	32	44
T	6	27	33
			n = 941

system of given-new can be investigated. The amount of each type of cohesion found in the new parts of clauses is calculated as a percentage of all occurrences of that type of cohesion (Table 6-17). The data permit the comparison of how each type of cohesion is coded in the clause. Cataphora, lexical cohesion, and reference are the types of cohesion most frequently coded as new information (25% to 70% of their use is in the new part of the clause). These types of cohesion are also the most frequently coded as unmarked new rather than marked new. Marking seems to be less frequent for cataphora, reference, and lexical cohesion since these types of cohesion frequently do occur in the new part of the clause. The other types of cohesion (substitution, conjunction, and exophora) are less frequently assigned the status of new information, but are relatively frequently encoded as marked new. That is, when a type of cohesion is unlikely to be coded as new, the probability of marking increases as a means of drawing attention to the unusual encoding. We thus have a reasonable functional explanation of the relationship between the encoding of a stretch of language as given or new information and the probability of a specified type of cohesion.

CONCLUSIONS

These data on the relationship of one linguistic system to another raise some important issues about how functional distinctions should be represented and how these representations relate to the use speakers make of language. Systemic grammar represents options of a system paradigmatically. Options may be related to other systems or subsystems by being

Table 6-17. Each type of cohesion in the new parts of clauses as a percentage of the total use of cohesion in all parts of the clause

	Cataphora	*Lexical*	*Reference*	*Exophora*	*Conjunction*	*Substition*
New Unmarked	58	32	19	12	9	8
(as % of all new)	(83)	(80)	(76)	(67)	(53)	(67)
New Marked	12	8	6	6	8	4
(as % of all new)	(17)	(20)	(24)	(33)	(47)	(33)
Total	70	40	25	18	17	12
					n = 1811	

an entry condition or part of an entry condition. There are also proposals and data that suggest that the relations of one system or option to another may be probabilistic (see Fawcett, 1990; Fawcett, van der Mije, & van Wissen, 1988; Fine, in press-b; Nesbitt & Plum, 1988).

The data discussed earlier suggest that the probabilities are sensitive to the functions of the options in question and how the functions of options from different systems may be congruent in some sense. The coding of the clause into given and new information, and in particular the assignment of the feature GIVEN, is not independent of the use of certain kinds of cohesion. Cohesion that also signals to the hearer that some needed information is present in the verbal environment sends a message to the hearer that is similar, but not identical to the feature of GIVEN in clause structure. The relationship between GIVEN and cohesion is not formalized in linguistic theory, but nevertheless should be stated, since the relationship of the systems may have a communicative effect. Minimally there may be difficulty in processing an unexpected mapping of one system onto another. However, there may be a more serious impact on communication if there is an apparent and consistent clash between the semantics of different systems. At the moment, this "clash" cannot be stated in formal terms since the names of features on different systems are distinct. However, the empirical data suggest that systems are related to each other and that this relationship is not arbitrary. Rather, the probabilities seem to reflect constraints that derive from the functional value of the options in the system. To the extent that the theory is accurate, this probabilistic relationship of systems should be expected. The basic paradigmatically defined distinctions represented as features in a system need to be associated (most likely, probabilistically) to other distinctions that carry congruent communicative loads. The degree of coherence may be measurable by the strength of the probabilities. Strong association (near a probability of 1) or strong dissociation (near a probability of 0) would indicate that a functional relationship exists between the two distinctions from different systems. If the probability were near 1, then there may be a functional reason for the co-occurrence of the options. Similarly, a very low probability of co-occurrence would suggest a functional basis for a constraint.

As well as the direct association between cohesion and the systems of given-new and theme-rheme, all these systems together are related to the length of the cohesive link. As this study is concerned with dialogue and how speakers interact, cohesive links were measured in terms of the turn. The turn is defined as the talk of one speaker that is bounded by the talk of another speaker (or the beginning or end of the conversation). Thus the length of the cohesive link is a measure of the number of turns by successive speakers. The length of cohesive links is presented in Table 6-18. Links that send the hearer backward from the given part of the clause have somewhat longer links (lower percentage of links of zero (0) length, higher percentages of links of 1 and 2 turns) than links from the new part of clauses. Put differently, what has been mentioned sometime ago is established and coded as being part of what speakers share. What is nearer (both in speaker's and interlocutor's language) is more likely coded as new. There is little difference between cohesion in the given theme or rheme.

Looking at cohesion found in the new parts of the clause, the marked new establishes shorter links than the cohesion found in the unmarked new. The special device of marking for new is used to draw attention to a relatively near antecedent. The message to the hearer is "you do not expect a link to *x* since *x* has just been explicitly mentioned, but nevertheless I would like you, the hearer, to regard this as new or different information." The gloss is not absolute but is used more frequently than for given parts of clauses. This interpretation of the difference between marked and unmarked new is broadly consistent with the interpretation of the difference in lengths of cohesive links from given compared to new parts of clauses. When information is expected or coded as in the verbal context, then the link can extend slightly further back in the immediate conversational context. It is the unexpected (either coded as new or, moreso, coded as marked new) that is associated with

Table 6-18. Length in turns of cohesive links as a percentage of all cohesive links, by part of clause

Distance to cohesive partner (in turns)	*No Thematic Structure*	*Given*			*New*		
		Theme	*Rheme*	*Total*	*Unmarked*	*Marked*	*Total*
0	52	38	35	36	38	45	40
1	34	27	24	25	22	20	22
2	8	15	15	15	11	13	12
3	1	5	5	5	6	6	6
4 +	1	4	5	5	5	2	4
					n = 4817		

somewhat shorter cohesive links. That is, one of the values of new and marked new is to draw attention to in order to add to information already in the near-explicit verbal context.

The information structure of given-new functions in the context of conversation and works with cohesion in managing the flow of information the speaker is designing for the hearer. The relation of information structure and cohesion is probabilistic and so the hearer comes to expect certain co-occurrences across the two systems. For linguistic theory, the relation between information structure and cohesion reveals tendencies of how the functions (in the technical semantic sense of functional role, see Butler, 1985, pp. 48-49) are combined to encode the overall meaning of the text. The empirical data can also be a test of the systems and features proposed in the grammar. It would be unexpected to find systems and features co-occurring that work against each other. Such combinations would be highly marked and not communicatively useful (see the data and arguments in Fine, Bartolucci, & Szatmari, 1989).

7

DEVELOPMENT OF COHESION: TASK AND CLASS IN HEBREW

INTRODUCTION

The building of text by cohesion in the early years of school is an indication of the development of the social awareness and ability to communicate in the accepted ways. This learning to build text, though, is not a unitary phenomenon but involves the construction of text under a range of conditions. The school situation establishes a number of interactions involving differences of interactants and cognitive demands. There is evidence that the social and cognitive demands of situations are related to specific cohesion variables (Fine, 1985) and there is also a range of suggestions and evidence that social class may also be related to aspects of language performance.

The first year or two of formal schooling introduce situations and perhaps specific tasks that are new to the child and for which the child must develop the socially appropriate texts. The child must learn how to share information when required and to do it with different interactants. Cohesion, then, is not a series of variables that can simply be used as developmental indicators. Rather, cohesion indicates how a speaker constructs interpretable text in context (compare this approach to more narrowly conceived studies, e.g., Hemphill, 1989).

The study of cohesion in the language of young children provides information not just about how these speakers are entering into social and communication frameworks, but also shows how the linguistic system itself is used to construct and differentiate texts based on differences in situation. This study of Hebrew-speaking children, therefore, departs from the examination of relatively unconstrained informal conversation followed in most of this volume. A series of tasks is constructed to elicit language under different social and cognitive conditions. The construction of Hebrew text by children on these tasks also tests hypotheses of different coding orientations and language patterns based on class. The results show very few differences between speakers of the two social classes, but considerable differences from task to task.

This chapter is organized as follows. There is first an introduction to the social and cognitive variables that are built into the tasks used to gather the language data. Second, the method is presented, including details of subjects, materials, and the reliability of the cohesion measures in Hebrew. Third, the results are presented, followed by a discussion and conclusion.

BACKGROUND TO TASK AND SPEAKER DIFFERENCES

Task Differences

It is by now common knowledge that the use of language changes with differences in context, and specifically the social identity of interactants and the cognitive demands of the situation (see, for example, Cole, Dore, Hall, & Dowley, 1978; Dore, 1977; Gee & Michaels, 1989; and for systemic approaches, Fine 1978, 1985; Martin, 1983b). Three different dimensions of task are used in this study: (a) whether the visual information that is the basis for a description is shared by both speaker and hearer, (b) whether the visual information is presented in full detail or just by a minimal outline, and (c) whether the task involves a description of a single picture or the retelling of a story with the assistance of pictures. If the information in the picture to be described is shared (joint vs. single viewing), this sets up a difference in the situation that the speaker must consider. In the single-viewing situation, the hearer does not have the same visual information as the speaker, and so the speaker's description must be more independent of the specific context. In the joint-viewing task during which speaker and hearer both can see the picture being described, the speaker is only verbalizing information that is already shared (Bokus & Shugar, 1979). The joint- compared to single-viewing task sets up different possibilities for exophoric reference. Exophoric reference can be appropriately more frequent in the joint-viewing task (Edwards, 1976). Exophoric reference has been shown to separate lower or working-class speakers from middle-class speakers. Working-class speakers produce more exophoric reference and more context-dependent texts than middle-class speakers in studies of a number of ages and languages (Adlam & Turner, 1977; Cais, 1983; Hawkins, 1973; and see review in Hemphill, 1989). Using joint- and single-viewing tasks provides a test of whether the two socially defined groups adjust their language in the same way to accommodate the information that the hearer does or does not share.

A second dimension of the tasks is the variation of the amount of information in the pictures to be described. Cohesion is specifically affected by the cognitive load of tasks and by the cognitive abilities of the speakers (Fine, 1985, 1988; Martin, 1983b; Rochester & Martin, 1977, 1979). Thus the formation of text is related to the complexity of the task and the cognitive resources the speaker can draw on to complete the task. In this study, the cognitive load is varied by manipulating the abstractness of the stimuli. A black-and-white line drawing is assumed to be more difficult to describe than a fully detailed colored picture of the same setting. The line drawing provides less specific information to the describer, requiring the speaker to infer or even invent details appropriate to the skimpy information presented.

A third dimension of the study contrasts picture description with the retelling of a story. Stories have underlying organizations that aid in their recall (see the classic studies of Mandler & Johnson, 1977; Stein & Glenn 1979; Stein & Nezworsky, 1978) and contribute to the building of text through cohesion (Fine, 1985; Rochester & Martin, 1979). Furthermore, appropriate pictures make the story-recall task easier (Moerk, 1985).

Class Differences

A large number of studies have documented a difference in the use of language between lower and middle-class speakers, including children (see Hemphill, 1989, for a survey). Lexical, phonological, morphological, and syntactic differences have been identified (see Farbey, 1987, for a review). In a specific study of picturebook reading comparing higher and lower class Israeli children (mean age about 19.5 months), Ninio (1980) found few differences in the language of the children, although there were more important differences in the language addressed by mothers to their infants. The lower class children had smaller productive vocabularies and larger initiative vocabularies but the speakers from the two social groups were equal in "the readiness of infants to initiate or to participate in book reading, to emit vocalizations, and to emit well-formed labels in various types of [interaction] cycles" (Ninio, 1980, p. 588).

Characteristics of the speech of lower class children are the use of pronouns rather than full nominal groups and the use of exophoric reference. These patterns are taken as features of a restricted code that is more appropriate for concrete, "here-and-now" situations for which certain information is left implicit (Bernstein, 1973; see also Gregory & Carroll, 1978). The details of the following study of Hebrew-speaking children from two social classes do show differences in pronominal usage and particularly in the use of exophoric reference. However, the differences do not generally line up with class differences, but rather with the differences in task. Although major class differences were not found, it is interesting to note that the task differences are in areas of the cohesive system where class differences have been found in other studies.

METHODOLOGY

Subjects

The subjects for this study were 32 children from 5-and-a-half to 6-and-a-half years of age. Half the subjects belonged to a high socioeconomic status group (H-SES) and half to a low SES group (L-SES). Each group of 16 was half male and half female. All the subjects were residents of a small town in the center of Israel. The subjects were in the oldest groupings in their nurseries and had been in nursery school for at least 2-and-a-half years. The schools were secular, as opposed to religious, with experienced teachers. To select subjects, the teachers were interviewed and asked to identify children of at least average ability with respect to the school. This procedure was adopted to eliminate children with emotional or learning problems.

Socioeconomic status was based on scales from Kraus (1979) and Weintraub and Kraus (1981) designed for Israel. The scales produce a numerical weighting of father's occupation, number of children in family, housing (from detached house to tenement blocks), size of housing relative to number of people, father's income, and parents' level of education. The information was supplied by the child's teacher. The high SES and low SES groups showed a significant difference on the SES scale (one tailed t-test $p < .025$).

In order to assess possible group differences based on language ability, the subjects were tested on the Reynell Developmental Language Scales-revised (Reynell, 1977). This test assesses language comprehension and production and is highly correlated with scores from general intelligence tests (Reynell, 1977). The test has not been formally standardized in Hebrew but a comparison on a small sample shows a high correlation between the Hebrew and English versions (Fishman, Fredman, Hamburger, Janko, & Nay, 1981). The two groups did not differ on the Reynell scale (two-tailed t-test, $p > .05$).

Materials

Two pictures and a story illustrated with pictures were selected to elicit the language samples. The pictures were chosen to meet the following criteria: unbiased with respect to class, easily identified and comprehended objects and activities, and sufficient amount of information to describe. After a pilot study, two pictures of everyday activities were chosen. These pictures produced relatively long and cohesive responses. The first picture is a scene in a home kitchen with five people. A young woman is cooking at the stove, an elderly woman is washing dishes in the sink, a boy is unpacking groceries, and a girl is opening an outside door for a man wearing a coat and hat and carrying a bag. The second picture shows several children in a playground. They are involved in a number of activities including swinging, running, sliding, flying kites, riding a scooter, playing marbles, and playing in sand. Two elderly people are sitting on a bench to one side of the playground. One is watching the children and the other is reading a book.

Each picture was presented in two formats: a detailed colored format and a black-and-white line drawing outlining the objects and background of the full picture.

A story was chosen for retelling by the subjects. As with the pictures, the story was chosen to be culturally unbiased and easily understood. The story was from a book published just before the data was gathered (Meir, 1986) to minimize the chance of familiarity with the story. The story was a repetitive story about a child who was afraid to sleep alone. Each night over a week, the child brings in an additional toy to his bed. In the end, the child sleeps on the floor since there is no more room in the bed. The toys then decide to return to their shelf and do so one by one in the course of the second week. The child realizes that he is no longer frightened and sleeps happily alone in his bed. The presence of a number of toys (parallel to the several participants in the picture tasks) places a particular demand for the proper use of personal and demonstrative reference. The story could easily become ambiguous and unclear if the reference links are not constructed appropriately. To prompt the retelling of the story, two pictures from the book were used. One picture showed the child sleeping on the floor with the toys in the bed and the second picture showed the toys back on the shelf.

Procedure

The subjects were tested individually on four occasions with two weeks between sessions to minimize familiarity with the pictures. The recording was done in a quiet room in the nursery schools. The sessions coincided with the first free-play period of the school program in order to minimize any disruption of routine and to record the children when they were not tired. The experimenter and subject sat together at a small table with an external microphone present. At the beginning of each session the subject was told that he or she would be able to hear some of the recording at the end of the day's session.

There were nine tasks that were presented in a random order for each subject. Each of the two pictures was described under each of the following conditions:

1. joint viewing, full picture;
2. joint viewing, outline picture;

3. single viewing, full picture;
4. single viewing, outline picture.

The ninth task was the recall of the story read to the subjects. Details of these tasks follow.

The joint-viewing tasks enabled both the subject and experimenter to see the pictures being described. A pile of pictures was placed face-down on a table in view of both the experimenter and subject. One of the stimulus pictures was picked up from the pile and the subject was told: "Tell me a story about all that is happening in the picture that we can see." As the subject responded, the experimenter encouraged the subject with minimal verbal clues and also thus indicated understanding. The experimenter did request clarifications if the subject was inaudible. Each description was commended equally on completion.

The single-viewing task was identical to the joint-viewing task with the exception that the subject was given the stimulus picture to hold in a way that it was hidden from the experimenter. The instruction was: "Only you can see the picture. I cannot see it. Tell me a story about all that is happening in the picture."

The story recall task was as follows. Before the story was read, the experimenter said: "I am going to read you a story about a boy who did not want to sleep on his own. When I have finished, you will retell whatever you can remember of the story." When the experimenter read the story, she pointed to relevant parts of the two stimulus pictures to help the subject understand the story and to establish the pictures as memory prompts for the retelling task. During the retelling the experimenter showed encouragement but only prompted with "and" or "and then." If the end of the story was omitted, the experimenter prompted with "and in the end."

Transcripts of the sessions were made and the coding was done from the transcripts. Nineteen measures of cohesion were found to be relatively frequent in the data. These measures are presented in Table 7-1. A proportion measure was calculated for each reference variable and for ellipsis by dividing the raw frequency by the total number of nominal groups. For the conjunction scores, the frequency for each type was divided by the total number of conjunctions. A similar procedure was used to determine the proportion of each type of lexical cohesion.

To establish differences between the two socially defined groups of speakers and across conditions, two-tailed t-tests were

Table 7-1. Cohesion variables used in Hebrew language analysis

Personal reference
Demonstrative reference
Exophoric reference
Speech role reference – first person
Speech role reference – second person
Bridging
Ambiguous reference
Inappropriate reference – no previous referent
Inappropriate reference – single viewing
Ellipsis
Additive conjunction
Temporal conjunction
Adversative conjunction
Causative conjunction
Continuative conjunction
Synonym
Collocational word
Subordinate word
Superordinate word

used. Since the direction of difference was predicted for exophoric reference, additioning, and bridging, one-tailed tests were used for these variables across groups. Similarly, since it was predicted that the joint-viewing tasks would produce more exophoric reference than the story retelling task, one-tailed tests were used for the comparison of these tasks.

Reliability

The reliability of the coding of cohesion in Hebrew was established by the recoding of one text from each subject group for each of the five tasks. The overall reliability (agreements divided by agreements and disagreements) was 90.5%, with a range from 88% to 93%.

RESULTS

Overall the results show few differences between the two groups of speakers but substantial differences in the use of cohesion in the variety of tasks. These variations included the joint-viewing single-viewing dimension and the full or outline picture dimension. The results are presented in the above order, starting with each of the cohesion variables.

Personal Reference

There were no significant differences in the use of personal reference between the two groups of subjects. The results for the subject groups were then pooled. The picture description tasks also did not differ significantly from each other. However, the picture description tasks resulted in a rate of personal reference (5.85%) that was less than ($p < .001$) a quarter the rate compared to the story retelling task (26.7%).

Demonstrative Reference

The results for demonstrative reference are the same as for personal reference. There was no difference between the groups and among the picture description tasks but a much higher rate ($p < .001$) of demonstrative reference in the story retelling task (26.5%) compared to the picture description tasks (7.2%).

Bridging

Unlike personal and demonstrative reference which are explicit, bridging is an implicit cohesive link. There were very few uses of bridging in the picture description tasks (a range of 0.5% to 1.9%) and none at all in the story retelling. This low rate of bridging may be due to the age of the subjects or perhaps the resources available in Hebrew and the acceptability of those resources.

Ambiguous Reference

Ambiguous reference was used relatively infrequently in the picture descriptions (mean of 0.73% of nominal groups) but more frequently ($p < .05$) in the story retelling mean (6.06%). In all the tasks there is a tendency for the low-SES group to use more ambiguous reference than the high-SES group.

Additioning

Additioning, like ambiguous reference, is an uninterpretable signal for the hearer. For all tasks, the low-SES group used more additioning than the high-SES group. These differences were significant ($p<.05$) for the outline picture and for the single-viewing tasks. There were also substantial differences across tasks. The single-viewing task resulted in a high rate of additioning (10%) compared to the joint-viewing task (1%) ($p<.001$). Speakers did not take into consideration that in the single-viewing task, the interlocutor did not share the information in the picture. The story retelling task produced a low level of additioning (0.5%) that was significantly less than the single-viewing task (10%) ($p<.001$) and the outline and full-picture tasks (5.7% and 5.3%, respectively) ($p<.05$ in both cases). The story retelling task produced interpretable text as did the joint-picture description. That is, when the task does not require special estimation of the information needs of the interlocutor or in the case that a semantic unity is ensured by the nature of the task, then the text is most interpretable.

Exophoric Reference

The subject groups tend to be different in their use of exophoric reference, with the low-SES group using more exophoric reference on all tasks. However, these differences do not reach significance. The joint-viewing task led to more exophoric reference (26%) than the single-viewing tasks (7.8%) ($p<.01$). The speakers evidently exploited the shared visual information in the joint-viewing task.

Conjunction

There were no significant differences between the groups in the use of conjunction. The picture-describing tasks, though, differ from the story retelling. In the picture-describing tasks, additive conjunction is the predominant variety of conjunction (90–93% of all conjunction depending on the task), whereas additive conjunction is used as only 39% of the conjunction in story retellings ($p<.05$). Rather than additive conjunction, the story retelling makes substantial use of temporal conjunction (41%)

and causal conjunction (16%). Temporal and causal conjunction are rarely used in the picture descriptions (between 1% and 4% of conjunction) and the difference between the frequency in picture descriptions and story retelling is significant ($p<.001$) for both variables.

Lexical Cohesion

As with most studies, the overwhelming type of lexical cohesion was found to be lexical repetition. There were no significant differences between the subject groups or across tasks.

As well as presenting the results according to the linguistic variables, the results are now restated according to tasks. There are substantial differences between the storytelling and picture descriptions both in reference and in conjunction. The storytellings are characterized by high levels of personal reference, demonstrative reference, and ambiguous reference. Although there is a relatively high level of ambiguous reference in the storytelling, there is a relatively low level of additioning, the other type of unclear reference. In terms of conjunction, the picture descriptions are constructed with mainly additive conjunction, whereas the stortyellings substantially use temporal and causal conjunction as well. The other difference among tasks is that the picture descriptions during which both parties could see the pictures ("joint" descriptions) produced more exophoric reference than the single-viewing descriptions when only the subject could see the picture.

There are two findings of significant differences based on class. The low-SES group used more additioning than the high-SES group on the outline pictures and in the single-viewing task.

DISCUSSION

The empirical results for cohesion pertain to a number of issues in the study of text formation and in the use of language under various conditions. This discussion first deals with the linguistic variables and the issues they raise and then treats the task-related issues. Finally the issue of class differences is discussed.

Cohesion

Reference (Phoricity). Two areas of cohesion show variation in the data: reference and conjunction. Personal and demonstrative reference are means of continuing the identity of participants in a text. The story task produced considerable personal and demonstrative reference in contrast to the picture descriptions. The picture descriptions were more characterized by shifts in participants and indefinite participants (e.g., and then a boy . . . a girl . . . and X is . . .). Speakers typically did not construct narratives from the picture descriptions, despite the instruction to do so.

Once a number of participants are introduced, it is necessary to carefully separate the participants when using the reference system. The substantially higher rates of ambiguous reference in the storytellings compared with the picture descriptions indicates that the speakers do not fully control the reference system when it is used in contexts with the potential of misidentifying participants.

Although the study of reference in psychiatric patients has sometimes grouped additioning and ambiguous reference into a more general category of "unclear" (Rochester & Martin 1977, 1979), the current data on storytelling and picture description show high levels of ambiguous reference and low levels of additioning in the storytelling. There was little difficulty constructing implicit reference in most tasks including the storytelling. Speakers did not attempt to add new participants that were not interpretable. Rather than general problems in constructing interpretable reference links, the speakers in this study had a specific difficulty with reference only when the task introduced participants that were potentially difficult to separate by the reference system. These findings show the value in considering the regrouping of reference variables according to the context of use. In studies of some psychiatrically impaired speakers additioning and ambiguity can be sensibly grouped as forms of unclear reference. However, the number of participants and their continuing identification by reference creates an increased rate of ambiguous reference for storytelling with no similar difficulty with additioning. The specific demands of a task may affect only one part of the reference system; the functional basis of the reference system reveals the relationship between the crucial characteristic of the task and the part of the reference system that varies or is at stake.

Although not directly related in the data to ambiguous reference or to a general category of unclear reference, additioning is an option in the reference systems that is sensitive to a number of differences in task. Additioning is a failure in constructing a referential link that could have been either explicit or implicit. The picture descriptions generally have more additioning than the storytellings. The storytellings have a set number of participants that are referred to explicitly, whereas the picture descriptions involve a number of potential participants that may or may not be introduced by the speaker. If a participant is not specifically introduced but the speaker later attempts to use a personal or demonstrative reference to identify that participant, then uninterpretable additioning results.

One picture description task, the joint-viewing, is similar to the storytelling in having low levels of additioning. In the joint-viewing task, the speaker and hearer have the same access to the visual information that is the basis for the text. Similarly, the storytelling task involves the description of pictures that both speaker and hearer can see. The problem of additioning does not arise in the joint-viewing task since all the relevant information is shared. Additioning is relatively rare in the storytelling task since the story genre is known to the speakers and they display reasonable skill in using the reference system. The participants are limited and recur in the story line. The characteristics of the tasks can contribute to relatively greater or lesser uses of additioning. Additioning reflects a lack of shared information when the participants being referred to are not explicit and central to a story line.

Additioning is the one cohesive variable that shows a difference between the low- and high-SES groups. The low-SES group uses more additioning than the high-SES group on the two tasks that are more demanding socially and cognitively: picture outline and single viewing. The picture-outline task requires the speaker to infer information that is not visually explicit and to then provide a verbal description. The single-viewing task requires that the speaker present information explicitly and not assume that the hearer shares or can infer necessary information. Additioning as an unclear signal to the hearer is not an undifferentiated marker of class differences. Rather additioning is one part of the use of the textual system that creates difficult-to-interpret stretches of language under conditions that impose specific demands for processing and presenting information for social interaction.

Exophoric reference is the final part of the reference system to be considered. Exophora is insensitive to the task variables except for the most directly relevant component of situation present in the contrast between single viewing and joint viewing. The speakers appropriately exploited the visually shared information in the joint-viewing task. The speakers can construct descriptions without exophora but exploit the possibility of exophora when possible. The single-viewing task shows a high level of additioning perhaps as an attempt to continue the identity of participants that were not explicitly presented. In contrast, exophora offers a means of clearly and repeatedly identifying participants in the joint-viewing task.

The use of the reference system is thus not a unitary phenomenon. Different parts of the reference system have different text-forming functions. These functions are closely related to the characteristics of the situation of language use. A situation with the possibility of two participants is associated with higher levels of additioning. Situations with a number of potential noncentral participants are associated with additioning references that are uninterpretable since speakers improperly assume that participants have been introduced or are retrievable by inference when they are not. Changes in the use of exophora are narrowly based on the amount of visually shared information that can serve as referent for the exophora. As well as such direct relationship between the reference system and components of the situation, there are more complex relationships involving more than two factors. Additioning as a problematic kind of relationship is used differentially by the two socially defined groups only on tasks which themselves present special problems in processing. That is, the group difference emerges on a specific use of cohesion only under particular task conditions.

Conjunction. Despite the instruction to tell a story about the pictures in the picture-description tasks, the overwhelming use of additive conjunction indicates that speakers do not construct a temporal or causal story line. In fact, most speakers do not provide recognizable stories but, rather, lists of statements about the pictures. Additive conjunction is the unmarked choice for conjunction and merely signals to the listener that the following stretch of language is connected to the prior stretch without further specifying the semantic relation. The two stretches of language are to be interpreted as belonging to the same text. In the picture-descriptive tasks, the additive conjunction signals minimally that the description is of the same picture. The unity of text created by additive conjunction can be seen as imposed by the task itself. The experimenter has requested that the subject perform some verbal task. The subject does not seek temporal or causal relationship in the picture but just connects one piece of information to another as the task proceeds. The storytelling task, on the other hand, provides the subject with recognizable and typical temporal and causal relations in the story line. It is possible that with more prompting and a sense of greater time for the task, subjects would use their evident skill in stating temporal and causal relations to construct more elaborated picture descriptions with less additive conjunction.

The use of conjunction can be better understood by comparing the results from a number of studies. When normal readers retell a story that they originally composed when looking at a sequence of pictures, the retelling uses more temporal and causal (nonadditive) conjunction than the initial production from pictures (Fine, 1985). The recall task enables the speaker to integrate all the information and express temporal and causal relations between pieces of information that the story line organizes. In the picture descriptions by the Hebrew-speaking children, all the information is presented at once and is available for organization by the speaker. However, the low levels of temporal and causal conjunction suggest that without some sequential visual organization and/or a second opportunity to develop the material, verbally specific relations are relatively rare.

Martin (1983b) also presents data on conjunction in children's story telling and recall. The recall of an orally presented fable contains less explicit additive conjunction than the recall, without the aid of pictures, of a story initially developed by following a series of pictures. Since both kinds of tasks in Martin's study involved stories rather than static pictures that only implicitly embody a story line, the differences in the use of additive conjunction are not so overwhelming as in the task presented to the Hebrew-speaking children. The recall of the fable shows explicit marking of temporal and causal conjunction since the relations cannot be left implicit or merely indicated by the unmarked additive relation. That is, the importance of the marked conjunctive relations to certain tasks is associated with the explicit and more frequent use of those marked conjunctions compared to both implicit conjunctions (as formulated in Martin,

1983b) and the unmarked additive conjunctive relation. Martin's data show the description from the sequence of pictures to have the least amount of nonadditive explicit conjunction. Since conjunctions link information to come to current information, when the information to come is not available, the speaker is restricted to unmarked additive conjunction.

There are thus two general factors influencing the choices from the conjunction system: (a) the availability of information, and (b) the kinds of semantic relations that must be made explicit in the task. The picture description tasks provide the speaker with all the relevant information at the same time and in this respect are parallel to the recall task in Martin (1983b) and Fine (1985). In these tasks the speaker realizes that text must be produced and so conjunctive links are required. However, for the picture descriptions there is no special need to mark temporal and causal relations since there is no clear temporal or causal organization in the pictures. The instruction to create a story from the static pictures was not successful. In Martin's (1983b) story-creation task (Task 1), the sequence of pictures and the directions indicated also that a single text should be produced. Nevertheless, without the availability of prospective information, additive conjunction tended to be used. For increased uses of marked conjunction (causal and temporal), prospective and retrospective information must both be available. Furthermore, the task must impose the necessity of using marked conjunction; that is, if the task were accomplished with unmarked additive conjunction, the necessary relations between stretches of language would not be stated (as in Martin's task 3).

Lexical cohesion. As in other studies, there is little variation in the use of different forms of lexical cohesion. Overwhelmingly, speakers use repeated forms of lexical roots rather than use lexical subordinates, superordinates, synonyms, and so on. There is little variation in lexical cohesion across both speakers and tasks. The choice of subtype of lexical cohesion is not an area of linguistic potential that reflects differences in the coherence of text, genre, or register. Ultimately, the lexical cohesion shares in a system with reference as means for continuing the identity of participants. Once the choice of lexical cohesion is made, however, further choices at greater levels of delicacy are rarely exploited to signal different kinds of texts.

In summary, the measures of cohesion show specific and

functional relationships to the tasks used to produce language samples. Close examination reveals that the variation in the use of cohesion is on certain choices under specific circumstances. Notions of more or less cohesion are too general and do not reflect the intricate and functional relationship between aspects of the nonlinguistic situation and the choices available from the various cohesion systems.

Task

Joint and single viewing. It was expected that the joint- and single-viewing contexts would reveal differences between the high- and low-SES groups. The joint-viewing task is more typical of interactions between young children and adults than the single-viewing task (Moerk, 1985) and has simpler requirements for referential cohesion. In the single-viewing task the speaker must realize that the hearer does not have access to the visual information on which the description is based. The message must be specific, and not rely on either the visual information or what the hearer may infer from such information. However, it is just this sort of task that young speakers must master in order to extend their own knowledge into that of others creating a shared social reality.

Of the tasks, the single-viewing task produced the greatest number of trends toward differences between the two subject groups. The extra cognitive load of having to account for the hearer's lack of information may have contributed to both groups using most additioning in the single-viewing task and for the low-SES group using more additioning than the high-SES group in the single-viewing task. Although speakers relatively frequently did not accommodate to the information needs of hearers in the single-viewing task, the relatively frequent use of exophora in the joint-viewing task suggests an asymmetry in the appropriate use of reference options. Speakers do exploit exophora appropriately when it is possible, but do not appropriately adjust to explicit identification of participants when the sharing of information must be made explicit. It is in this second kind of adjustment that the low-SES group shows a modest but significant difference from the high-SES group.

Full and outline pictures. There were not substantial differences in the language produced in the full- and outline-picture tasks. The only significant difference was that the low-SES group used more additioning than the high-SES group on the picture-outline task but not on the full-picture task. This difference supports a view that the greater cognitive demands of the outline-picture task are associated with less interpretable messages from the low-SES group. The increment in the cognitive demands of the task is thus a contributing factor to the clarity of the text produced. The relationship between cognitive demands and additioning is not direct and strong, but rather is mediated by the group difference defined in the study and is even then of only moderate strength. Perhaps parallel tasks with greater differences in cognitive demands would result in more substantial differences in the nature of the text produced (see Fine, 1985, for a study with such clearer results based on cognitive demands).

Story retelling and picture description. The story retelling and picture descriptions both derive from visual material but involve crucially different organizations of verbal material. The story retelling task provides an organization of material that is predictable in terms of story structure and the genre of children's stories. The subjects were presented with the message as a verbally organized unit with the pictures serving to clarify the participants and changes in the location of participants. The picture descriptions, in contrast, required the subjects to impose their own organization of material and then to actualize that organization verbally. There were accordingly substantial task effects on a number of cohesion variables including personal reference, demonstrative reference, ambiguity, additioning, and conjunction.

The story retelling task was the only condition that produced a significant shift away from additive conjunction—the default choice. With a memory of all the parts of the story and one example of how the information can be interrelated verbally, the subjects do indeed introduce considerable temporal and causal conjunction. In view of the parallel findings of Martin (1983b) and Fine (1985) that more nonadditive conjunction is used in story retelling compared to storytelling tasks, the current results must be interpreted as reflecting the prior nonverbal and verbal organization of the material presented to the subjects in the story task.

The patterning of reference in the story retelling also shows the strong influence of a clear story line. Compared to the picture descriptions, the story retellings have a greater proportion of personal and demonstrative reference, more ambiguous reference, and less additioning. The storytelling task led to texts with participants—the protagonist and the series of animal friends—that are continued through the story. Since there are several animals that perform similar actions, the speakers must use reference carefully to correctly reidentify the participants. This nature of the story is associated with high levels of ambiguity as speakers fail to express that they are keeping accurate track of the participants. However, there is no general difficulty in presenting interpretable messages. Story retellings have no more additioning, and sometimes less, than the picture descriptions. The high rate of ambiguous reference is related to the presence of several participants in the story task and the need to keep them distinct. The rates of exophora for the picture descriptions and storytelling were parallel, indicating that the creation of semantic continuity in the story retelling task was done verbally rather than by referring nonverbally to the pictures. This strategy contributed to the higher levels of ambiguity. Subjects attempt to establish the continuity of participants by referential means and so also fail verbally. The story task was appropriately interpreted as a verbal task, despite the presence of pictures as prompts. The use of the various options in the reference system are thus dependent on a combination of factors, including the participant structure of the text to be created, the presence of a clear story line that organizes the participants, and the task characteristics that influence the use of nonverbal information.

Class Differences

In general the two groups of subjects differed little on the cohesion variables. The high-SES group was somewhat more verbal than the low-SES group but the use of cohesion to create text differed minimally. The use of cohesion by the two groups is discussed, followed by some accounting of why class differences reported in other studies were not apparent. Some studies (Haslett, 1983; Liles, 1985a, 1985b) report greater use of personal pronouns by girls, older children, and normal children compared to children with language disabilities. Personal pronoun usage, on this evidence, is thus an indicator of better developed language skills, with demonstrative reference used proportionately more by boys, younger children, and the language disordered. If there were to be class differences, the lower SES group would be expected to use less personal reference and more demonstrative reference. These differences were not found.

Rather than the explicit cohesion of personal and demonstrative reference, bridging creates an implicit cohesive link between two stretches of language. If the link cannot be reconstructed, then additioning results: The receiver recognizes that a cohesive link is being established but cannot recover the information that the sender codes as recoverable. Although the differences did not reach significance, the high-SES group used bridging relatively more frequently than the low-SES group in all the picture-description tasks except the joint-viewing task. In the joint-viewing task, the information that can be referred to is explicitly shared and so there is little need or possibility for bridging. Additioning—"failed" bridging—is found more frequently in the language of the low-SES group for all the picture-description tasks, with the difference between the low- and high-SES groups reaching significance for the single-viewing and outline-picture description tasks. The single-viewing and outline-picture tasks are the most difficult both in estimations of what the hearer knows and in demands of explicitness in language. Other evidence (Pratt & MacKenzie-Keating 1985; Rochester & Martin 1977, 1979) shows that additioning decreases developmentally and with increased sanity. Certainly less additioning is the sign of more interpretable messages. In the context of these studies, the current moderate differences in the language of the two socially defined groups of subjects suggest modest differences in the cognitive maturity or ability to assess the communicative needs of others. In particular, the group differences appear only in the more demanding situations and only in a very limited set of cohesive variables.

The failure to find clear differences in the language of the two socially defined groups needs explanation. The socially based differences in language reported for British and American populations were not replicated here. The theoretical basis for the social differences, for example, elaborated and restricted codes, should hold for languages other than English. The first difference between the studies that found marked class differences and the current data is the nature of the classes themselves. The British class structure is a self-perceived social fact as well an economic fact. In Israel there are clear economic differences that are overlaid with differences in ethnicity and ultimate country of origin. However, most children are from families with only a generation or two of history in the country and in a Hebrew-speaking society. Thus, distinct social patterns and associated communication patterns are unlikely to have developed. There are also language enrichment programs targeted at "deprived" neighborhoods, so that class differences would be attenuated in school-age populations. Those studies that found socially based differences in Israeli school populations were based on either written texts (Stahl, 1977) or older children (Cais, 1983) where the effect of differential educational opportunity or a divergence in later socialization and language development may have played a role.

CONCLUSION

The data in this chapter point to specific relations between uses of cohesion and the nonlinguistic social and cognitive components of the situation. There are both simple relations between a particular cohesion measure and a nonlinguistic factor (e.g., more exophoric reference in the joint picture-description task) and more complex relations interrelating one or more cohesion measures with one or more components of the situation. In all cases, there is a clear functional basis for the relationship of the cohesion measures and the situational components. Cohesion is more than a convenient and objective method for assessing the relative development of language skills. Cohesion in its functional character reflects the kind of information that speakers can clearly convey to others.

The direct functional basis of cohesion suggests educational implications for groups of speakers. The cohesion variables indicate specific kinds of miscommunication that are likely under very specific social and cognitive conditions. As well as straightforward cases of miscommunication, the cohesive variables describe the kinds of information (e.g., anaphoric or exophoric, temporal or additive) that are presented by different speakers in various circumstances. These different typical ways of presenting information can then serve as a basis for instruction or the reorientation of certain educational practices and materials. See Mohan (1989) and Ventola (1987), whose ultimate motivations derive from language teaching.

APPENDIX

Two examples of texts in picture description tasks

Example 1.

Text of a low-SES girl - Joint-Viewing, Outlined-Picture Context. Picture number 1.
(S = Subject; E = Experimenter).

Transliteration

S> Ha'ima ... shemvashelet ... mxasa et hasir ve holexet.

E> Ken.

S> Vehamgirot boltot. Hem ptuxot kulam. Vehate al ha'aron.

E> Ken.

S> Ve'kol hakosot muxanot al hashulxan le'yom shabat. Ve'hem osim oxel le'yom shabat. Veha'yeladim ozrim.

E> Mmhhmm.

S> Ha'yalda holexet le'saxek. Ima lo marsha la likanes labayit ve'la'azor ki hi kvar rotsa lalexet.

E> Ken.

S> Ve'haya'eh zaruk al haritspa. Ve'ha ... hamatateh al ha'ritspa.

E> Ken.

S> Ve'hasakin be'yaxad al hashulxan. Ve ... hatsalaxot al hashulxan.

E> Mmhhmm.

S> Ve'hamenora boletet. Ve'kol, kol, kol hadevarim ve'haberez bolet. Kol hadevarim. Ve'hi shotefet hakelim.

E> Mmhhmm.

S> Ve'hayeled hive ta'sak ... hiniax oto vehalax la'azor le'ima. Ve'zehu.

Translation

S> The mother ... who is cooking ... covers the pot and goes.

E> Yes.

S> And the drawers are sticking out. They are all open. And the tea is on the table.

E> Yes.

S> And all the cups are ready on the table for the sabbath. And they are making food for the sabbath. And the children are helping.

E> Mmhhmm.

S> The girl is going to play. Mother does not allow her to go into the house and help because she wants to go.

E> Yes.

S> And the dustpan is thrown on the floor and the broom is on the floor.

E> Yes.

S> And the knife is together on the table and ... the plates are on the table

E> Mmhhmm.

S> And the light is sticking out. And all, all, all the things. And the tap is sticking out. All the things. And she is washing dishes.

E> Mmhhmm.

S> And the boy brought the sack, put it down and went to help mother. And that's all.

Example 2.

Text of a high-SES girl - Single Viewing, Full-picture Task. Picture number 2.

Transliteration

S> Yesh po sha'on.

E> Mmhhmm

S> Im shte kapiyot mitaxat la'sha'on, ve shne kumkun ... kumkumim munaxim be'aron. Ve shne bakbukim ... eh ... shne kosot im bakbut ... im bakbuk munaxim bifnim. Ve ... eh ... sh ... milx ... tsa ... milxiya munaxat leyadam.

E> Ken.

S> Ve'isha mv ... ve'ima mvashelet. Ve'yesh al yad hasir gam max ... ve'yesh al yad hasir she'ima mvashelet maxvat.

E> Ken.

S> Ve'im ... ve'savta roxetset kelim.

E> Mmhhmm.

S> Ve'yalda potaxat hadelet ve'ish ba. Ve'yeled orex shulxan. Ve'reshet kazoti ve'yesh betoxo m...dvarim. Ma ze? Duvdevanim? Lo! Kadurim adumim - ze ma she' efshar le'hagid - al hakise. Ve'mivreshet ... mivreshet im kaf ve'matateh munaxim batsad shel habayit.

E> Ken.

S> Ve'sal im ... im tapuxe ets batsad. Lemala yesh aron kelim. Kruv baxuts, xatux, sakin le'yado ve'ke'arot.

E> Ken.

S> Ve'bakbuk ... min bakbuk kaze im berez ma'yim ve'megirot al yad hatanur.

Translation

S> There is a clock.

E> Mmhhmm.

S> With two teaspoons below the clock, and two ke ... kettles placed in a cupboard. And two bottles ... eh ... two cups with a bottle ... with a bottle placed inside. And ... eh ... t ... sal ... pl ... a salt shaker is standing next to them.

E> Yes.

S> And a woman i ... a mother is cooking. And next to the pot there's also a fr ... and next to the pot that mother is cooking there's a frying pan.

E> Yes.

S> And m ... a granny is washing dishes.

E> Mmhhmm.

S> And a girl is opening the door and a man is coming. And a boy is laying the table and a sack next to ... and a sack is next to a chair and ... and ... and a sort of net and in it m ... things. What's this? Cherries? No! Red balls - that's what one can say - on the chair. And a brush with a pan and a broom are on the side of the house.

E> Yes.

S> And a basket with apples is on the the side. There's cabbage outside that's cut up, a knife next to it and bowls.

E> Yes.

S> And a bottle ... a sort of bottle with a water tap. And there are drawers next to the oven.

8

COHESION IN BILINGUAL CONVERSATION

INTRODUCTION

The immediately preceding chapters have dealt with cohesion in the spoken language of children. In developmental studies there is a natural sense of direction: Children emerge into adultlike interactions in the adult linguistic community. The current chapter examines cohesion in the context of second-language learning. Again, there is a clear goal: The speakers should use the second language appropriately in the situations they find themselves in.

As with first-language acquisition, the use of cohesion in second-language acquisition is related to a series of social and interactional factors. The use of cohesion varies with the identity of the interlocutor (peer or nonpeer in the data), the turn-taking organization of the conversation, and the choice of native or second language. These factors all have specific roles in influencing how speakers construct text. As has been shown for first-language development, the use of cohesion reflects the functions of cohesion and the relation of those functions to factors of linguistic and nonlinguistic context. The study is of the functions of cohesion rather than a quantitative analysis of the use of certain cohesive items or relations by certain speakers.

The learning of a second language in a naturalistic situation involves the social nature of language, the dialogue nature of interaction, and the resources of language that must be used. The social context of language, and, in this particular case, of language learning, is not peripheral but central to the use of language by specific speakers. The study of such language then requires a view of language that addresses the connection of language to its social context. This chapter examines the use of second language (French for native speakers of English) in a naturalistic setting (an immersion French-speaking day camp).

For any given speech event, a great deal of common reality can be assumed by each, speaker. A speaker has knowledge of common social patterns, common cultural and physical artifacts, and the conventional use of language. However, the speakers must themselves build a relationship with each other through language. They must display that they are connected to the specific situation in a similar way. If speakers do not code the relation between language and the situation similarly they will find that they will misunderstand each other: "the president" for one speaker will be different than "the president" for another speaker; "now" will include the past ten years for one speaker and the past ten days for another speaker. Speakers must relate their language to the social situation and to each other's speech for a shared reality to develop. To hint at a subsequent discussion, the process of second-language learning and the use of a second language in naturalistic situations involves using the target language to construct a shared reality between speakers. If interaction is to take place, then speakers must construct a shared reality by using a first language, second language, or some other signaling system. If the educational task at hand is learning the second language, then it is the process of building and sharing reality in this second language that must be examined. Again, the focus must be on those parts of the linguistic system that develop and display connections from speaker to speaker and from speakers to situation. By looking at such specific parts of language, the processes of learning to use the second language appropriately in situations can be better understood.

The building of social reality through language in dialogue is dynamic. Each successive utterance and turn by successive speakers is dependent on prior speech. However, as has been discussed in earlier chapters, language and dialogue are organized by simultaneous principles. Turns at talk are organized by mechanisms such as adjacency pairs, repair strategies, and conventional and nonconventional codings of speech functions. The language within those turns is also organized by other principles, such as syntax and cohesion. The speaker is therefore required to use language in a dynamic system and to fashion utterances to conform to a number of organizing principles simultaneously. This study examines two of these organizing principles (cohesion and turn taking) in the context of dialogue which is necessarily dynamic and in the context of each other. The dynamic nature of dialogue requires examination of the social roles that are expressed in the dialogue and the changing of those roles from speaker to speaker. This dynamic is also important from the point of view of learning. In a naturalistic setting and in first-language learning in normal cases, emerging speakers must enter and maintain social dialogue.

Studying the effect of social role on language in dialogue would seem to involve measuring of the effect of one set of variables on another (in this particular case, turn taking as representing social role and the cohesion represented by lexical repetition).

To return to the use of L1 and L2 in a naturalistic situation, the focus will be on the socially affected use of language. By choice of language, a speaker indicates ability in L2 (assuming L1 can always be used) and also an assessment of the social situation. Part of the social assessment will be an estimate of how hearers will socially assess the speaker's use of L1 or L2. Will a certain degree of "accent" or grammatical or vocabulary errors carry a valued or disvalued assessment? On the other hand, a speaker may be positively valued for attempting to use L2 even with errors. The choice of L1 or L2 thus displays a speaker's place in social interaction. This choice is within the context of dialogue where social role is also created and displayed by the use of turn-taking mechanisms. In the dynamic of conversation, social roles controlling the direction of talk can be negotiated and exchanged. Thus the choice of language is in a context of social interaction that can be partly understood in terms of turn taking.

This chapter is concerned with two specific devices for building and signaling text (the pair "building and signaling" is intended as a reminder of how messages are constructed out of linguistic features and then display their semantic unity as text by those features): lexical repetition and explicit exophoric references to the situation. These two kinds of signals enable us to examine how text is constructed in dialogue by two speakers. (For the development of text from dialogue ontogenically, see Halliday, 1975).

Repetition of lexical items signals semantic continuity from one stretch of language to another by the mere identity of the signals. There may or may not be identity of reference. For example, the second occurrence of "balloon" below does not indicate identity of reference but nevertheless contributes to the construction of text and signals to the hearer that speaker and hearer are still continuing in the same text.

Speaker A: Yesterday I saw the biggest balloon I've ever seen.
B: Balloons are a bore. Don't you have anything better to do?

In the language activity of the students in this study it is likely that much of the lexical repetition is in fact signaling an identity of reference, but such a condition is not necessary. Lexical cohesion exists between lexical items with the same lexical root even if the part of speech is different. For example, "pay" and "payment" in the following constructed conversation are linked by cohesion and signal a continuity of text.

Speaker A: You should pay the bill by the first of the month.
B: No, I think the payment can be as late as the tenth.

In a study of monolingual children of about the same age as those in this study, it was found that lexical cohesion (overwhelmingly repetition) was used principally to show continuity within the speech of single speakers. The repetition was much more of lexical items the speaker had already used rather than of lexical items found in the speech of other participants in the conversations (Fine, 1978, and Chapters 5 and 6, this volume).

Exophoric reference helps create by signaling the connections between language and the nonverbal environment of language use. An important distinction in the nonverbal environment signaled by language is between speech roles and nonspeech roles. The linguistic signals of speech roles (e.g., I, we, you, mine, ours, yours, my, yourself, etc.) make a direct reference to the participants in a conversation. Continued use of these items maintains the identification of participants. The identity of participants may be made overt by using these speech role references as address terms ("You really should change that shirt."), or as actors in ongoing events ("I think that John is looking younger," compared to "George thinks that John is looking younger," in which the actor "George" is not referred to by an exophoric speech role reference). Nonspeech role exophoric references specify nonparticipant features of the environment. Time (now, later, today, next year), location (here, there) or identity of objects (this book, that man) may be referred to. These references establish the nonverbal common environment of speaker and hearer. Together speech role and nonspeech role references indicate the relation of participants in a conversation to their environment. Different kinds of texts (compare service encounters to political interviews, for example) may be connected to the environment by different exophoric devices. One question that is relevant is: How important are the speakers for the unity of any particular type of text? Phrased differently, the issue is how important is the intrusion of the speakers in a conversation to the reality being created through language?

Turn-taking organization is the reflection of social roles in dialogue. One basic mechanism of turn taking is the construction of local dependence from one turn to another (see Fine, 1978; Garvey, 1975; Sacks, Schegloff, & Jefferson, 1974; and Chapter 5, this volume). Most often the dependence is between pairs of adjacent turns (adjacency pairs). Commonly, the first turn in an adjacency pair (a first-pair partner) is a question, command, suggestion, or invitation. Speakers of first-pair partners have the role of defining the turn of the other speaker. The turn after a first-pair partner will be heard as a response to it, whatever the semantic content of this second-pair partner (e.g., "get lost," "let's talk about the weather," "when did George's dog become sick"). The speaker of a first-pair partner is exerting local control over the conversation. The speaker who responds to a second-pair partner may regain local control by using the second-pair partner to initiate a conversational set and thus require the original speaker to fill the conversational slot of a second-pair partner. The continuity and shifting of local conversational control is part of the dynamic development and displaying of social roles in conversation.

A BILINGUAL STUDY

Data Collection

The data for this study comes from a day camp designed to teach French to English-speaking children from the ages of 6 to

12. The camp uses native or nativelike French-speaking staff. The children are encouraged to speak French but there are no formal rules for language use and no specific instructional sessions. The campers come with a wide range of experience in French. They are divided into groups for the purposes of the camp on the basis of age rather than ability in French. Le Camp (as the camp is called) is in an English-speaking city and there is no significant exposure to French outside of the camp. Although intended to be an instrument for the teaching of French, the emphasis at Le Camp is on the conduct of a summer camp. That is, all activities are real camp activities and thus all uses of language are real functional uses of language, rather than uses for the specific purpose of language teaching.

A number of the activities of the camp setting were videotaped and then transcribed as part of the research program associated with Le Camp. The data reported in this study come from two types of situations. The most uncontrolled situation is that of an arts-and-crafts session. The campers stand or sit around a table with a least one and sometimes two staff members present to help and to some extent guide the campers in making small objects. There is considerable interaction among the campers and with the staff. Two such videotaped sessions are included in the current analyses: one is of a younger group of 6- and 7-year-olds and the second is of an older group of 10- and 11-year-olds. Each tape lasts about one-half hour. The second type of situation is part of a drama workshop in which the campers are given a situation to act out. In the case of the younger group, the campers are in a restaurant and must order food from a cooperative but monolingual French waiter played by a staff member. In the case of the older group, the campers are the survivors of an airplane accident and must explain their predicament to the inhabitant of the nearest house, who once again is cooperative but a speaker of only French and played by a staff member. This latter type of situation is termed improvisation and lasts about 15 or 20 minutes. One session from the older group of campers and one session from the younger group of campers is included in the data for this study.

Analysis of Data

This study analyzed: (a) the repetition of lexical items in the context of the identity of the speakers involved and the language that they use to form text, and (b) the use of exophoric reference to the nonverbal situation. To study text formation by lexical means it is necessary to exclude grammatical items, that is, words from closed lexical sets. These words do not create the continuity of meaning of textness since their appearance in a stretch of language is determined by grammatical considerations and not by text-forming semantic considerations. Furthermore, these grammatical words usually have minimal semantic value on their own. Grammatical words from closed sets include articles, pronouns, auxiliary verbs, prepositions (although at least some prepositions have a reasonable amount of semantic content), complementizers, relativizers, negative particles.

Each lexical item not excluded by the above rules was regarded as potentially a repetition. An earlier use of the same lexical root was searched for in the situation being studied. The earlier use of the word (called the "source") was identified and coded in terms of the speaker of this source word. The language of the source word was also coded as either L1 (English) or L2 (French). Thus for every repetition, the source could be identified in terms of language and speaker. The issues of moving from language to language or remaining in a given language can then be addressed. The following conversation exemplifies the method. Speakers X and Y are French-speaking staff members; speakers a, b, c, and d are campers.

1 - X) où elle est ta manche toi - where is it your sleeve, you
2 - a) quoi manche - what sleeve?
3 - X) c'est grand ça on pourrait - that's great that it could
4 - le donner à Danielle ... - be given to Danielle
5 - où est-ce quelle est ta - where is your
6 - manche... oui - sleeve yes
7 - Y) c'est difficile, oke, comme - that's difficult, OK. like
ça that
8 - b) that way - that way
9 - Y) mais coupe-le ... oui - but cut it ... yes
10 - c) regarde ... y-il va... - look ... he is going to
y manger eat
11 - les ciseaux - the scissors
12 - X) oke - OK
13 - c) raaaaa - raaaaa
14 - a) what's this line for - what's this line for
15 - X) oke - OK
16 - b) oh ssss-excuse moi - oh excuse me

17 - d) ça c'est ... ça c'est une ..- that's that's a ...
une - a

18 - ligne pour les ciseaux? - line for the scissors?

In this example, camper a repeats "manche" (line 2) from the staffer X speaking French (line 1). Camper d repeats "line" (line 18) from the English source "line" spoken by camper a (line 14). In this case, camper d moves from the English of camper a to French. Camper d also repeats from a French source in repeating "ciseaux" (line 18) from the source by camper c in line 11. As well as the language of the repeated words, its location in one of three kinds of turns was coded. A turn was defined as the uninterrupted speech of one speaker. As soon as another speaker spoke, the turn of the first speaker was considered as ended. Turns were classified as initiating (first-pair partners) if they started a conversational set (see Garvey, 1975, Ch. 5, this volume). In practice, most initiating turns were questions with a small number of imperatives and suggestions. The turns after initiating turns were defined as responding turns (second-pair partners). These turns were defined by their position in relation to initiating turns. Turns that neither initiate nor respond to other turns were defined as unconstrained turns.

Exophoric references require the hearer to interpret certain words by searching the nonverbal situation for information. Exophoric references were coded as one of two kinds: (a) speech roles, or (b) nonspeech roles. Speech role exophoric reference included references to first- and second-person participants in a conversation. Each nominal group with such a reference was coded. Nonspeech role reference specifies to the hearer that the information needed from the physical environment is not the identity of the speaker or hearer but is related to the space or time of the conversation. Each speech role and nonspeech role reference was identified and coded as being in L1 or L2 and as being in a first-pair partner, second-pair partner, or an unconstrained turn.

Results and Discussion

The first set of results answers two specific questions: (a) When a camper repeats in French (L2), what earlier language is the source? and (b) When the naturalistic situation of the use of language includes substantial amounts of English (L1), is there

Table 8-1. Sources of repetitions in L2 (French) by campers as a percentage of all repetitions in L2

Repetition in L2 from camper L1	7%
Repetition in L2 from camper L2	64%
Repetition in L2 from counselor L2	29%

a detrimental effect of this use of L1 on the use of L2? Table 8-1 addresses the first question by showing the sources for the lexical items repeated by campers in L2 (French). Clearly the largest source for campers in L2 is earlier L2 spoken by campers (64%). The next largest source is the L2 spoken by French-speaking staff (29%). Only a small amount (7%) of the repetition in L2 has a source in L1. These results are rather surprising given the relative weakness of the campers' L2 and their infrequent use of it. In sum, there is relatively little translation from L1 to L2 in the formation of text by the campers but substantial continuation in L2 once it has been introduced into the language context.

If there is little translation from L1 to L2 in these situations, it could be the case that the presence of L1 may lead to transitions from L2 back to L1. This second question may be answered from the data in Table 8-2. As long as there is a source in the L2 of campers, the repetition remains overwhelmingly in L2 (85%). Translation from camper L2 back to L1 occurs relatively rarely (15%). When the source of a repetition is the staff's L2, there is considerable translation by the campers back to L1 (38%). Comparing these results, then, there is a greater likelihood to revert to L1 from the staff's L2 than from camper L2. At present, the reason for the relatively frequent translation from staff L2 back to L1 is not clear. It may be due to the difficulty of the L2 used by the staff, such that campers find it easier or more practical to use the L1 equivalent of more difficult vocabulary.

Rather than looking at repeating in one language or another

Table 8-2. Sources of repetition in L2 (French) and L1 (English) by language of repetition and source of repetition

Source – camper L2 (French)	
Language of repetition L2 (French)	85%
L1 (English)	15%
Source – counselor L2 (French)	
Language of repetition L2 (French)	62%
L1 (English)	38%

Table 8-3. **Repetition in a given language as a percentage of all repetitions by speaker and language of source lexical item.**

	Language of Repetition	
	L1	*L2*
(1) Repetition of own L1	83%	17%
(2) Repetition of own L2	27%	73%
(3) Repetition of other camper's L1	86%	14%
(4) Repetition of other camper's L2	20%	80%
(5) Repetition of counselor's L2	38%	62%

from a source that is either one's own language or another's language, we can examine in more detail five possible continuities in language. A camper may (a) repeat his own L1, (b) repeat his own L2, (c) repeat another camper's L1, (d) repeat another camper's L2, or (e) repeat a counselor's L2. Counselors as a matter of policy do not speak L1 and no instances of counselor L1 were found in the data. A camper who repeats L1 of his own speech displays a clear continuity of meaning but does not take into consideration the L2 speaking environment (especially when such L1 repetition is in the context of a dialogue involving both languages). In Example 1, the camper's second and third uses of "job" are repetitions of her own L1. Given that one participant in the dialogue speaks only L2, this continuity of L1 ensures that the text is continuing but ignores that the social interaction is occurring in two languages. Table 8-3 shows that campers repeat in L1 once they have started in L1 at a relatively high rate (83%), compared to switching from their earlier L1 to L2 (17%).

A camper may also show continuity of text by continuing in L2. Compared to continuing in L1 (83%), the data show that the campers continued in L2 when they themselves started in L2 73% of the time. That is, a camper will revert to L1 for repetition (although he has earlier used L2) 27% of the time. In the first utterance of Example 2, camper 1 uses "besoin" ('need') and

Table 8-4. Repetition in the same language as the source lexical item as a percentage of all repetition from the speaker of the source items

(1) Repetition in L1 of own L1	83%
(2) Repetition in L2 of own L2	73%
(3) Repetition in L1 of other camper's L1	86%
(4) Repetition in L2 of other camper's L2	80%
(5) Repetition in L2 of counselor's L2	62%

"bleu" ('blue') in L2, but a few turns later repeats both these lexical items in L1. In such cases it is clear that the camper knows the L2 word but nevertheless only uses it 73% of the time. The process is one of returning to L1 probably to ensure that another camper will not misunderstand. Texture is retained since the repetition will be understood by both campers and counselors; the latter understand the camper's L1 but do not use it. Table 8-4 presents the percentage of repeated items that retain the language of the source lexical item. The consistency in L1 (83%) is somewhat higher than the consistency in L2 (73%) from a speaker's own earlier utterances. The difference between these two levels of consistency may represent a judgment that the social context does not demand a display of L2 as much as it demands the continuity of text by a display of semantic continuity, whatever the language used to achieve it. This suggestion can be made since the difference between the two levels of consistency is not attributable to the camper's lack of knowledge of L2: The camper has just used the L2 lexical item in question.

As well as repeating lexical items from his or her own speech, a camper may repeat lexical items spoken by another camper. In these cases the speaker must demonstrate a continuity in text across speakers and not merely with the speaker's own earlier utterances. As Table 8-3 shows, the rate of repeating in L1 from another camper (86%, compared to 14% shifting to L2) is about the same as repeating one's own L1. The continuity in L1 is then strong and about the same, independent of the speaker of the earlier language. These two measures are somewhat higher than the rate for staying in L2 when that L2 is spoken by the speaker himself. A shift from the L1 of a speaker to L2 by a second speaker may mark that second speaker as not demonstrating solidarity with a peer—another camper. Rather, shifting to L2 is the typical pattern of counselors who do not speak L1 but nevertheless interact with L1-speaking campers in dialogue.

Repeating in L2 what another camper has said in L2 is perhaps the best indication that effective L2 dialogue is taking place. In fact, 80% of the repetition of other camper L2 is in L2 (Table 8-3). There is then a high rate of continuing the L2 of another camper once the language is present in the environment. The rate of continuing another speaker's L2 seems to be higher than a speaker continuing his own L2. A suggestion for the difference is that there is a social reason for retaining the L2 of another speaker that is not present for one's own language.

A speaker may repeat the L2 of another speaker to show clear continuity of meaning but also to give the social message of solidarity in the prestige language of the situation. Continuing the L2 of another speaker is a sign of solidarity with a speaker in the more highly valued of the two socially possible languages. That this rate of continuing in L2 is about as high as the rates for continuing in L1 suggests that the social value of continuing in L2 is sufficient to overcome the strong preference for campers to use L1 in many intercamper transactions. Once a camper has entered L2, there is a substantial tendency for other campers to build text by specific repetition of the L2 that is available in the verbal environment.

There is only a 62% rate of repeating the counselor's L2 in L2. Over 35% of the repetition of a counselor's speech in L2 is translated back to L1 by the campers. This failure to remain in L2 is the lowest of the repetitions within a single language (Table 8-4). Just as the repetition of a camper's own L2 must be relatively low for social reasons rather than cognitive ones (the lexical item is known), so the movement away from the counselor's L2 lexical items is probably for interactional reasons. From the camper's perspective, continuing another camper's L2 may display solidarity, and show understanding of the L2. Continuing in the counselor's L2 may lead the camper into an undesirable situation in which the counselor increases the level of difficulty of the L2 and the camper displays inappropriate solidarity with the counselor. Overall, the rates for remaining in each of the languages based on the speaker of the earlier language (Table 8-4) suggest that continuing in L2 is not as consistent as continuing in L1—not a surprising finding. More interesting, however, is the relatively strong tendency to repeat the L2 of another camper, compared to repeating L2 from a counselor or even one's own earlier speech. This is an indication of the importance of the interaction between peers in establishing the use of L2. To be understood by a counselor, a camper may use L1; however, to be identified by a peer as being able to continue a dialogue in the prestige language, the camper must use L2.

The process of moving away from the L2 of the counselor involves a translation of apparently difficult L2 into L1 and then the use of the L1 by the campers. Example 3 shows the counselor asking the camper a question in L2 with the lexical item "fini" and the camper replying in L2 repeating the counselor's lexical item "fini." This is perhaps a case of learning by the camper or at least using L2 in context. However, shifts from counselor L2 to camper L1 may also be a matter of translating into L1. Example 1 shows the counselor using "travailler" and "payée" in L2 but the camper translating them into L1: "job," "paid." Similarly, in Example 4 there is repetition of the counselor's L2 "colle" by the camper in L1, "glue." In this case the construction of text is almost without awareness by the camper of the interrelationship of the linguistic items. The camper has not made an overt connection between "colle" and "glue." Nevertheless, the repetition indicates that camper and counselor are talking about the same thing in the same situation, but in different languages.

The study of repetition involves not only the speakers and languages of the original and repeated items, but also the conversational turn in which the repeated item was used. Of the over 200 instances of repetition, 60% were in unconstrained turns with the remainder about equally divided between first-pair partners and second-pair partners. A detailed analysis is presented in Table 8-5. What is interesting conversationally and educationally is the distribution of repetition according to language in each of the three types of turns. As Table 8-5 shows, there is considerably more repetition in L2 in constrained turns compared to unconstrained turns. The stronger preference for L2 is clear for both first-pair partners and second-pair partners, suggesting that it is not just the locus of control in a conversation but the degree of conversational constraint that is associated with L2 repetition. The controlled dialogue of the dramatic improvisations is a possible explanation for the higher use of L2 in constrained turns. Therefore, the free settings of the arts-and-crafts activities were analyzed separately. The results are given in Table 8-6. Even in this quite free-flowing setting with no specific social constraints imposed by a structuring of the situation, the constrained turns have a higher proportion of repetition in L2 than the unconstrained turns. There is a tendency for campers to repeat and thus construct continuous text by using L1. However, the force of this tendency can be altered by changing the nature of the conversation to one more structured by the dependence of one conversational turn on another.

Speakers brought together in conversational structure are necessarily more responsive to each other and to the situation. The situation of Le Camp is designed to build a social reality in L2 and the campers react to the situation by using L2. The

Table 8-5. Repetition in L1 and L2 for each type of turn as a percentage of repetitions in the turn type (all situations)

Language of Repetition	*Type of turn* First-pair partner	*Second-pair patner*	*Unconstrained*
L1	38	47	64
L2	62	53	36

Table 8-6. Repetition in L1 and L2 for each type of turn as a percentage of repetitions in the turn type (arts-and-crafts situations)

Language of Repetition	*Type of turn* First-pair partner	*Second-pair patner*	*Unconstrained*
L1	44	47	65
L2	56	53	35

basis of most of the social interaction in the camp setting is interaction among campers. In general, repetition in L2 is from other camper language (64% of all L2 repetition). This result confirms that there is an effort to speak and construct continuity among campers in L2. The high rate of L2 repetitions in constrained turns (first- and second-pair partners) is not a simple effect of counselor talk, since campers rarely ask counselors questions and the overall picture is of campers repeating L2 from campers rather than from counselors (see Table 8-3).

The study of lexical repetition is a study of continuity from one stretch of language to another. In situations where more than one language is spoken, continuity of meaning, the creation of text, is still necessary. The results show that repetition does serve this function but in complex ways. The social identity and roles of the speakers (camper or counselor) and the conversational turn-taking (also an indication of social role) influence how repetition is used. That is, language, and specifically repetition, is a tool for the creation of interaction and reflects the social nature of interaction.

The creation of text involves situating the language in the nonverbal context as well as in the context of other stretches of language. Connections between language and the nonverbal situation signal to the speakers in a dialogue that they share the same nonverbal situation and that they share the encoding of the nonverbal situation. For example, it is by exophoric references such as "here," "now," "yesterday," or "soon" that speakers establish that they share a time and space frame. The arts-and-crafts sessions, but not the improvisation setting, is located in a real time and space frame. The improvisation settings require that "here and now" be agreed upon by imagination. Therefore the study of reference to the nonverbal situation is restricted to the arts-and-crafts sessions. Of the two types of reference to the nonverbal situation, reference to speech roles will be dealt with first, followed by reference to nonspeech role aspects of the situation.

Speech role references (e.g., "I," "your," "ours") identify the speakers in a conversation. In the arts-and-crafts sessions studied, 72% of the speech role references were in L1 and 28% were in L2. This level of L1 is roughly similar to the rates for continuity in L1 obtained when examining repetition (Table 8-3): 83% repetition in L1 of own L1, 86% repetition in L1 of other camper's L1. However, repetition in L2 of previously used L2 varies from 62% to 80% (again, see Table 8-3). Thus the use of L1 for speech roles seems particularly strong since it is not based on earlier L2. The existence of L2 in the environment is important for the continuation in L2. Speech role references draw a connection not between one stretch of language and another but between the nonverbal situation and language. Furthermore, references to speech roles are made by closed grammatical systems such as personal pronouns and adjectives, and possessives. These closed systems may be controlled relatively late in the learning of language in naturalistic situations. The above results from the analysis of speech role references suggest that L2 use can be encouraged more through situations that require internal links from one stretch of language to another rather than links to the speakers in conversation.

The use of speech role references takes place in the context of the turn-taking structure of the conversation. The percentage of speech role references spoken in L1 is given in Table 8-7 for each type of turn. Example 5 shows a segment of conversation classified into conversational turn types with a number of speech role references. In first-pair partner turns there is the use of "your" (lines 7, 8) and "mon" ('my;' line 20). In second-pair partner turns, note the use of "you" (line 14—a turn that starts by being a second-pair partner but is also a first-pair partner to the following turn) and "I" (line 16). Example 5 has one instance of a speech role reference in a camper's unconstrained turn, "je" ('I;' line 19). There is then a similarity in the relative frequency of choice of L1 and L2 speech role references in the different turn types. The addressing and identifying of functions of speech role references are necessary in conversation and the choice of language seems to be derived from the knowledge of L2 and the appropriateness of L1 or L2 in the situation, rather than from the internal structure of the conversation. This independence from conversational structure is in contrast to the choice of language for lexical repetition. That is, the exophoric connections of speech references imply an independence from conversational structure, whereas the endophoric connections of repetition imply a dependence on language both in terms of lexical similarity and in terms of the conversational structure of the dialogue.

Nonspeech role exophora signals a link between language and aspects of time and space in the external situation apart from the speakers themselves. As with speech role exophora, the appropriate data to examine are the arts-and-crafts situations for which there is no doubt about the reality of the external world. There is no imagining of time or space. The uses of exophoric references such as "today," "soon," and "this" are wholly determined by the physical world and are not dependent on any sharing of an imaginary world. In these situations, 82% of the nonspeech role exophoric references are in L1 and only 18% in L2. These results indicate slightly greater use of L1 for speech role exophoric references (L1, 72%). There are just less than 50 occurrences of nonspeech role reference in the arts-and-crafts settings and so an analysis by type of turn is not possible. The effect of this type of reference is given in Examples 5 and 6. In example 5, line 14, the camper is responding to the counselor's request for permission ("oke?") and asks a question herself ("You see this"). The use of "this" is nonspeech role exophora as the speaker requires that the hearer see the fingers being displayed in order to interpret "this." In Example 6 there are two occurrences of a camper using L1 nonspeech role exophoric reference ("this," line 1; "that," line 4). Both these occurrences are found in first-pair partners (question turns in these cases). These uses of L1 are in contrast to the counselor's use of L2 for the same referring

Table 8-7. Speech role reference in L1 as a percentage of all speech role references, by turn type (arts-and-crafts situations)

Type of turn		
First-pair partner	*Second-pair partner*	*Unconstrained*
77	69	69

functions in adjacent turns. In Example 6, the counselor uses "c'est" (line 2) and "c'est" (line 5) to correspond to the camper's use of "this" (line 1) and "that" (line 4), respectively. These examples show the lack of carryover of L2 from counselor to camper. Exophora of this kind is expressed through grammatical systems with closed sets of options. Use of such systems would seem to be different from relatively open systems of lexical items for which there tend to be substantial levels of influence from the L2 of one speaker into the L2 of another speaker.

In general, the results for speech role and nonspeech role exophoric references are similar. Speakers code the external situation largely in L1 and this use of L1 is not affected by the turn-taking organization of conversation. The preponderance of L1 is perhaps due to the limited choices from closed sets (largely of pronouns and determiners) that express exophoric reference. Exophoric reference contrasts with lexical cohesion which is a signal of continuity of meaning within language. The continuity of meaning expressed by exophoric reference is established by speakers identifying the same elements in the external environment. The identity of such elements by L1 and L2 leads to rather simple understanding of the common element. In contrast, lexical cohesion (and endophoric cohesion in general) establishes a link between one stretch of language and another and so different surface forms in L1 and L2 may weaken the intrinsically linguistic link being created.

CONCLUSIONS

This study is concerned with the building and sharing of reality in a setting designed to teach L2. The setting of a camp requires purposeful communication and there is a constant necessity to attend to social interaction and social roles as well as conveying meaning. Campers could choose to speak in L1 or L2. The choice of language and the fitting of language into the context contributes to the construction of shared information but also shared understanding of the social roles in the situation. The aim of speakers, and therefore the aim of creating a situation for the learning of L2, must be to create text. Text is the use of language that is appropriately tied to its verbal and nonverbal context in terms of speakers, social roles, and the verbal cotext. One of the choices in the situation studied is the choice of L1 or L2. This choice itself reflects social role and the use of verbal cotext. This study has shown that the learning of text can be examined in detail by focusing on cohesion variables that signal and construct texture. Furthermore, these variables can be considered in relation to the structure of conversation which is itself sensitive to and constructive of the social roles in dialogue.

Conversation is constructed by simultaneous and interlocking systems of language and conversational organization. Some systems of language (such as lexical cohesion and anaphora) connect stretches of language to each other. Other systems (exophoric reference) connect language to the nonverbal environment by referring hearers to the nonverbal environment for information needed to interpret the language. The task for a learner of L2 is to be able to use L2 systems to build text being sensitive to and constructive of the social roles in conversation as the L2 is used.

Language actualizes conversational structure at the same time as it displays the creation of text. For example, repetition (part of cohesion) may be in L1 or L2. The choice combines with the social structuring displayed by turn taking to help create the social relationship between speakers. The results show that the dependence of conversational turns within sets of adjacency pairs combines with a relatively strong tendency to continue in L2 to construct text among campers. The link of one stretch of language to another (by repetition) becomes socially relevant and a means of displaying social facts of solidarity and identification. On the other hand, signals in language to the external environment do not show an independence of language choice and turn taking. The nonverbal environment itself provides a continuity of meaning and makes choice of L1 or L2 more independent of the other choices that contribute to the flow of conversation. Since the meanings are available in the environment, there seems to be less influence of the socially negotiated structure of turn taking. Although the signaling of social role by turn taking, the use of endophoric cohesion and exophoric references, and choice of language are interrelated, the relationship is not fixed. Rather, these three factors interrelate in different ways and to different degrees in the construction of ongoing conversation. The goal of communication by the formation of text remains constant in real and cooperative situations. It is the way this goal is realized that changes.

There are a number of educational implications of the methods and results of this study. The educational goal is the use of L2 in real situations. The learning must then be a process of doing things with language. That is, the goal and the processes to attain it are identical. Rather than a statement of hope or dogma, this study has provided specific evidence that it is the use of L2 by peers in conversation that contributes to the use of L2 by campers. It is the necessity for interaction and for contributing to social reality that is associated with the use of L2. If specific suggestions can be made it is that learners of L2 must be given the necessity and social circumstances to communicate to the speakers of L2 even if those speakers are primarily speakers of L1 and frequently use L1. In the data examined there was relatively little translation back from L2 to L1 when the social roles favored L2. Rather, L1 aids in the formation of text and thus promotes the social interaction that can become the basis for using L2. The overall social setting gives a value to communication in L2 and a motivation for using L2 when possible. The measurement of cohesion in dialogues with L1 and L2 is not merely a convenient and quantifiable gauge of language use. Rather, cohesion is an important device for displaying how language is operative in its verbal and nonverbal context. It is this functional use of language that speakers must achieve in L2 while being fully appropriate to the social and conversational aspects of interaction.

In the setting studied, speakers of different abilities in L2 were placed in the same group for day-to-day activities. It would seem that this policy is constructive since there is a tendency to move from L1 to L2 and a weaker tendency to move from L2 to L1 in the forming of text. However, specific studies of students at different levels of L2 are needed to corroborate this suggestion. Further studies are also needed concerning the social meanings conveyed in L1 and L2 (see Halliday, 1984). The linguistic measures of text formation can also be expanded to include conjunction, anaphoric references, and perhaps systems of information distribution. It is through detailed studies of language use in real situations that we can understand the principles of the relationship of language to social reality and the educational processes involved.

Example 1

Counselor: travailler toute la journée tu ne veux pas que je sois payée un peu ... pour vous endurer toute la journée il faut bien que je sois payée un peu.

Camper: and that's a job, it's a job and a job you have to get paid.

Example 2

Camper 1: bleu j'ai besoin bleu
Counselor: oh c'est beau ... tu veux le coller maintenant ... tu veux le coller avec de la colle
Camper 2: oui
Camper 1: I need the blue.

Example 3

Camper 1: qu'est-ce qu'il est le temps?
Counselor 1: l'heure?
Camper 1: yeah.
Counselor 1: tu veux savoir l'heure qu'est qui a l'heure?
Counselor 2: il est deux heures vingt-cinq
Counselor 1: tu a fini Allan
Camper 1: fini oui

Example 4

Camper 1: What's that?
Counselor: c'est de la colle pour coller la petite attache pour pouvoir la mettre
Camper 1: It looks like glue.
Counselor: oui oui c'est de la colle

Example 5

(1=first-pair partner, 2=second-pair partner, X=unconstrained turn, [= overlapped turns)

Line	Turn Type	
1	1	Counselor (to Camper 1): Il faut, est-ce que tu peux lui
2		dire pour moi est-ce que tu peux lui dire qu'on ne doit
3		pas écrire son numéro de téléphone on doit écrire le
4		numéro de téléphone du camp dis-lui.
5	2	Camper 1: [oh d'Anglais
6	X	Counselor: [oui en Anglais
7	1	Camper 1 (to Camper 2): Don't write the number of your

8		house write the number of your camp
9	2	Camper 2: oh
10	X	Counselor: oh tu comprends maintenant, tu comprends oui
11		c'est pas grave
12	2	Camper 2: oui
13	1	Counselor: je vais l'écrire pour toi oke?
14	2+1	Camper 1 (to Camper 2): [you see this (indicates
15		successively all his fingers)
16	2	Camper 2: [oh I didn't realize that ah ah
17	1	Counselor: eh voilà oke
18	2	Camper 2: oke
19	X	Camper 1 (to Camper 2: Je peux voir
20	1	Camper (identity uncertain): regarde mon main regard mon
21		main

Example 6

(1 = first-pair partner, 2 = second-pair partner, X = unconstrained)

Line	Turn Type	
1	1	Camper 1: oh who did this?
2	2	Counselor: c'est celui d'Elliot
3	X	Camper 1: aha
4	1	Camper 2: what's that?
5	2	Counselor: c'est de la colle pour coller la petite
6		attache pour pouvoir la mettre

9

CONCLUDING REMARKS WITH A NEUROLINGUISTIC STUDY

INTRODUCTION

The preceding chapters have viewed cohesion as a linguistic resource that is used to create interpretable language in context. Cohesion works with other elements of language to accomplish this function and so the study of cohesion must involve other areas of language. One of the purposes of the empirical study of cohesion is then to explore the role of cohesion in relation to other linguistic systems. As well as relating to other linguistic systems, cohesion is crucially important in the understanding of the relation of language to the verbal and nonverbal contexts. The interpretability of language is an issue which can only be addressed in contexts since language's principal use is in context (as text) and not as citation. Cohesion displays links to both verbal and nonverbal contexts and the variation in the use of cohesion is variation in how language is fitted to the context. Ultimately, this fitting of language to context contributes to the interpretability of the language. The study of cohesion is thus to a considerable extent the study of the interpretability of speakers in various contexts. Throughout the earlier chapters, the data have indicated how speakers differ in interpretability and in the strategies they require the hearer to follow for interpretation. Depending on context and social and cognitive characteristics of the speaker, hearers must adopt different strategies of interpretation.

This final chapter explores some of the implications of cohesion for a theory of language. The emphasis is on the role of cohesion in a wide view of language rather than on the categories of speakers. The social and cognitive considerations that have been presented so far are extended in the last section of this chapter to a neurobiological level. A case study is presented that suggests a relationship between cohesion and certain cognitive processes that can be influenced pharmacologically.

COHESION AND ASPECTS OF LINGUISTICS THEORY

Probabilities

The quantitative data in the previous chapters and in other studies show that the categories of cohesion are not used in categorical ways. There is usually a greater or lesser use of cohesion rather than the presence or absence of the particular categories and subcategories. Although options in the systems of language, including cohesion, are seen as paradigmatic, contrasting, and categorical, the use of the options is mainly probabilistic. Not only is the use of one option from a particular system probabilistic in relation to the other options from that system, but the use of an option from one system may be probabilistically related to the use of an option from another system.

The probabilities of using different cohesion options is not just a fact about linguistic systems themselves. Rather, these probabilities reflect what speakers typically do with language and how they typically mean. The probabilities take the 'can mean' potential of language (Halliday, 1973) and related it to what speakers 'typically mean.' Furthermore, we can learn what meanings are typically combined in language use. The next step is to relate the probabilities of different options to the contexts and specifically to various kinds of speakers. The questions then are: what systems and specific options tend to show variability across speakers and contexts? What is the direction and range of this variability? What functional role does the variability carry? How can the variability be explained in social, cognitive or even neurobiological terms?

In terms of the hearer and the language community in general, the probabilities reflect the expected and agreed things that people say. Departing from the expected probabilities suggests to the hearer that the speaker (a) is not parsing or cannot parse the verbal or nonverbal situations in accordance with the norms of the community, (b) is intentionally constructing a message that departs from those norms for some rhetorical purpose, or (c) perhaps is not aware of how the systems of language are used in relation to the context. In some cases, the hearer may not be able to determine the reason for the departure from the expected probabilities: the speaker does not seem otherwise socially inappropriate, there seems no rhetorical value in the atypical uses of language, and the speaker seems to be a sane native speaker, thus excluding apparent problems of cognitive processing or the use of a partially acquired language.

Relative Importance of Options in Systems

Certain parts of the cohesion system repeatedly distinguish speakers and contexts; for example, the choice of endophoric reference as contrasted to exophoric reference. This part of the cohesion system frequently shows how different texts are formed. The reasons for a high functional load being placed on the endophoric-exophoric contrast are found in two areas. First, the continuity of the participants in text (in the sense of Grimes, 1975; Martin, in press) is very important in conversation. The speakers must identify and reidentify what they are talking about in relation to the verbal and nonverbal contexts. As these contexts differ, so must there be adjustment to how participants are identified. Second, for part of a cohesion system to carry a functional load, there must be a reasonable frequency of occurrence. An option that rarely occurs will show a floor effect such that the variability will be constrained in at least one direction: Using the option even less frequently cannot make much difference. An exception is the use of an option such as ambiguous reference whose effect is jarring and disrupting even at low frequencies. These relationships between functional load and frequency are also found for systems of intonation (see Fine et al., 1989).

The variability in reasonably frequent options also opens up the possibility of conveying quite subtle meanings. The speaker, knowing the typical probabilities of using a certain option, can use a different rate in order to highlight the message as different from the expected in certain respects. The speaker can set up a counterpoint against the background of the typical. The background of the typical may be in terms of the verbal or nonverbal contexts, or in terms of selection of options from simultaneous systems. Placing sentence stress on a pronoun is an infrequent set of simultaneous options from the intonation system and the nominal group system. Both sentence stress and choosing a pronoun are frequent, but their simultaneous choice is unusual and can be used for specific rhetorical effect.

As well as probabilistic relations between options, the empirical data on cohesion suggests a hypothesis of functional congruence between options from different systems and from a linguistic option to an element of the nonlinguistic context. (These points are made in a somewhat different form in Halliday's (1984) claims about typical mappings of lexicogrammar and speech functions.) For example, anaphoric reference is usually encoded in the information system as given rather than new. This congruence of phoric with given can be violated as in: It was HIM I saw in the park, compared to: It was JOHN I saw in the park. However, such violations are statistically rare and send the hearer searching for a reason for the unusual combination of functions. Here we have a use of counterpoint not just against the background of the typical but against the background of congruent options: anaphoric reference carries a function quite close to information coded as given in the information system. The congruence of a linguistic function may also be with an aspect of situation, as exemplified in Chapter 6. When visual information is available to both speaker and hearer, nonspeech role exophoric reference can be effectively used. This kind of exophoric reference is appropriate to a particular aspect of the situation: shared visual information. To take another example, turn-taking organization and the social roles of speakers provide constraints on cohesion (see Chapters 4 and 5).

In some cases, the functional congruence between options from different linguistic systems suggests a suprafunction whose selection is realized in more than one system. The relation between phoric nominal groups and given information is one kind of example. In this case the probabilities cut across the two systems such that phoric nominal groups are usually found in the given parts of clauses. However, another relationship is also possible. If there is less phoric reference of certain types in dependent turns, it appears that a suprafunction of dependence is realized by either the phoricity system or by the turn-taking organization but not simultaneously by both. The dependence function leads to an inverse relation between phoricity and the constraint imposed by turn-taking organization. That is, the inverse quantitative relationship is not an accident.

The relations between linguistic systems and between aspects of context are areas that show development as children become full members of a society. Children increasingly vary more aspects of linguistic systems for functional ends. They learn both the functionally congruent mappings and the atypical mappings that function in terms of a counterpoint against the typical. Psychiatric disturbances that effect language, on the other hand, can be characterized by the use of atypical mappings that are not functional (see Fine et al., 1989, in press).

The importance of linguistic systems and options in distinguishing speakers or contexts is not directly related to what the hearer can report. The relative frequency of endophoric compared to exophoric reference is difficult for a hearer to report yet seems quite important in creating different texts (or different textures, to be only slightly metaphorical). On the other hand, unclear reference is relatively infrequent, a marginal option that is uninvolved with many other systems, but is disruptive and easily identified by hearers. The specific-generic distinction occurs with some intermediate level of frequency compared to the endophoric-exophoric distinction and the unclear option, but is reportable. The term "vague" speech in some clinical descriptions may be the result of a skewing of the specific-generic options. Thus the importance of particular contrasts or of individual options may be related to the direct and reportable reaction of the hearer or may have a more subtle role in creating text that is appropriate to context

Dynamics of Conversation

As convenient as it is to create rates of cohesion for a speaker or a conversation, the dynamic nature of conversation must not be ignored. In conversation a speaker uses cohesion in a cotext that is constantly being built by at least one other speaker.

Speakers are using cohesion in part to display the mutual construction of the conversation. Cohesion enables speakers to connect their speech to each other and to mutually known entities. This signaling, however, is subject to constant adjustment and reassessment. The dependence of language on context and situation must be accomplished by both speakers. This dependence is not a static structural feature of a conversation, but is built up interactively. The dynamic construction of conversation in any specific case is not random and unpredictable but follows patterns learned by the speakers as members of the speech community. Speakers can predict to some extent what another speaker will say and how the conversation will develop. The interpretation will be constructive and dynamic, but in relation to a background of expectations.

The dynamic perspective also has implications for the cognitive processing of conversation. Speakers must be able to monitor conversations at a specific rate and have the ability to plan their contributions in relations to the changing context. They must also be able to generalize from other conversations based on relevant recurring features. Each contribution to conversation is a particular selection of options against the background of the typical choices. Speakers must be able to processes the relevant probabilities and aspects of context that they are associated with. The dynamic perspective requires that all this processing and constant updating be done in real time as conversation develops.

SOME NEUROLINGUISTIC DATA AND SPECULATIONS

Although most of this volume has implicated, to various degrees, social and cognitive connections with cohesion, there is yet a further set of possible connections with cohesion: the neurolinguistic. Although these connections are explored thoroughly in the second volume of this set, some neurolinguistic processing that nevertheless also involves social and cognitive factors is documented below. As with other empirical studies in this volume, a series of different tasks are used to attempt to understand the use of cohesion and its relation to different factors. In addition, there is a drug condition which suggests the kind of processing involved in using cohesion.

COHESION AND THE EFFECTS OF MEDICATION ON COGNITIVE PROCESSING

The following study is concerned with specifying cognitive processes in the reading disabled by investigating cohesion and the effect of a drug treatment on underlying cognitive functioning. A given cognitive function may underlie a number of behaviors and may be affected by a number of factors. In this study of a reading-disabled subject, the chief behavioral measures are the use of oral language on a number of different tasks, and responses on standardized neuropsychological tests. The effects on the cognitive processing were produced by social characteristics of the tasks and drug treatment with piracetam, a psychoactive substance tested for possible use with learning disabilities. A single subject is carefully compared on a number of tasks with and without drug treatment, and is compared to a matched control and a group of similar reading-disabled subjects.

The biological and cognitive roots of the reading disabled have been the focus of numbers of studies and discussions concerning methodology as well as substance. In a review Galaburda (1985) suggests that developmental dyslexia ('reading disabled' will be the term generally used here) may have a number of biological sources, including unusual cerebral dominance and lateralization, changes in the development of the cerebral cortex, hormone abnormalities, and immune system abnormalities. With a such a variety of possible substrates, there is clearly a difficulty in determining how to specify the cognitive processes contributing to the deficit. Ellis (1985) also notes that reading-disabled subjects are not homogeneous, suggesting that the cognitive deficits leading to developmental reading disorders cannot be specific to reading since reading is an evolutionarily late skill. Rather, the deficits should be discoverable in nonreading tasks including oral language tasks. In order to uncover the underlying processes, Ellis argues not for typologies of the reading disorders but rather analyses of behavioral characteristics that can then serve as the basis for speculation about brain function. A substantial number of studies in such a direction which focus on close study of one or a few cases have identified specific cognitive and related processes (see for example the studies of Coltheart, Patterson, & Marshall, 1980; Patterson, Marshall, & Coltheart, 1985; and Siegel, 1985).

Evidence (Galaburda & Kemper, 1979; Holmes & McKeever, 1979; McKeever & Hulings, 1970; McKeever & Van Deventer, 1975) suggests a specifically left-hemisphere problem in reading disabled subjects. Nonreading linguistic deficits reported for the reading disabled include using proportionately more pronouns without a concrete antecedent in narratives (Feagans & Short, 1984), tolerating more ambiguous messages than a control group (although not all subjects were specifically reading disabled; see Donahue, 1984) and having difficulty with cohesive devices in narrative (here again there is some question about whether the subjects were only reading disabled; Liles, 1985b).

In terms of nonreading activities, the reading disabled have been found to have a number of deficits. These include poor short-term memory (Rudel & Denckla, 1974) and poor coding and naming abilities (Denckla & Rudel, 1976; Symmes & Rappaport, 1972). The goal of the present study is to investigate use of cohesion by reading-disabled children in order to draw inferences about possible neuropsychological deficits and their relation to cohesion.

The drug treatment in this study is with piracetam. Piracetam is structurally related to gamma-aminobutyric acid (GABA) and is thought to selectively improve the efficiency of higher cognitive function (Giurgea & Salama, 1977). It is relatively safe and free of side effects (Calliauw & Marchau, 1975; Stegink, 1972).

In a number of studies with children and adults with and without cognitive deficits, piracetam seems to improve performance on tasks associated with left-hemisphere functioning (Dimond & Brouwers, 1976). Epileptic children with learning difficulties treated with piracetam showed no change in tasks of spatial relationship (presumably requiring right-hemisphere functioning) but did show improvements in short-term memory, arithmetic, and school performance (Kunneke & Malan, 1979). Verbal learning, but not nonlateralized tasks, was found to improve in normal college students after piracetam treatments for 14 days (Dimond & Brouwers, 1976). Other studies have found improvements on a digit-symbol task (Mindus, Cronholm, Levander, & Schalling, 1976) and on the immediate recall segment of a verbal learning task and symbol-copying tasks (Wedl & Suchenwirth, 1977).

With regard to the specifically reading disabled, Dilanni et al. (1985) found that piracetam-treated subjects increased reading fluency without a decrease in accuracy and those with poor short-term memory increased their digit span scores. Chase,

Schmitt, Russell, and Tallal (1984) and Tallal, Chase, Russell, and Schmitt (1986) reported marked improvement in reading speed and writing accuracy with piracetam. Levi and Sechi (1987) found no effect of piracetam on tests of spatial ability or attention but there was improvement in recall of an oral story, ability to solve anagrams, and prose reading accuracy. A large-scale, double-blind, multicentered study of piracetam in reading-disabled children treated for 36 weeks was reported by Wilsher et al. (1987). This study showed that the treated group made significantly greater progress in reading ability (Gray Oral Reading Test) and reading comprehension (Gilmore Oral Reading Test). This latter finding of increased reading comprehension has only been evidenced in long-term studies and again points to an improvement in "left-hemisphere type" skills with piracetam treatment.

In summary, piracetam shows evidence of facilitating left-hemisphere function in reading disability as there is improvement of short-term verbal memory and of some increase on reading ability and comprehension. These trends are consistent with the hypothesis that reading-disabled subjects may have a specifically left-hemisphere deficit.

The linguistic analysis for the study is based on the concept of text as a meaning unit that is appropriate to both the linguistic and nonlinguistic context (Halliday & Hasan, 1976). If there are severe problems in the construction of text, then the listener may have difficulty in understanding the speaker. The analysis of the semantic signals in texts (in parts, cohesion analysis) has been used to investigate language and cognitive processing in a variety of subject groups and with a variety of tasks. Since cohesion analysis is sensitive to both the verbal and nonverbal contexts, variation in performance on different tasks is to be expected. That is, subjects may differ in their ability to adjust their language to different circumstances. This study will focus on a few of the signals of cohesion. These particular signals have been found to be useful in the study of other subject groups and are also interpretable in terms of cognitive processing. The signals are ambiguous reference, additioning (together composing a supracategory of unclear reference), endophoric reference, and exophoric reference. See Table 9-1 for definitions and examples. Harvey, Earle-Boyer, and Levinson (1986) studied reference failures (roughly, the above category of unclear reference) in manics and schizophrenics.

Table 9-1. Categories of signals of cohesion, definitions and examples

Endophoric

Endophoric reference—use of some (usually prior) piece of language is necessary for interpreting the nominal group.

TOM was sick. *He* had the flu. (Reference to TOM is necessary to interpret He)

Mary saw A LONG HALL. *The hall* was very dark.

Exophoric reference—use of some nonverbal (situational) piece of information is necessary for interpreting the nominal group.

Those trees (pointing) are going to be cut down.

I think that *you* are wearing *your best hat.*

Nonphoric reference—the nominal group is interpretable without recourse to information outside of itself.

John likes eating meat more than *bread.*

The fastest car I have seen is almost *an airplane.*

Unclear reference—insufficient information is given to interpret the nominal group.

Ambiguous reference—two or more possible antecedents.

My brother and father are tall. *He* likes basketball.

Additioning—no possible antecedent.

Tom saw *the other man* (when the first man has not been mentioned).

These reference failures differentiated the patient groups even when neuropsychological tests did not. Ulatowska, Hayashi, Cannito, and Fleming (1986), using similar principles of cohesion analysis, showed that the elderly use more ambiguous reference than younger subjects. They also found cognitive impairments in the same direction.

In a series of studies on language-impaired children, Liles (1985a, 1985b, 1987) found differences in the use of anaphora and conjunction. Subjects were asked to tell a story that they saw in a short movie. Subjects who were poor comprehenders on a test of the relationship between characters and events in the movie used more demonstrative reference, lexical cohesion, and made more conjunction errors. The language-impaired subjects as a group used more incomplete cohesive ties than normal subjects. These results suggest that underlying comprehension processes can have an effect on the use of cohesion and specifically on the presentation of interpretable messages. The group of language-disordered subjects in Liles's studies may be quite heterogeneous with respect to underlying cognitive processes and so direct inferences from the cohesion findings on the group data to cognitive processes is very difficult.

Method

The method of this study is that of a single-case design with a matched control. The two subjects serve as their own control and can also be compared to each other. The subjects were drawn from a large (257 cases) double-blind study of the effect of piracetam on reading-disabled boys (see Dilanni et al., 1985, for specific details). The entry criteria for the study were male, between the ages of 8 years 0 months and 13 years 11 months, with English as the primary language, full-scale I.Q. (WISC-R) of 80 or greater with a performance I.Q. score or a verbal I.Q. score of 90 or greater. A reading quotient of 0.85 or less was required. Reading quotient was defined as: (reading age x 100)/(chronological age x full-scale I.Q.). The reading age was obtained from the accuracy score of the Gilmore Reading Test. Patients had normal findings on audiologic, ophthalmologic, and neurologic examination prior to study entry. Patients with significant emotional problems or educational deprivation, and patients treated with psychostimulant medication within 6 months of the study or who required concomitant treatment with any psychoactive medication were all excluded from the study.

The subject of this study met the above entry criteria and was randomly assigned to the piracetam treatment group receiving piracetam in solution containing 0.33 grams per ml. The daily dose was 5 ml twice a day for a total of 3.3 grams of piracetam daily. The control subject was entered into the study but was randomly assigned to the placebo group. This subject was the closest match to the subject receiving piracetam based on age, I.Q., and reading quotient. Specific details of the two subjects are given in Table 9-2.

The oral language of the subjects was examined on a number of tasks (see Fine, 1985). Four of these tasks will be reported on here. Since the reading of printed material is so difficult for these subjects, only nonreading tasks were used to gather examples of oral language use.

Task 1 - Story recall. A story ("Tiger's Whisker" from Stein, & Glenn, 1979) was read to the subjects and they were then asked for an immediate recall.

Task 2 - Story telling. Sixteen scenes constituting a simple story were taken from a wordless book (Mayer & Mayer, 1975).

Table 9-2. Characteristics of piracetam-treated and placebo-treated subjects

	Piracetam-treated	*Placebo-treated*
Age at entry into study (months)	152	128
Sex	M	M
Performance I.Q.	130	114
Verbal I.Q.	97	96
Full-Scale I.Q.	113	105
Reading quotient	0.57	0.70

The subjects were told to go through the book page by page and to tell "the story." The subjects thus knew that the information would form a story but did not have an overview of all the information in the early stages of the task.

Task 3* - *Story retelling. The subjects were asked to retell the story from Task 2 without using the pictures. For Task 3 the experimenter went to another part of the room and the subjects were asked to retell the story for viewers of the video recording being made.

Task 4* - *Monologues. Subjects taped two monologues in the following way. Subjects were first asked to tell about the time they were most frightened and what it felt like. The subjects were to make a tape-recorded message while the experimenter went to a distant part of the room. For the second monologue subjects were asked to make a recording for a friend telling about the time the subject was maddest at someone or something. The topics of the monologues were chosen as emotional topics designed to reduce speakers' self-monitoring (parallel to Labov's, 1972, procedure for adults of asking about the time "you were in serious danger of being killed"). All the tasks were videotaped and transcribed into standard orthography.

The tasks were presented at the beginning of the study and again 12 weeks later after placebo or piracetam treatment. The language variables were scored before treatment conditions were decoded. A reliability check was done by having a second coder recode the relatively small amounts of data involved. All variables were coded at least 90% reliably across coders.

Results

Table 9-3 presents the frequency of the key language categories as a proportion of all nominal groups. The results are displayed graphically in Figure 9-1. The piracetam-treated and placebo subjects were quite similar at the beginning of the study. Over the 12 weeks of the study the subject receiving piracetam showed a notable decrease in unclear reference compared to his earlier performance and compared to the matched control. The exception is in the monologues where there is a floor effect.

The proportion of nominal groups that refer endophorically is generally greater with piracetam treatment. An exception is the performance in the monologues. As with the studies cited earlier, the relative stability of the measures suggests that they do not vary randomly and are measuring stable characteristics of language use. Differences in relative frequency of the measures on different tasks and complexity of tasks are consistent with the findings of Rochester & Martin (1979), Fine (1985), and Ulatowska et al. (1986). Cohesion is a means of creating continuity of meaning in context and as those contexts change the use of cohesion changes.

A number of calculations were made to determine if there was a practice effect of the linguistic tests. For five reading-disabled

Table 9-3. Frequency of language categories as a proportion of all nominal groups according to tasks, subject, and time of test

	Unclear reference		*Endophoric reference*	
	Piracetam	*Placebo*	*Piracetam*	*Placebo*
Task 1				
Story recall				
beginning of study	7	9	61	61
end of study	0	8	54	44
Task 2				
(storytelling)				
beginning	33	25	49	47
end	16	28	66	52
Task 3				
(story retelling)				
beginning	27	21	48	48
end	12	18	62	54
Task 4				
(monologues)				
beginning	0	2	24	36
end	0	1	14	39

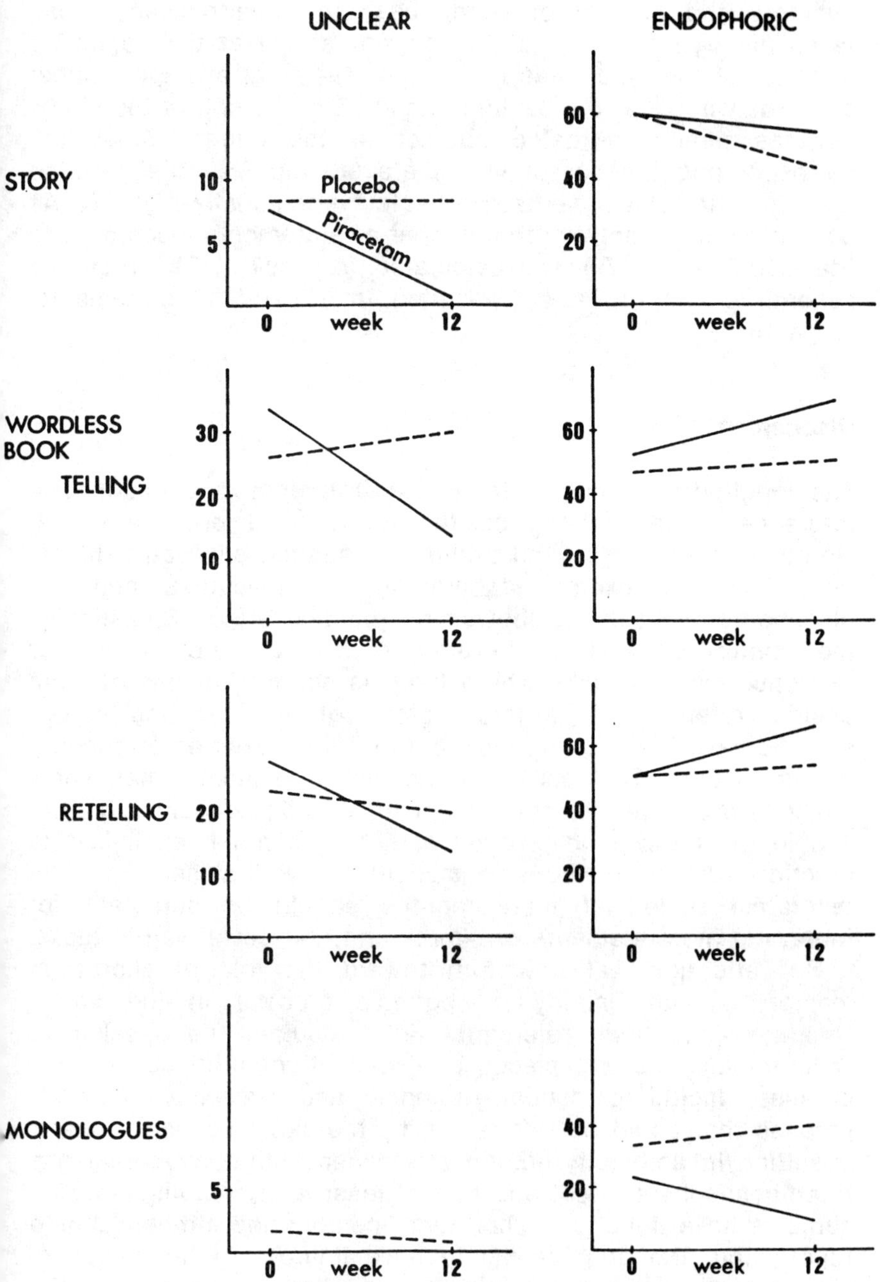

Figure 9-1. Unclear and endophoric phoricity as percentages of all nominal groups for two subjects, by task, over time.

subjects, the number of words used in three passage recall tasks (including Task 1 of the current study) at the beginning and end of the study was calculated. The total average number of words was 79 at the beginning and 77 at the end of the study. For the piracetam-treated subject of the current study the corresponding number of words are 96 and 95. This elevated level for our subject perhaps reflects his unusually high I.Q. As part of another analysis, the number of statements (according to Stein & Glenn, 1979) was calculated for Task 1. The first and second recalls of Task 1 resulted in 12 and 10 statements, respectively.

Discussion

The longitudinal changes in unclear reference and endophoric reference could perhaps be the result of a practice effect. However, there are several arguments against such an explanation. There is overall stability in the measures and the placebo-treated subject showed no practice effect. Specifically, the control showed no lowering in the amount of unclear reference even in tasks where there is substantial use of such unclear reference. In a larger group of subjects and in our specific case there is no practice effect for measures of quantity of production. The particular linguistic variables that show changes over time are not subject to specific conscious control and in the many studies cited earlier have not been linked to practice effects or conscious control by the speaker. The test-retest period of three months should be sufficient for forgetting most elements of simple and uneventful verbal tasks.

Our attention will now turn toward the role of short-term memory as an underlying cognitive process in the study. Creating endophoric referential links requires the speaker to keep track of several pieces of verbal information about noun phrases, including gender, number, and presence of noun phrases that could be referred to by the same cohesive marker (resulting in ambiguity). Given the evidence that piracetam has a left-hemisphere effect and that at least many reading-disabled subjects have deficits in short-term memory and left-hemisphere functioning, the drug seems to have improved left-hemisphere functioning. The lack of a clear direction of change in the linguistic variables on the monologue task can also be understood in the same terms. The monologue task is the only task in which the subject is completely in control of the verbal material to be presented. The other tasks require either following pictorially presented information or recalling information. There is thus less task-based stress in the monologues. Ulatowska et al. (1986) found a greater impairment of reference with increased complexity of the verbal task. Disabled readers have just such a difficulty in coping with linguistic tasks as they become more demanding cognitively or even in terms of social interactions (Fine, 1985). The reading-disabled subjects in the study have difficulty constructing connected language except under the least demanding situations. A drug effect on short-term verbal memory then can improve this particular aspect of linguistic output. That is, short-term memory is one cognitive process that underlies a specific method of creating connected text, and by improving this process the specific cohesion variables are affected.

The patient treated with piracetam had an unusually high performance I.Q. (130). This degree of ability is consistent with a view of reading as composed of many interrelated processes. Deficits in any one of the processes can lead to severe and distinct problems (Coltheart, Patterson, & Marshall, 1980; Patterson, Marshall, & Coltheart, 1985). The piracetam-treated subject in this study has many cognitive processes intact. This generally high level of cognitive functioning may have been helpful in compensating for a deficit in one area, especially when the subject was treated by a psychoactive drug with known left-hemisphere effects.

There are a number of theoretical points that lead from this case study. Oral language data are sensitive to cognitive processes and changes in those processes even when other elements of behaviors that initially identified the subjects (reading in this instance) show little change. Unlike studies of cohesion in the oral language of schizophrenics, the specifically reading disabled do not have noticeable difficulty in oral language. Nevertheless, the cognitive processes contributing to a difficulty in reading may also contribute to aspects of oral language use. In studying the oral language of speakers and the cognitive processes behind it, careful attention must be paid to the cognitive characteristics of the tasks used to collect the oral language. Studying subjects with specific language-related disabilities can help identify specific cognitive processes (see Caramazza, 1986). The addition of a drug treatment to this methodology, when appropriate, can also help to identify separable cognitive processes. The most secure method, however, is to have evidence for cognitive processes from a number of methodologies, including developmental and acquired language disorders, variations in tasks, treatment conditions, and different measures of language and cognitive functioning.

REFERENCES

Adlam, D. (Ed.). (I977). *Code in context.* Harmondsworth, England: Penguin.

Adlam, D., & Turner, G. (1977). Code in context. In D. Adlam (Ed.), Code in context. Hammondsworth, England: Penguin.

American Psychiatric Association. (I980). *Diagnostic and statistical manual of mental disorders (3rd ed.).* Washington, DC: American Psychiatric Association.

American Psychiatric Association. (1987). *Diagnostic and statistical manual of mental disorders (3rd ed., revised).* Washington, D.C.: American Psychiatric Association.

Asarnow, J. R., Goldstein, M. J., & Ben-Meir, S. (I988). Parental communication deviance in childhood onset schzophrenia spectrum and depressive disorders. *Journal of Child Psychology and Psychiatry. 29,* 825–838.

Bartolucci, G., & Fine, J. (1989). The frequency of cohesion weakness in psychiatric syndromes. *Applied Psycholinguistics, 8,* 67–74.

Bellack, A. S., Morrison, R. L., & Mueser, K. T. (1989). Social problem solving in schizophrenia. *Schizophrenia Bulletin, 15,* I01–116.

Benton, A.L. (I963). *The revised visual retention test (3rd ed.).* New York: Psychological Corporation.

Bernstein, B. (Ed.). (1973). *Class, codes and control, Volume 2.* London: Routledge and Keagan Paul.

Birchwood, M. J., Hallett, S. E., & Preston, M. C. (1989). *Schizophrenia: An integrated approach to research and treatment.* New York: New York University Press.

Bokus, B. , & Shugar, G. W. (I979). What will a three-year old say? An experimental study of situation variation. In 0. K. Garnica and M. L. King (Eds.), Language, children and society: the effect of social factors on children learning to communicate. New York: Pergamon.

Butler, C. S. (1985). *Systemic linguistics: Theory and applications.* London: Batsford.

Cais, J. (1983). Socialization and verbal behaviour: An Israeli example. *International Journal for the Sociology of Language, 41*, 57–75.

Calliauw, L., & Marchau, M. (1975). Clinical trial of Piracetam in disorders of consciousness due to head injury. *Acta Anaesthesiologia Belgica, 26*, 51–60.

Cancro, R. (1969). Psychological differentiation and process-reactive schizophrenia. *Journal of Abnormal Psychology, 74*, 415–419.

Caramazza, A., & McCloskey, M. (1988). The case for single patient studies. *Cognitive Neuropsychology, 5*, 517–528.

Caramazza, A. (1986). On drawing inferences about the structure of normal cognitive systems from the analysis of patterns of impaired performance: The case for single patient studies. *Brain and Cognition, 5*, 41–66.

Carpenter, W. T. Jr. (1987). Approaches to knowledge and understanding of schizophrenia. *Schizophrenia Bulletin*, 13, 1-8.

Chaika, E., & Lambe, R. (1985). The locus of dysfunction in schizophrenic speech. *Schizophrenia Bulletin. 11*, 8–15.

Chaika, E. (1974). A linguist looks at 'schizophrenic' language. *Brain and Language, 1*, 257–276.

Chase, C.H., Schmitt, R. L., Russell, G., & Tallal, P. (1984). A new chemotherapeutic investigation: Piracetam effects on dyslexia. *Annals of Dyslexia, 34*, 29–48.

Clark, H. H., & Clark, E. V. (1977). *Psychology and language: An introduction to psycholinguistics.* New York: Harcourt Brace Jovanovich.

Cole, M., Dore, J., Hall, W. S., & Dowley, G. (1978). Situation and task in young children's talk. *Discourse Processes, 1*, 119–176.

Coltheart, M., Patterson, K., & Marshall, J. C. (Eds.) (1980). *Deep dyslexia.* London: Routledge and Kegan Paul.

Crosson, B., & Hughes, C. W. (1987). Role of the thalamus in language: Is it related to schizophrenic thought disorder? *Schizophrenia Bulletin, 13*, 605–621.

Davies, M. (1989). Prosodic and non-prosodic cohesion in speech and writing. *Word, 40*, 255–262.

Davies, M., & Ravelli, L. (Eds.). (in press). *Selected papers from the Seventeenth International Systemic Congress.* London: Pinter.

Denckla, M.B., & Rudel, R. G. (1976). Rapid automized naming (R.A.N.) dyslexia differentiated from other learning disabilities. *Neuropsychologia, 14*, 471–479.

Di Ianni, M., Wilsher, C.R., Blank, M.S., Conners, C. K., Chase, C. H., Funkenstein, H. H., Helfgott, E., Holmes, J. M., Lougee, L., Maletta, G. J., Milewski, J., Pirozzolo, F. J., Rudel, R. G., & Tallal, P. (1985). The effects of Piracetam in children with dyslexia. *Journal of Clinical Psychopharmacology, 5*, 272–278.

Dimond, S., & Brouwers, E. Y. M. (1976). Increase in the power of human memory in normal man through the use of drugs. *Psychopharmacology, 49*, 307–309.

Donahue, M.L. (1984). Learning disabled children's conversational competence: An attempt to activate the inactive listener. *Applied Psycholinguistics, 5*, 21–35.

Dore, J. (1977). Children's illocutionary acts. In R. O. Freedle (Ed.), *Discourse production and cognition.* Norwood, NJ: Ablex.

Edwards, A.D. (1976). *Language in culture and class.* London: Heinmann.

Edwards, D., & Middleton, D. (1986a). Conversation with Bartlett. *Quarterly Newsletter of the Laboratory of Comparative Human Cognition, 8*, 79–89.

Edwards, D. & Middleton, D. (1986b). Joint-remembering: Constructing an account of shared experience through conversational discourse. *Discourse Processes, 9*, 423–459.

Ellis, A.W. (1985). The cognitive neuropsychology of developmental and acquired dyslexia: A critical survey. *Cognitive Neuropsychology, 2*, 169-205.

Farbey, D. (1987). *Cultural differences in the formation of texts within selected contexts.* Unpublished master's thesis, Department of English, Bar-Ilan University, Ramat Gan, Israel.

Fawcett, R. P. (1990). A systemic functional approach to selectional restrictions, roles and semantic preferences. Machine Translation.

Fawcett, R. P. (1988). The English personal pronouns: An exercise in linguistic theory. In J. Benson, M. Cummings, & W. Greaves (Eds.), Linguistics in a systemic perspective. Amsterdam: Benjamins.

Fawcett, R. P., van der Mije, & van Wissen, C. (1988). Towards a systemic flowchart model for discourse structure. In R. P. Fawcett & D. Young (Eds.), New developments in systemic linguistics: Volume 2, Theory and application. London: Pinter.

Feagans, L, & Short, E. J. (1984). Developmental differences in the comprehension and production of narratives by reading- disabled and normally achieving children. *Child Development, 55*, 1727-1736.

Feighner, J. P., Robins, E., Guze, S. B., Woodruff, R. A., Winokur ,G., & Munoz, R. (1972). Diagnostic criteria for use in psychiatric research. *Archives of General Psychiatry, 26*, 57-63.

Fine, J. (1978). Conversation, cohesive and thematic patterning in children's dialogues. *Discourse Processes, 1*, 247-266.

Fine, J. (1985). Cohesion as an index of social-cognitive factors: Oral language of the reading disabled. *Discourse Processes, 8*, 91-112.

Fine, J. (1988). Cognitive processes in context: A systemic approach to problems in oral language use. In E. Steiner & R. Veltman (Eds.), *Pragmatics, discourse and text: Some systemically inspired approaches.* London: Pinter.

Fine, J. (1991). The static and dynamic choices of responding: Toward the process of building social reality by the developmentally disordered. In E. Ventola (Ed.), Functional and systemic linguistics: Approaches and uses. The Hague, TheNetherlands: Mouton De Gruyter.

Fine, J. (1992). Functions of probabilities on linguistic systems. *Occasional Papers in Systemic Linguistics, 6*, 9-l8.

Fine, J., Bartolucci, G., Ginsberg, G., & Szatmari, P. (in press). The use of intonation to communicate in subjects with pervasive developmental disorders. *Journal of Child Psychology and Psychiatry, 32*, 771-782.

Fine, J., Bartolucci, G., & Szatmari, P. (1989). Textual systems: Their use in creation and miscalculation of social reality. *Word, 40*, 65-79.

Fine, J. & Freedle, R. (Eds.). (1983). *Developmental issues in discourse.* Norwood, NJ: Ablex.

Firth, C. D., & Done, D. J. (1988). Toward a neuropsychology of schizophrenia. British Journal of Psychiatry. *153*, 437-443.

Fishman, D., Fredman, M., Hamburger, H., Janko, D., & Nay, A. (1981). A comparison of norms for Hebrew-speaking children on the language test: Reynell Developmental Language Scales (Revised). [In Hebrew]. *DASH - Speech and Hearing Disorders (Israel)*, 10, 8-15.

Freedle, R. O. (Ed.). (1977). *Discourse production and comprehension.* Norwood, NJ: Ablex.

Freedle, R. O. (Ed.). (1979). *New directions in discourse processing.* Norwood, NJ: Ablex.

Galaburda, A.M. (1985). Developmental dyslexia: A review of biological interactions. *Annals of Dyslexia,* 35, 21-33.

Galaburda, A.M. , & Kemper, T. L. (1979). Cytoarchitectonic abnormalities in developmental dyslexia: A case study. *Annals of Neurology, 6*, 94–100.

Garnica, O. K. , & King M. L. (Eds.). (l979). *Language, children and society: The effect of social factors on children learning to communicate.* New York: Pergamon.

Garvey, C. (1975). Requests and responses in children's speech. Journal of Child Language. 2.41–63.

Gee, J. P., & Michaels, S. (Eds.). (1989). Discourse styles: Variations across speakers, situations, and tasks. [Special issne]. *Discourse Processes, l2.*

Giurgea, C., & Salama, M. (1977). Nootropic drugs. *Progress in Neuro-Psychopharmacology, 1*, 235–247.

Gregory, M. J. (1988). Generic situation and register: A functional view of communication. In J. Benson, M. Cummings, & W. Greaves (Eds.), *Linguistics in a systemic perspective.* Amsterdam: Benjamins.

Gregory, M. J., & Carroll, S. (1978). *Language and situation: Language varieties and their social contexts.* London: Routledge and Kegan Paul.

Gregory, M. J. (1967). Aspects of varieties differentiation. *Journal of Linguistics, 3*, 177–198.

Grimes, J.E. (1975). *The thread of discourse.* The Hague: Mouton.

Halliday, M.A.K., & Hasan,R. (1976). *Cohesion in English.* London: Longman.

Halliday, M.A.K. (1973). *Explorations in the functions of language.* London: Edward Arnold.

Halliday, M.A.K. (1984). Language as code and language as behaviour: A systemic-functional interpretation of the nature and otogenesis of dialogue. In R. P. Fawcett, M. A. K. Halliday, S. M. Lamb, & A. Makkai (Eds.), The semiotics of culture and language, Vol. 1: Language as social semiotic. London: Pinter.

Halliday, M.A.K. (1985). *Introduction to functional grammar.* London: Edward Arnold.

Halliday, M.A.K. (1967). Notes on transitivity and theme in English: Part 2. *Journal of Linguistics, 3*, 199–244.

Halliday, M.A.K. (1975). *Learning how to mean: Explorations in the development of language.* London: Edward Arnold.

Halpern, H. & McCartin-Clark, M. (1984). Differential language characteristics in adult aphasic and schizophrenic subjects. *Journal of Communication Disorders, 17*, 289–307.

Harvey, P. D., Earle-Boyer, E. A., & Levinson, J. C. (1988). Cognitive deficits and thought disorder: A retest study. *Schizophrenia Bulletin, 14*, 57–66.

Harvey, P. D. (1983). Speech competence in manic and schizophrenic psychoses: The association between clinically rated thought disorder and cohesion and reference performance. *Journal of Abnormal Psychology, 92*, 368–377.

Harvey, P. D., Earle-Boyer, E. A., & Levinson, J. C. (1986). Distractibility and discourse failure: Their association in mania and schizophrenia. *Journal of Nervous and Mental Disease, 174*, 274–279.

Haslett, B. (1983). Children's strategies for maintaing cohesion in their written and oral stories. *Communication Education,* 32, 91–105.

Hawkins, P.R. (1973). Social class, the nominal group and reference. In Bernstein (Ed.), *Class, codes and control,* Vol. 2. London: Routledge and Keagan Paul.

Hemphill, L. (1989). Topic development, syntax, and social class. *Discourse Processes, 12*, 267–286.

Hoffman, R.E., Stopek, S., & Andreasen, N. C. (1986). A comparative study of manic vs schizophrenic speech disorganization. *Archives of General Psychiatry, 43*, 831-838.

Holmes, D. R., & McKeever, E. G. (1979). Material specific serial memory deficit in adolescent dyslexics. *Cortex, 15*, 51-62.

Howlin, P., & Rutter, M. (1989). Mothers' speech to autistic children: A preliminary causal analysis. *Journal of Child Psychology and Psychiatry, 30*, 819-843.

Kraus, V. (1979). *Social gradings of occupations.* Unpublished Doctoral dissertation. Hebrew University of Jerusalem.

Kunneke, P.S., & Malan, G.M. (1979). A controlled clinical trial of the effect of Piracetam in epileptic children. *British Journal of Clinical Practice, 33*, 266-271.

Labov, W. (1972). *Sociolinguistic patterns.* Philadelphia: University of Pennsylvania Press.

Landry, S.H., & Loveland, K.A. (1989). The effect of social context on the functional communication skills of autistic children. *Journal of Autism and Developmental Disorders, 19*, 283-299.

Lanin-Kettering, I., & Harrow, M. (1985). The thought behind the words: A view of schizophrenic speech and thinking disorders. *Schizophrenia Bulletin,* 11, 1-7.

Lemke, J. (1991). Textproduction and dynamic text semantics. In Ventola (Ed.), *Functional and systemic linguistics: Approaches and uses.* The Hague, The Netherlands: Mouton.

Levi, G., & Sechi, E. (1987). A study of Piracetam in the pharmacological treatment of learning disabilities. In D. Bakker, C. Wilsher, H. Debruyne, & N. Bent (Eds.), *Child health and development, Vol. 5: Developmental dyslexia and learning disorders.* Basel, England: Kager.

Liles, B.Z. (1987). Episode organization and cohesive conjunctives in narratives of children with and without language disorder. *Journal of Speech and Hearing Research, 30*, 185-196.

Liles, B.Z. (1985a). Cohesion in the narratives of normal and language- disordered children. *Journal of Speech and Hearing Research, 28*, 123-133.

Liles, B.Z. (1985b). Production and comprehension of narrative discourse in normal and language-disordered children. *Journal of Communication Disorders, 18*, 409-427.

Lovett, M.W., Dennis, M., & Newman, J. (1986). Making reference: The cohesive use of pronouns in the narrative discourse of hemidecorticate adolescents. *Brain and Language, 29*, 224-251.

Mandler, J.M., & Johnson, N.S. (1977). Rememberance of things parsed: Story structure and recall. *Cognitive Psychology, 9*, 111-151.

Manschreck, T.C., Maher, B.A., Hoover, T.M., & Ames, D. (1985). Repetition in schizophrenic speech. *Language and Speech, 28*, 255-268.

Marshall, J.C. (1982). What is a symptom-complex? In M. Arbib, D. Caplan, & J.C. Marshall (Eds.), *Neural models of language processes.* New York: Academic.

Martin, J. R. (forthcoming). *English text: System and structure.* Amsterdam: Benjamins.

Martin, J.R. (n.d.). *Schizophrenia, language and reality.* Department of Linguistics. University of Sydney. Sydney, Australia.

Martin, J.R. (1983b). The development of register. In J. Fine & R. Freedle (Eds.), Developmental issues in discourse. Norwood, NJ: Ablex.

Martin, J.R. (1983a). Conjunction: The logic of English text. In J. Petofi and E. Sozer (Eds.), *Micro and macro connexity of texts.* Hamburg, Germany: Helmut Buske.

Martinsen, H., & Smith, L. (1989). Studies of vocalization and gesture in the transition to speech. In S. von Tetzchner, L.S. Siegel, & L. Smith (Eds.), *The social and cognitive aspects of normal and atypical language development.* New York: Springer Verlag.

Martinsen, H., & von Tetzchner, S. (1989). Imitation at the onset of speech. In S. von Tetzchner, L.S. Siegel, & L. Smith (Eds.), *The social and cognitive aspects of normal and atypical language development.* New York: Springer Verlag.

Matthysse, S. (1987). Schizophrenic thought disorder: A model-theoretic perspective. *Schizophrenia Bulletin, 13*, 173–184.

Mayer, Mercer, & Mayer, M. (1975). *One frog too many.* New York: Dial.

McCloskey, M., & Caramazza,A. (1988). Theory and methodology in cognitive neuropsychology: A response to our critics. *Cognitive Neuropsychology, 5*, 583–623.

McKeever, W.F., & Hulings, M.D. (1970). Lateral dominance in tachistoscopic word recognition of children at two levels of ability. *Quarterly Journal of Experimental Psychology, 20*, 600–604.

McKeever, W.F., & Van Deventer, A.D. (1975). Dyslexic adolescents: Evidence of impaired visual and auditory language processing associated with normal lateralization and visual responsivity. *Cortex, 11*, 361–378.

Meir, M. (1986). *A boy who did not want to sleep alone* [in Hebrew]. Tel Aviv: Sifriat Hapoalim.

Mindus, P., Cronholm, B., Levander, S.E., & Schalling, D. (1976). Piracetam-induced improvement of mental performance: A controlled study on normal aging individuals. *Acta Psychiatrica Scandinavica, 54*, 150–160.

Moerk, E. L. (1985). Picture-book reading by mothers and young children and its impact upon language development. *Journal of Pragmatics, 9*, 547–566.

Mohan, B. (1989). Knowledge structures and academic discourse. *Word, 40*, 99–115.

Morrison, R.L., & Bellack, A.S, (1987). Social functioning of schizophrenic patients: Clinical and research issues. *Schizophrenia Bulletin, 13*, 715–725.

Nesbitt, C., & Plum, G. (1988). Probabilities in a systemic functional grammar: The clause complex in English. In R.P. Fawcett and D. Young (Eds.), *New developments in systemic linguistics, Vol. 2: Theory and application.* London: Pinter.

Ninio, A. (1980). Picture-book reading in mother-infant dyads belonging to two subgroups in Israel. Child Development, *51*, 587–590.

Nuechterlein, K.H., & Dawson, M.E. (1984). A heuristic vulnerability/stress model of schizophrenic episodes. *Schizophrenia Bulletin, 10*, 300–312.

Oshima-Takane, Y., & Benaroya, S. (1989). An alternative view of pronominal errors in autistic children. *Journal of Autism and Developmental Disorders, 19*, 73–85.

Patterson, K., Marshall, J.C., & Coltheart, M. (Eds.). (1985). *Surface dyslexia.* London: Routledge and Kegan Paul.

Petofi, J., & Sozer, E. (Eds.). (1983). *Micro and macro connexity of texts.* Hamburg: Helmut Buske.

Pratt, M., & MacKenzie-Keating, S. (1985). Organizing stories: Effects of development and task difficulty on referential cohesion in narrative. *Developmental Psychology, 2*, 350–356.

Prizant, B., & Wetherby, A. (1987). Communicative intent: A framework for understanding social-communicative behavior in autism. *Journal of the American Academy of Child and Adolescent Psychiatry, 26*, 472–479.

Rapaport, D., Gill, D., & Schafer, R. (1968). *Diagnostic psychological testing.* New York: International Universities Press

Reynell, J.K. (1977). *Manual for the Reynell Developmental Language Scales* (Revised). Windsor, England: NFER Publishing.

Roberts, J. M. A. (1989). Echolalia and comprehension in autistic children. *Journal of Autism and Developmental Disorders, 19*, 271–281.

Rochester, S., & Martin, J.R. (1979). *Crazy Talk: A study of discourse of schizophrenic speakers.* New York: Plenum.
Rochester, S., & Martin, J.R. (1977). The Art of referring: The speaker's use of noun phrases to instruct the listener. In Freedle R.O. (Ed.), *New directions in discourse processing.* Norwood, NJ: Ablex.
Rosenberg, S. (Ed.). (1982). *Handbook of applied psycholinguistics: Major thrusts of research and theory.* Hillsdale, NJ: Erlbaum.
Rosenberg, S., & Abbeduto, L. (1982). Adult schizophrenic language. In Rosenberg (Ed.), *Handbook on applied psyaholinguistics: Major thrusts on research and theory.* Hillsdale, NJ: Erlbaum.
Rudel, R.G., & Denckla, M.B. (1974). Relation of forward and backward digit repetition to neurological impairment in children with learning disabilities. *Neuropsychologia, 12,* 109-118.
Rund, B.R. (1986). Communication deviances in parents of schizophrenics. *Family Process, 25,* 133-147.
Rund, B.R. (1988). Cognitive disturbances in schizohrenics: What are they, and what is their origin? *Acta Psychiatrica Scandinavica, 77,* 113-123.
Rutter, D.R. (1985). Language in schizophrenia: The structure of monologues and conversations. *British Journal of Psychiatry, 146,* 399-404.
Sacks, H., Schegloff, E.A., & Jefferson, G. (1974). A simplest systematics for the organisation of turn-taking for conversation. *Language, 50,* 696-735.
Schaffer, H.R. (1989). Language development in context. In S. von Tetzchner, L.S. Siegel, & L. Smith (Eds.), *The social and cognitive aspects of normal and atypical language development.* New York: Springer-Verlag.
Service, V., Lock, A., & Chandler, P. (1989). Individual differences in early communicative development: A social constructivist perspective. In S. von Tetzchner, L.S. Siegel, & L. Smith (Eds.), *The social and cognitive aspects of normal and atypical language development.* New York: Springer-Verlag.
Siegel, L.S. (1985). Deep dyslexia in childhood? *Brain and Language, 26,* 16-27.
Sinclair, J. McH., & Coulthard, R.M. (1975). *Towards an analysis of discourse: The English used by teachers and pupils.* London: Oxford.
Smith, L. (1989). Case studies of maternal speech to prelinguistic children in the format of object transfer. In S. von Tetzchner, L.S. Siegel, & L. Smith (Eds.), *The social and cognitive aspects of normal and atypical language development.* New York: Springer-Verlag.
Solovay, M.R., Shenton, M.E., & Holzman, P.S. (1987). Comparative studies of thought disorders: I Mania and schizophrenia. *Archives of General Psychiatry, 44,* 13-20.
Sparrow, S., Balla, D., & Cicchetti, D. (1984). *Vineland Adaptive Behaviour Scales* (survey form). Circle Pines, MN: American Guidance Service.
Sperber, D., & Wilson, D. (1986). *Relevance: Communication and cognition.* Cambridge, MA: Harvard University Press.
Sperber, D., & Wilson, D. (1987). Precis of Relevance: Communication and Cognition. *Behavioral and Brain Sciences, 10,* 697-754.
Spitzer, R.L., Endicott, J., & Robins, E. (1978). Research diagnostic criteria. *Archives of General Psychiatry, 35,* 773-782.
Stahl, A. (1977). Language and thought of culturally deprived children in Israel [In Hebrew]. Tel Aviv: Otsar Hamoreh.
Stegink, K.J. (1972). The clinical use of Piracetam, a new nootropic drug. The treatment of senile involution. *Arzneim Forsch* [Drug Research], *22,* 975-977.
Stein, N.L., & Glenn, C.G. (1979). An analysis of story comprehension in

elementary school children. In R.O. Freedle (Ed.), *New directions in discourse processing.* Norwood, NJ: Ablex.

Stein, N.L., & Nezworski, T. (1978). The effects of organization and instructional set on story memory. *Discourse Processes, 1*, 177–194.

Steiner, E., & Veltman, R. (Eds.). (1988). *Pragmatics, discourse and text: Some systemically-inspired approaches.* London: Pinter.

Sudhalter, V., Cohen, I., Silverman, W., & Wolf-Schein, E. (1990). Conversational analyses of males with fragile X, Down syndrome, and autism: Comparison of the emergence of deviant language. *American Journal on Mental Retardation, 94*, 431–441.

Symmes, J.S., & Rappaport, J.L. (1972). Unexpected reading failure. *American Journal of Orthopsychiatry, 42*, 82–91.

Szatmari, P., Bartolucci, G., Bremner, R., Bond, S., & Rich, S. (1989). A follow-up study of high-functioning autistic children. *Journal of Autism and Developmental Disorders, 19*, 213–225.

Szatmari, P., Bartolucci, G., & Bremner, R. (1989). Asperger's Syndrome and autism: Comparison of early history and outcome. *Developmental Medicine and Child Neurology, 31*, 709–720.

Szatmari, P., Bremner, R., & Nagy, J. (l989). Asperger's Syndrome: A review of clinical features. *Canadian Journal* of *Psychiatry, 34*, 554–560.

Tallal, P., Chase, C., Russell, G., & Schmitt, R.L. (1986). Evaluation of the efficiency of Piracetam in treating information processing, reading and writing disorders in dyslexic children. *International Journal of Psychophysiology, 4*, 41–52.

Ulatowska, H.K., Hayshi, M.M., Cannito, M.P., & Fleming, S.G. (1986). Disruption of reference in aging. *Brain and Language, 28*, 41–52.

Ventola, E. (Ed.). (in press). *Recent systemic and other functional views on language.* The Hague: Mouton De Gruyter.

Ventola, E. (1988). Text analysis in operation: A multilevel approach. In R.P. Fawcett & D. Young (Eds.), *New developments in systemic linguistics: Vol. 2, Theory and application.* London: Pinter.

Ventola, E. (1987). *The structure of social interaction: A systemic approach to the semiotics of service encounters.* London: Pinter.

von Tetzchner, S., Siegel, L.S., & Smith, L. (Eds.). (1989). *The social and cognitive aspects of normal and atypical language development.* New York: Springer-Verlag.

Wechsler, D. (1974). *The Wechsler intelligence scale for children - revised.* New York: Psychological Corporation.

Wechsler, D. (1944). *The measurement of adult intelligence.* Baltimore: Williams and Wilkins.

Wedl, W., & Suchenwirth, R.M.A. (1977). Effects of the GABA-derivative Piracetam: A double-blind study in healthy probands. *Der Nervenarzt, 48*, 58–60.

Weintraub, D., & Kraus, V. (1981). *Social differentiation and locality of residence: Spatial distribution, composition and stratification in Israel* [in Hebrew]. Rehovot, Israel: Settlement Study Centre, Working paper no. 3.

Wilsher, C.R., Bennett, D., Chase, C.H., Conners, C.K., Di Ianni, M., Feagans, L., Hanvik, L.J., Helfgott, E., Koplewicz, H., Overby, P., Reader, N.J., Rudel, R.G., & Tallal, P. (1987). Piracetam and dyslexia: Effects on reading tests. *Journal of Clinical Psychopharmacology, 7*, 230–237.

Yang, A.W. (1989). Cohesive chains and writing quality. *Word, 40*, 235–254.

Zurif, E.B., Gardner, H. & Brownell, H. (1989). The case against the case against group studies. *Brain and Cognition, 10*, 237–255.

Author Index

Subject Index